WAR
WITHOUT
END

Books By Robert Shogan

Bad News: Where the Press Goes Wrong in the Making of the President

*The Double-Edged Sword: How Character
Makes and Ruins Presidents from Washington to Clinton*

Fate of the Union: America's Rocky Road to Political Stalemate

*Hard Bargain: How FDR Twisted Churchill's Arm,
Evaded the Law and Changed the Role of the American Presidency*

Riddle of Power: Presidential Leadership from Truman to Bush

None of the Above: Why Presidents Fail and What Can Be Done About It

Promises to Keep: Carter's First 100 Days

*A Question of Judgment: The Fortas
Case and the Struggle for the Supreme Court*

The Detroit Race Riot: A Study in Violence (with Tom Craig)

WAR
WITHOUT
END

Cultural Conflict and the Struggle
for America's Political Future

ROBERT SHOGAN

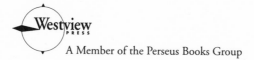

Westview
PRESS

A Member of the Perseus Books Group

Westview Press books are available at special discounts for bulk purchases in the United States by corporations, institutions, and other organizations. For more information, please contact the Special Markets Department at the Perseus Books Group, 11 Cambridge Center, Cambridge MA 02142, or call (617) 252-5298.

Published in 2002 in the United States of America by Westview Press, 5500 Central Avenue, Boulder, Colorado 80301-2877, and in the United Kingdom by Westview Press, 12 Hid's Copse Road, Cumnor Hill, Oxford OX2 9JJ

Find us on the World Wide Web at www.westviewpress.com

Library of Congress Cataloging-in-Publication Data
Shogan, Robert.
    War without end: cultural conflict and the struggle for America's political future / Robert Shogan.
    p.   cm.
    Includes bibliographical references and index.
    ISBN 0-8133-9760-X (alk. paper)
    1. United States—Civilization—1970–. 2. Culture conflict—United States—History—20th century. 3. Politics and culture—United States—History—20th century.   I. Title.
E169.12 .S515—2002
973.92—dc21

Text design by Trish Wilkinson

The paper used in this publication meets the requirements of the American National Standard for Permanence of Paper for Printed Library Materials Z39.48–1984.

10   9   8   7   6   5   4   3   2   1

For Ellen, Cindy and Amy

CONTENTS

AUTHOR'S NOTE

In the 1992 presidential election Democrat Bill Clinton's drive for victory was fueled by a campaign slogan coined by his chief consultant, James Carville: "It's the economy, stupid." As everyone in both parties later agreed, the pain from a severe recession overrode concerns about Clinton's values as reflected by his personal behavior. Republicans were stunned that a candidate whom they viewed as a philanderer and a draft dodger would occupy the office first held by George Washington. And that made it clear to all that economic conditions ruled the struggle for political power in the United States. Or so it seemed.

Fast forward eight years to the election of 2000. The economy was roaring along in high gear. By all the laws of politics, journalists and scholarly prognosticators agreed, Vice President Al Gore, the candidate of the incumbent party, would succeed Clinton in the White House. It was the economy, stupid. No doubt about it.

Except that Gore lost. To be sure, it was the narrowest of defeats, one that will be disputed for years to come. But he did lose. And the reason, as many politicians and independent analysts came to conclude, was the troublesome cultural profile of Bill Clinton. The misgivings and contradictions about his values that voters were willing to overlook in 1992 now came back to haunt and defeat Clinton's hand-picked legatee, Al Gore.

The economy was no longer king. It had been trumped by morals and values. As James Carville might have put it: "It's the Culture War, stupid." In fact, the 2000 campaign was another engagement in the prolonged Culture War that has helped to shape and define U.S. politics since the 1960s. Cultural factors are not as easy to measure as gross domestic product, the inflation rate, or unemployment. And they are harder to define. They have to do with religion and morality, race and gender, sex and crime, and sundry other aspects of human behavior, which tend to be amorphous in contrast to the cold calculus of the dismal science of economics. But cultural issues are nonetheless real. Sometimes they stand on their own, as with the seemingly never-ending battle over abortion. Sometimes they blend in with economic pressures, as with issues of racial and gender discrimination. One thing is certain: Any understanding of modern U.S. politics must begin with a recognition of the major role that cultural issues play, a reality underlined by the durability of cultural tensions even after the nation, in September of 2001, plunged tragically into another kind of conflict, a shooting war against terrorism.

It is with the hope of contributing to that understanding that I have written this book. Much of what is presented within these pages was drawn from my own experience as a political journalist for more than four decades. But of course I could not have completed this work without incurring a huge debt to the work of fellow journalists and of scholars, as the reference notes at the end of the book demonstrate.

I am obligated to more people than can be named here, but I want particularly to thank John Green, director of the Ray C. Bliss Institute for Applied Politics at the University of Akron, who provided me with information and advice, both invaluable, and David Keene, chairman of the American Conservative Union, who searched obscure archives to provide me with a better understanding of the birth of the New Right. For encouragement and wise counsel I am grateful to Leo Wiegman, my first editor at Westview Press; my agent Carl Brandt; and my wife, Ellen S. Shogan, who as usual served as first reader and best friend.

Robert Shogan
January 2002, Chevy Chase, Maryland

PART ONE
IMPEACHMENT

CHAPTER 1

"DOES THE
TRUTH MATTER?"

No one could blame Eric Holder for ignoring his pager. The deputy attorney general of the United States had decided he deserved a night on the town, and he had reason to feel that way. It was January 14, 1998, and Holder was forty-seven years old. For six months he had had his hands full getting accustomed to being the number two man at the Justice Department, where he had been buffeted by the controversies generated by the White House of Bill Clinton. He could only hope that his quota of on-the-job headaches had already been filled. But when Holder finally responded to his pager later that night, the message he received would set in motion events that would plunge him into the thick of a new presidential storm transcending all previous ones, a political and cultural cyclone that aside from clouding his own future would consume official Washington and divide the entire country.

Holder was the third person to serve as understudy to the nation's first woman attorney general, Janet Reno, whose tenure had come to be dominated by the problems beleaguering the president who had appointed her. The cross-pressures flowing from those problems had already been immense. Reno had been charged with political bias by Republicans because she had refused to appoint an independent counsel to investigate allegations that both Clinton and his vice president, Al Gore, had violated the campaign finance laws during the 1996 campaign. To Clinton and his aides the criticism leveled against Reno seemed like a bad joke. They could not forget that she had authorized six other probes by independent counsels, all of which had added to the discomfort of a chief executive who had begun his presidency under a lingering cloud from scandals raised during his campaign. It was common gossip in Washington legal circles that Clinton had picked Holder in the hope that he would be more tractable than the standoffish Reno. For his part, Holder, as he neared the age of fifty, always kept his eye on the future and the main chance. He had reason to suppose that if all went smoothly with his service as deputy, he would be the logical person to succeed Reno, plagued not only by criticism but also by Parkinson's disease, should she decide to resign.

Holder had already borne out the White House's faith in him by helping to persuade Reno to disregard the demands for an independent counsel to probe the fund-raising charges. And to avoid other potential headaches he had assumed the particularly sensitive task of serving as liaison to the office of Independent Counsel Kenneth Starr, whose relentless and fitful pursuit of Clinton had created additional tensions for Justice.

But even a man as ambitious as Holder needed a break once in a while. And on this night, hoping to escape from the burdens of office for a few hours, he had taken himself and an old friend to the MCI Center, recently installed in the nation's capital in an attempt to breathe some life into its moldering urban core. But Holder found no joy in Mudville this evening. Whatever benefit the multimillion-dollar arena had achieved for city life, it had failed to improve the fortunes of its most important tenant, the Washington Wizards of the National Basketball Association. For years the Wizards had been among the doormats of the NBA, and on this night, pitted against the San Antonio Spurs, the home team was turning in an all-too-typical performance. The Wizards were already well on their way to what would turn out to be their third successive defeat by the time Holder's pager first went off, about 9:30 P.M.

Holder had chosen to ignore it, even though he suspected, correctly as it turned out, that it was the night duty officer at the Department of Justice who was trying to reach him. Time enough for that; he wanted to watch the game. When the pager went off again, a little after 10, the Wizards were attempting to stage a comeback, and Holder once more disregarded the page, even though the message line flashed the word "urgent." The game over, with the Wizards on the wrong end of the 89–79 score, he headed down to the locker room. As the nation's number two lawman, and as the first African American to hold that post, Holder inevitably enjoyed some perks. Tonight he was taking advantage of his position to hobnob with the visiting team and chat with David Robinson, the Naval Academy graduate who had become one of the NBA's biggest stars playing center for the Spurs.

But first, duty called. Holder found a pay phone in the basement of the MCI Center and returned the page. The number he was given was all too familiar to Holder. It was the number of Jackie Bennett, who as deputy to Kenneth Starr was Holder's counterpart at the Office of Independent Counsel. Bennett and Holder had some things in common. Both had put in time at the Justice Department's Public Integrity Section, pursuing wrongdoers among the wielders of power. In their off-hours, they had played pickup basketball together. But their styles differed. Holder tended to be restrained and correct. Jackie Bennett was more of a free-wheeling operator. A big, husky man who had played tackle on his college football team, he used his bulk to intimidate recalcitrant witnesses. While some of his colleagues at Starr's office had given up their pursuit of the Clintons, discouraged by the frustrations of the Whitewater inquiry, and found lucrative spots in private practice, Bennett seemed to become more determined and dedicated than ever. And now at last he was convinced that he was onto something, a lead that would finally break through barriers of dissemblance and deception that he believed had so far shielded the Clintons in the Whitewater probe.

Bennett's excitement and intensity came across in the brief phone conversation. "We are sort of into a sensitive matter," Bennett told Holder. The information was still developing, he said, adding, "It involves people at and associated with the White House." The FBI already had been called on to help. The inquiry was "highly sensitive," he emphasized. "We need to meet with you in person."

Holder said nothing while he collected his thoughts. At moments like this he tried to draw on the lessons he had learned during his twenty-year law career. He had been raised and educated through law school in New

York City, where his father, an immigrant from Barbados, sold real estate and his mother kept house. In 1976, when he was barely twenty-five, he had come to Washington to work in the Justice Department, then served five years on the D.C. bench as a Superior Court Judge before Clinton made him U.S. Attorney for the District of Columbia. Five years later came his big opportunity to be Reno's deputy.

He was used to sensitive investigations, first in the Public Integrity Section at the Justice Department, where he prosecuted a Philadelphia judge and a Florida insurance commissioner, both of whom had taken money they should not have. Later, as a U.S. attorney, his first target had been the tarnished baron of Capitol Hill, Daniel Rostenkowski, the congressman from Illinois who was indicted on corruption charges in 1994. "People were afraid that Eric Holder might back down," Janet Reno had recalled at Holder's swearing in as deputy attorney general a few months earlier. "People didn't know Eric Holder, didn't know that he was committed to doing the right thing, regardless of the consequences, and he was going to do it the right way."

Rostenkowski had come to Congress when Dwight Eisenhower was still in the White House and most people were sure he would stay until he was good and ready to leave. As chairman of the House Ways and Means Committee he exuded clout. But Holder pushed him against the wall and sent him to federal prison. He had been a big tree to fell. Now Holder sensed from his conversation with Bennett, as much from the tension in his voice as in the words he uttered, that he would be walking in even taller timber now. And he knew that whatever he did here might jeopardize his delicate relations with the White House. But he also knew he could not disregard the urgency of Bennett's request. Holder was in a pickle.

Gauging Holder's concern from his hesitation in responding, Bennett felt impelled to break the silence. "I know this is vague," he said. "I apologize."

"No kidding," Holder replied. He had recovered from his initial shock at Bennett's veiled revelation and now began to think clearly and respond professionally.

"Can I call the AG?"

Now it was Bennett's turn to hesitate. He wanted to believe that Holder would respond as a lawyer, not as a politician. But Holder's boss, Attorney General Janet Reno, was another matter. For the past six years, through one embarrassment after another, she had stood loyally by the president, at no small cost to her own prestige and reputation. Bennett, with the paranoia characteristic of all investigators, had to consider her a potential threat to his nascent inquiry. Yet as a practical matter he knew he could not impose unreasonable conditions on the man on the other end of the line.

"I don't want to tell you not to," he offered.

"Jackie, this is Eric," Holder said, reminding the prosecutor that they went back a long way together.

"I know that," Bennett conceded, "but this is dicey enough. I called *you*," Bennett said, by his stress on the personal pronoun implying his mistrust of others in the Justice Department.

In the end, Bennett got from Holder what he wanted. A promise to meet the next night in Holder's office to discuss the "sensitive matter" he had mentioned.

Preparing for that visit with Holder, Bennett and the other senior lawyers from the independent counsel's office could hardly be faulted for feeling a measure of excitement, even grim satisfaction. More than once over the preceding four years, as they met with frustration after frustration, it had seemed such a day might never come. Then a flurry of telephone calls over a long weekend produced the information that gave Bennett reason to seek this meeting. The gist of it was that President Clinton had carried on a clandestine affair with a young White House intern named Monica Lewinsky. But the secrecy that had shrouded their liaison was now threatened because Lewinsky had been subpoenaed in the long-pending Paula Jones sexual harassment suit against Clinton and was being asked to lie about their relationship to protect the president.

Starr's team could hardly believe their good fortune. Murder and mayhem generally get the headlines and bring glory to cops. But men and women who make their living enforcing the law know that white-collar crime is the toughest nut of all to crack. The perpetrators are often persons of wealth, privilege, and power, well able to fend off the minions of the law. The circumstances of their suspected wrongdoing are always murky and shaded in gray rather than outlined in stark black and white.

And a heads-up about a crime still in progress is almost unheard of. "Usually in white-collar crime, you arrive and the body is already dead," one of Starr's subordinates said. "This was an ongoing enterprise. It was like we got a tip there's going to be a bank robbery and if you're outside, you're going to see guys going in with ski masks," he added. And what no one on Starr's team could forget was that one of the guys in a ski mask was alleged to be the President of the United States. No wonder then that the investigators sensed that with this lead they now had a chance to make history.

They could not have imagined, however, the impact of the history they would create. The information that Jackie Bennett would take to the Justice Department would set off one of the great commotions in the annals of twentieth-century America. The fierce constitutional and political battle to come would not only threaten Clinton's own future and stain his legacy but in addition shake the institution of the presidency to its foundations. Also unleashed would be an even more impassioned struggle— one over moral standards and individual behavior that would give a new dimension to the Culture War that had raged nonstop in American politics since the 1960s, the longest sustained struggle over culture and politics in the nation's history.

Arrayed on one side in the clash over impeachment would be conservatives bent on ridding the country of Clinton because they viewed him as embodying the erosion of values rooted in the turbulent Sixties. The "nub of the question" raised by the charges against Clinton, Republican Representative Bob Inglis would claim on the floor of the House, is, "Does the truth matter or is everything relative? Is there any truth or is my truth different than your truth?"

Rising up in the president's defense would be liberals who feared the assault on Clinton would demolish the advances made by feminism, gay rights, and other lifestyle changes wrought by the baby boom generation.

Speaking of Clinton's right-wing foes, Harvard University law professor and defense lawyer Alan Dershowitz would say, "I think they are dangerous. . . . I think they would like to impose a theocracy on America, they would like to have thought police and sex police."

In theory at least, politics and culture exist in two separate domains. The world of politics is ruled by governance, the making and mending and enforcing of the laws that order American society. Culture's realm is the social order, customs, manners, values and mores, how Americans feel about themselves and each other and how they behave in their personal lives. In the real world, just by the very nature of things in a country with tens of millions of inhabitants with competing needs and concerns, the distinction between culture and politics is hard to maintain, particularly during times of stress and change.

One such period occurred following World War I when Americans, uneasy with their country's new role as a world power, had also to confront tensions at home between several opposing forces: a polyglot flood of immigrants and the old stock citizenry, the settled countryside and encroaching urban centers, and deep-rooted religious faith, along with its concomitant values, and the tides of change spurred by commerce and technology. Those were turbulent times as culture spilled over and at times dominated politics. Prohibition and its attendant by-products, the speakeasy and the gambler, split the nation between Wets and Drys. These tensions engulfed the Democratic Party and turned its 1924 nominating convention into the longest, and up until that time, most acrimonious and self-destructive in political history. The very next year, Americans were transfixed by the drama that took place in a courtroom in a little town in Tennessee that no one had ever heard of. There Clarence Darrow argued the case for evolution against William Jennings Bryan, who defended the story for creation as set forth in the Bible. In 1928 Al Smith's candidacy for president, the first by a citizen of Catholic faith, set the tradition-bound Protestants of the rural South and West and the teeming immigrant masses of the cities at each other's throats. The white-sheeted Knights of the Ku Klux Klan marched down main streets across the land and rode out at night, leaving flaming crosses in their wake.

Over time these cultural conflicts subsided, not so much because they were resolved but rather because they were overshadowed by the Great Depression and the Second World War. These two seismic events brought with them overpowering impulses for national unity and survival which transcended cultural differences, but which dissolved with the return of peace and relative prosperity. In the years after World War II sweeping social and economic changes sowed the seeds for a renewal of cultural conflict in the political arena, in some ways different and in some ways similar to what had gone before.

During the postwar decades Americans became a people on the move, in several directions at once—upward, in educational as well as in economic status; outward, from the cities to the suburbs; and westward and southward, to the inviting climes of the Sunbelt states. Between 1940 and 1960 the population jumped by more than one-third, from 132 million to 179 million, with nearly all of the growth in the metropolitan areas of big cities. During the same twenty-year period the gross national product increased fivefold, from $100 billion to more than $500 billion, and family income soared. Educational levels advanced. More Americans completed high school and more went on to college, and even to graduate school, than ever before.

Changing constituencies with increasingly complex interests made it harder for party leaders to define and dominate the political debate. Voters with higher levels of education and more leisure time to find out things for themselves declared themselves independent. Compounding the other difficulties of the old bosses, the mass media, riding a wave of technology, had taken control of political communication. "Men still talk to each other," the social scientists Joseph Bensman and Bernard Rosenberg observed. "But what we say to each other is very often no more than an extension of facts and feelings relayed to us by the mass media."

Debate over so-called substantive issues became moot because of a sort of vicious circle. Since politicians could not mobilize support, they could not deliver on promises; since they could not keep their promises, they could not find supporters. Searching for ways to win votes, politicians turned to cultural concerns that stirred the emotions and passions.

And the citizenry, with their world in ferment and flux, resorted to politics to promote their own cultural values and to defend them against hostile forces.

It is the mission of this book to visit the events that have been the main flash points in the collision of culture and politics over the past four decades, the most deeply rooted and far reaching in importance. In doing so, I will try to explain the most encompassing of the grievances and forces on each side as well as the principal personalities who have shaped these episodes, demonstrating how their political roles both reflected and shaped the cultural environment. The narrative begins with the struggle over President Clinton's impeachment which complicated Eric Holder's career. But this battle had its roots in "the Sixties," that tumultuous decade which actually stretched for almost twenty years, from the mid-Fifties into the early Seventies, and pitted a resentful and raucous younger generation against a grimly determined middle class.

In reexamining the Sixties, it is useful to consider how much some things about cultural politics have changed during the course of the century, and how much some other things have stayed the same. The controversy over the teaching of evolution that consumed the nation in 1925 was renewed by Ronald Reagan in his 1980 drive for the presidency and returned to confront George W. Bush and Al Gore in their 2000 contest. Yet the bigotry of 1928 that hounded Al Smith, the first Catholic to run for president, had no echoes in the reaction to Joseph Lieberman, the first Jew to run on a national ticket in 2000. On the other hand, the national capacity for outrage on both sides of cultural issues which scarred and split the nation in those bygone days seems in no way to have diminished in the current battles over the cultural issues that divide the country in the new millennium.

The cultural skirmishes of the Twenties were purely domestic in origin while the Culture War that started in the Sixties was linked to the disastrous war in Vietnam. Still, the protest movement against the war took its cues from the civil-rights revolution and embodied a panoply of other domestic cultural forces, notably the drive for sexual liberation. All this ferment triggered a prolonged conflict with strong generational overtones, reaching an apotheosis in the 1968 Democratic Convention in Chicago when Richard Daley squared off against Abbie Hoffman in a battle that took a heavy toll on both sides.

But if the youthful protesters began the Culture War they did not finish it. They were met with a counter-onslaught. The first blows came from the middle class, mobilized first by Richard Nixon, who hailed it as the Silent Majority, and then reenergized behind Ronald Reagan, the Great Communicator. And its numbers were enlarged by the return to the political arena, led by the likes of Pat Robertson, of millions of Christian conservatives, some of whose not-too-distant forebears undoubtedly cheered for Bryan in his contest against Darrow and donned hoods and robes to march with the Klan against Al Smith.

The political victories achieved by this counterrevolutionary force would bring about a cultural transformation of the Democratic Party which helped pave Bill Clinton's path to the White House. This makeover began after the 1988 presidential campaign when the party suffered its third consecutive presidential defeat, a string of debacles unmatched in sixty years. Democrats had blamed their first two presidential defeats in the Eighties on the magic of Ronald Reagan, whose talents as a political performer they joined in praising as a way of excusing their own failings. They also held culpable their last president, Jimmy Carter, whose ineptitude during his ill-fated four-year tenure was blamed for wrecking the nation's economy at home and lowering its prestige abroad.

But this formula failed to explain what happened in 1988. Reagan was gone from the scene, memories of Carter had faded, and the Republicans chose as their standard-bearer a dithering, aging preppy given to spastic outbursts of mangled sentence fragments. Nevertheless, George Bush easily bested the Democratic nominee, Michael Dukakis.

Clinton's victory in 1992 was made possible largely by a strategy devised by Democratic pollster Stanley Greenberg, who, in response to Dukakis's defeat, sought to help the Democrats regain ground they had lost in the Culture War during the past generation. Greenberg had been frustrated by Dukakis's failure to respond to the cultural attacks mounted against him by George Bush. Greenberg's research in this area had begun after the 1984 election. In overwhelming Walter Mondale that year Reagan drained blue-collar voters, Catholics, and southern whites away from their traditional home in the Democratic Party, creating a new coalition of his own.

What was striking about this group of voters, Greenberg found, was that they had turned to Reagan even though they objected to some of his most significant economic policies, including his tax cuts, which, as the Democrats liked to say, favored the rich and were the foundation of Reaganomics. "He has guts," the blue-collar defectors told Greenberg about Reagan. Others said, "He's honest"; "He shoots from the hip, but whatever he says he will stick by"; "He has very high morals"; "Reagan is straight as an arrow. He reminds you of John Wayne."

Despite their sharp policy quarrels with Reagan, these voters saw in him, in contrast to Democrat Mondale, "a sense of strength and unity that is more important than specifics," Greenberg concluded. Though lacking Reagan's combination of charisma and convictions, Bush, in 1988, had picked up on these cultural themes where Reagan left off by pounding away at Dukakis's values. Focusing on several alleged blemishes on Dukakis's gubernatorial record—his veto of the law requiring teachers to lead their classes in the Pledge of Allegiance, his opposition to capital punishment, and the weekend furlough he had granted to convicted killer Willie Horton—Bush sought to define his opponent as outside of what Bush called "the mainstream" of American beliefs and values—to demonstrate, in other words, that he was not culturally fit to be president.

As a consultant to Dukakis, Greenberg had tried to warn him of the disastrous image Bush was painting, but Dukakis shrugged him off. Indeed, Clinton himself, as he later said, told Dukakis, "Where I come from people won't vote for you for President if they think you don't like to pledge allegiance to the flag." But again Dukakis shrugged off the advice.

But now Greenberg was determined that the next Democratic nominee would benefit from the error of Dukakis's ways. In the wake of Dukakis's defeat, Greenberg pointed out in a landmark article in *American Prospect*, which would have a profound impact on the Clinton campaign, that Dukakis's inarticulateness in the face of Bush's assault had left

Lee Atwater's "savage caricature" as the dominant image of the Democratic Party.

It was a political party, as depicted by Bush and Atwater, that was short on patriotism, weak on defense, soft on criminals and minorities, indifferent to work values and family. It was a party, Greenberg wrote, that could now depend really only on Jewish, black, and Hispanic voters. The historic models for the party's liberals, the New Deal and the Great Society, had become discredited and irrelevant. Yet Greenberg's surveys on 1988 voting turned up the same paradoxical pattern he uncovered in his studies of the 1984 Mondale-Reagan campaign. Even though the country was supposedly caught up in a pervasive conservative mood, Greenberg's data showed that voters favored an activist agenda for government, supported more spending for a range of supposedly out-of-favor social programs, from day care to Social Security to AIDS research, and wanted to help pay for it by boosting taxes on corporate polluters and the wealthy.

What was needed to take advantage of these liberal impulses, Greenberg argued, was a new model to replace the New Deal and the Great Society, a model which could be made vital and compelling by linking it to the nation's common cultural experience "and explaining it with a convincing story which could reach the middle class voters who had left the party." "Middle class voters, the heart of American culture," he continued, "saw themselves as squeezed between the rich and the poor, neither of whom play by the rules, but seek their rewards through short cuts and special claims—tax breaks, windfalls, and welfare." Even though they "play by the rules," he said, middle-class voters believed they were getting few of the benefits. From this diagnosis emerged the New Democrat model for the 1990s, which Bill Clinton rode into the White House.

Greenberg's new paradigm consisted not only of a policy agenda—proposals such as health care, education, and welfare reform, most of which had been part of the Democratic canon since Jimmy Carter—but also a "convincing story," in Greenberg's phraseology. And this story, constructed of clues from Greenberg's polling, relied heavily on cultural values as embodied by Clinton for emotional impact.

The seed work for Clinton's campaign began long before the official announcement of his candidacy when the Democratic Leadership Council (DLC), the self-styled centrist group which Clinton had helped found after Mondale's defeat, designed its new Democratic Agenda. Proclaimed in 1990, it affirmed support for "the moral and cultural values that most Americans share." Al From, president of the DLC, explained, "We wanted to make it clear that Democrats believed in those values."

Echoing Greenberg, Clinton and other DLC leaders argued that Dukakis's failure to make that point clear had brought on his doom. To avoid repeating Dukakis's mistakes, Clinton had spelled out his New Democratic principles in an address to the DLC convention in the spring of 1991, a talk which would actually serve as the keynote for his as-yet unannounced candidacy. "Why have the Democrats been shut out of the White House for all these years?" Clinton asked. "I'll tell you why," he said. "Because too many of the people who used to vote for us, the very burdened middle class we're talking about, have not trusted us in national elections to defend our national interests abroad, to put their values in our social policy at home or to take their tax money and spend it with discipline."

To get back into the good graces of the electorate, Clinton urged his party to lean heavily on cultural themes. Democrats, he said, must insist on greater responsibility from citizens—for example, welfare mothers. "We must demand that everybody who can go to work do it," Clinton said. "For work is the best social program this country has ever devised." His performance was more of a sermon than a political speech. It was part of an effort to rehabilitate the Democrats' reputation as cultural scalawags. Mainly Clinton wanted to convince the "middle class," i.e., white voters—only once since FDR left the White House, in LBJ's 1964 landslide, had their party won a majority of the white vote—that at last Democrats had broken with the soft-headed permissiveness that had marked their past.

That speech and similar Clinton utterances during this period leading up to the announcement of his candidacy were designed to inoculate Clinton against the kind of cultural warfare Bush had waged on Dukakis.

But still another, more specific, type of cultural inoculation was needed—against revelations of the womanizing that had long marked Clinton's personal life and had even kept him from running for president four years earlier.

In the past when this issue had been raised, Clinton had brushed off the questions, contending that candidates should be allowed "a privacy zone." But that defense had not really settled anything, and now that he was about to formally declare himself, his advisers convinced him that something more ought to be done—all the more so because any hint of personal scandal would certainly undercut his appeal to the middle class and give ammunition to the GOP's culture warriors.

In midsummer he arranged to be the guest at a press breakfast in Washington, surprising his hosts by bringing with him his wife Hillary. Clinton was clearly braced for questions about his personal life, and when the first one was asked, he jumped on it like a cleanup hitter going after a fat pitch. First he dismissed the question as unworthy of discussion in a presidential campaign. "This is the sort of thing they were interested in (in) Rome when they were in decline, too," he said. Then, with Hillary Rodham Clinton at his side, he laid down his position:

> What you need to know is that we have been together for almost 20 years and have been married almost 16, and we are committed to our marriage and its obligations, to our child and to each other. We love each other very much. Like nearly anybody that's been together 20 years, our relationship has not been perfect or free of difficulties. But we feel good about where we are. We believe in our obligations. And we intend to be together 30 or 40 years from now, regardless whether I run for president or not. And I think that ought to be enough.

And yet the problem would not go away. It was not only the journalists who were interested in Clinton's past. So were the leaders of his party. "A lot of us are worried that this could turn out to be a problem," Jeff Neubauer, the Wisconsin Democratic state chairman and a Clinton admirer, told me, referring to Clinton's womanizing. "If this stuff is going to come out we would rather it come out now than when he is so far in front that it would be too late to do anything about it."

Which is more or less what happened. The "stuff" Neubauer feared about Clinton's extramarital activities came to light—his alleged relationship with a Little Rock nightclub singer named Gennifer Flowers. And so did other "stuff" that Neubauer had not even imagined, disclosing Clinton's tortured but ultimately successful efforts to avoid military service while the Vietnam War raged. And yet Neubauer and his Democratic colleagues concluded that it was too late to turn their backs on Clinton, whom polls showed to be well in front in New Hampshire's first-in-the-nation presidential primary, and whose face already was on the cover of the newsmagazines. It was a decision that was less reflective of their commitment to tolerance and fair play than of their dedication to avoiding controversy and their fear of deserting a frontrunner.

Even with the willingness of the Democratic leadership to close their eyes to his past behavior, Clinton would not have survived the womanizing controversy without the forceful support of his wife and future First Lady. Fully as ambitious as her husband, Hillary Rodham Clinton had promised him in advance that she would stand by him if scandal broke to defend his White House candidacy. And she proved to be as good as her word, providing him with the cover he needed to withstand the onslaught of the Republican culture warriors. "From my perspective, our marriage is a strong marriage. We love each other," she said in response to a question planted by Clinton aides during the New Hampshire primary. "We support each other and we have had a lot of strong and important experiences together that have meant a lot to us. In any marriage, there are issues that come up between two people who are married that I think are their business."

Blessed with remarkably weak opposition, and bolstered by the reluctance of political leaders to resist inertia, Clinton stumbled through to the nomination. But he was "damaged goods," as his pollster, Stanley Greenberg, later admitted, and to repair that damage, his advisers set out by hook and by crook to change the public's view of his cultural values. Clinton himself played the dominant role in this makeover. Whereas once he had complained that "too much of this election has been about me," now he could hardly get enough of himself into his speeches. At every turn he stressed his humble origins and the fortitude he displayed in rising above such handicaps. "My life is a testament to the fact that the American dream works," he cried in the idiom of the middle class. "I got to live by the rules that work in America and I wound up here today running for President of the United States of America."

Once in office, Clinton's behavior pattern continued. The old allegations, though never fully resolved, seemed to fade in the public's mind, yet they were replaced by a flood of new charges. But as the controversy surrounding Clinton shifted from Gennifer Flowers and the draft to Paula Jones and the assortment of alleged misdeeds falling under the rubric of Whitewater, Clinton continued to maintain that his critics were trying to distract him from serving the good of the middle class.

"Our internal mantra was 'public values trump private character,'"—a refined version of the formula that had worked ever since Gennifer Flowers and the draft—George Stephanopoulos later recalled. "For us it was now an article of faith that Clinton could overcome personal attacks as long as he kept addressing the 'real problems of real people.'" Thus, in the face of the contradictory disclosures of his conduct, Clinton continued to present himself as the champion of middle-class people "who play by the rules," a phrase right out of his pollster's lexicon.

Godliness was also part of Clinton's middle-class values mantra as he extended the presidential bully pulpit to the clerical pulpit, where he often deplored how far national life had strayed from the influence of the Almighty. "I think God wants us to sit down and talk to one another and see what values we share and see how we can put them inside the millions and millions of Americans who are living in chaos," Clinton told fellow Yale Law School alumni. He called for a national discussion of religious values to help "heal this land." In a television interview he lamented the "decline of the family," and told religious journalists that the United States needed "almost a spiritual change" to fight violence. At a National Prayer Breakfast Clinton talked of the need for humility, honesty, and forgiveness in politics: "Sometimes I think the commandment we most like to overlook in this city is 'Thou shall not bear false witness.'"

"He may well be the greatest practitioner of civil religion and of public theology of any president we've ever had," said Clemson University political scientist Charles Dunn, editor of the anthology *American Political Theology.*

On occasion Clinton seemed to contradict himself with his own words. Early in his first term in a talk to junior high school students in Washington's inner city, the president made a moving plea for sexual restraint and family values, stressing that sex was not "sport" but a "solemn responsibility." But five days later, talking to autoworkers in Shreveport, Louisiana, Clinton recalled owning a pickup truck with Astroturf in the back. Amid laughter from the audience, Clinton added: "You don't want to know why, but I did." Later he tried to explain away the lubricious implications of that remark. "I carried my luggage back there," he said. "It wasn't for what everybody thought it was for when I made the comment, I can tell you that."

And so Clinton's efforts to make himself into a symbol of middle-class culture went on in the face of evidence to the contrary. "What we have tried to do and what Clinton has tried to do with us is articulate values which are the underpinning of a public agenda," Al From, head of the Democratic Leadership Council, which had helped to develop Clinton's middle-class appeal, told me. "I think he's changed the agenda dramatically in the way he's conducted his office. I'm not going to talk about his personal conduct."

But if From and his compatriots would rather not discuss Clinton's personal conduct, there were some politicians who never wearied of the subject. They were the leaders of the Christian Right, and for them, Clinton, warts and all, but especially the disfigurements of his personal behavior, had become a powerful motivating force—a rallying point to draw millions into the political arena.

2

GOD'S OWN GUERRILLA

"I paint my face and travel at night," Ralph Reed said while he was building his army of Christian Crusaders. "You don't know it's over until you're in a body bag. You don't know until election night."

Afterward, when trying to cast himself as a born-again moderate, Reed had reason to regret such macho posturing. But his words captured the spirit of his early leadership in the Culture War. If his rhetoric sounded ruthless and out of keeping with his altar-boy visage, it was because he modeled himself after his cultural enemies, who as he saw it let little stand in the way of their thrust for power. Barely out of his teens when he arrived in Washington and became head of the College Republicans, he and his activist cohorts pored over the works of such left-wing prophets of protest as Saul Alinsky and Tom Hayden and sought to emulate their impact. "We viewed ourselves as the mirror image of the leaders of the New Left of the Sixties," Reed said. "We saw ourselves as building a new generational consciousness that was pro-Reagan, conservative, very aggressive, very creative."

Born in Portsmouth, Virginia, the second of three children of a Navy doctor, Reed spent his formative years in the Bible Belt of northwest Georgia. In his first campaign, running for student council president at Cutler Ridge Junior High School in the small town of Toccoa, he threw away a prepared speech to a student group and spoke extemporaneously. "I learned I had an ability to connect with an audience—that moment when you know you have to say what they need to hear," he recalled. It was a skill he never lost as he began his climb up the conservative political ladder. Early in the game, Reed, who had been raised in a devout Methodist family, concluded that his own lifestyle as a smoker and social drinker did not conform to the family values he was urging on the electorate. He made what he called "a faith commitment" in 1983, when he began regularly attending an evangelical church in the Washington suburbs and gave up drinking and smoking. One thing did not change—his vocation as a political operative. "I'm a political strategist," he said. "I just happen to be a committed Christian."

His career took a decisive turn in 1989 when Reed, then a graduate student in history at Atlanta's Emory University, met the religious broadcaster and erstwhile presidential candidate Pat Robertson, with whom he shared his ideas about the organizing potential of the Christian Right. Robertson was impressed enough to ask Reed to head a new group that would enlist the involvement of activists who had toiled for his losing 1988 presidential bid. They called it the Christian Coalition.

Reed realized from the first that he could not afford to depend on some other organization's mailing lists. The key to the Coalition's future, he believed, was grassroots organizing. The Moral Majority and other Christian Right groups had tried this tactic since 1980—and even before. Reed just did it better because he was a political organizer at heart. Starting with the remnants of Robertson's failed presidential campaign as a nucleus, Reed reached out to conservative parents disheartened with their local schools' disregard for their own values. Not only was prayer banned, but sex education classes that often emphasized condoms instead of abstinence had been introduced, along with courses seeking to familiarize youngsters with gay lifestyles. Reed's genius was to convert the discomfort these families felt with their schools and other elements of the rapidly coarsening popular culture into the fuel to drive political campaigns. Using voter guides and legislative scorecards—backed up by the technology of phone, fax, computer, and satellite dish—sifting through church directories to develop phone lists, and distributing material in church parking lots on the eve of the elections, Reed steadily built his army. Within a year the Coalition had 125 chapters and 57,000 members nationally and was ready to take on its tasks of rewarding and punishing elective officials according to how they rated on the Christian Coalition's own scorecard.

Along with the nuts-and-bolts labor in the fields, Reed was aided by the energies that had been mobilized by Robertson's candidacy. When Ronald Reagan, hero of the Christian Right, departed the political scene in 1988, he left his supporters fragmented and confused. By running for president in 1988, even though his effort fell short, Robertson kept hopes and spirits up among members of the Christian Right. Beyond that, Reed contended, Robertson did for religious conservatives what Barry Goldwater, Reagan's predecessor as icon of the Right, had done for secular conservatives during his presidential campaign in 1964. In Reed's view, broadened by a Ph.D. in history from Emory, political movements have to run and lose to learn what it takes to win. Robertson "was a midwife who took what was largely a social protest movement and transformed it into a political movement that elects candidates."

Perhaps just as important, although certainly unintended, was the help Reed and his allies got from Bill Clinton. Clinton's emergence as a particularly controversial president came at a particularly auspicious time—just as the Christian Right was trying to shake off the effects of Bush's 1992 defeat and shed the blame many Republicans assigned to its ranks for that debacle. Clinton immediately became the prime target of the Christian Right.

For the faithful of the Christian Right those 1992 returns had represented their darkest hour. The blow fell even harder because the election was the first setback most had experienced since being drawn into politics on Ronald Reagan's 1980 coattails. Reagan's landslide reelection, and Bush's triumph in 1988, made some analysts speak of a Republican "lock" on the electoral college—and that of course was good news for the Christian Right, since the vast majority of its members had found a home in the GOP.

Few were prepared for Bush's ignominious defeat at the hands of a politician whose dossier of draft dodging and womanizing mocked all their basic values. Democrats themselves had no trouble figuring out the reason for this turn in political fortunes. "It's the economy, stupid," was the watchword of their campaign. And they had little difficulty finding fault with Bush's handling of economic policy as Americans suffered through a vicious recession. A grim new term, "downsizing," crept into the public's vocabulary, and familiar ones, like "bankruptcy," took on a more urgent meaning.

Nevertheless, many in the media, and in their own Republican Party, pointed the finger at the cultural conservatives as accessories to Bush's downfall, citing the strident rhetoric from their leaders at the 1992 nominating convention at Houston. For this, Bush and his strategists had partly themselves to blame. Uneasy about dealing with the Christian Right and other cultural conservatives, whom they had mainly ignored during the 1988 general election campaign, and worried about Bush's faltering candidacy, the Bush high command tried to make amends by allowing conservative leaders to sound off at the convention. Patrick Buchanan set the ferocious tone by declaring: "There is a religious war going on in this country for the soul of America." Then, using a term few Americans had heard before, he declared: "It is a cultural war, as critical to the kind of nation we shall be as the Cold War itself. And in this struggle for the soul of America, Clinton and Clinton are on the other side and George Bush is on our side."

Though not quite as bellicose, other cultural conservatives also bared their teeth. Pat Robertson denounced Bill Clinton's values, warning that Clinton's election would undermine the American family. The Democratic nominee, he charged, would "make sexual preference a privileged minority under our civil rights laws" and was "running on a platform that calls for saving the spotted owl, but never once mentions the name of God." Marilyn Quayle's combative speech, which raised once again the old dividing lines of the 1960s between those who joined the counterculture and those who did not, managed to attack both Bill Clinton and Hillary Rodham Clinton, at least by inference. She criticized Vietnam War protesters and dope smokers, which took care of Bill Clinton. She then dealt with Hillary's well-established determination not to be a homebody by contrasting career women with women who "love being mothers or wives, which gives our lives a richness that few men or women get from professional accomplishment alone."

Trying to sustain the mood after the convention ended, House Republican Whip Newt Gingrich, another icon of the Christian Right, sought to exploit the then much-publicized custody battle between Woody Allen and his former inamorata Mia Farrow. Alluding to Allen's profession of love for one of Farrow's adopted daughters as reflecting the "weird values" represented by the Democratic opposition, Gingrich declared, while stumping for Bush: "Woody Allen having non-incest with a non-daughter to whom he was a non-father because they were a non-family fits the Democratic platform perfectly."

Immediately after the convention a hue and cry went up denouncing the voices of the Right for the harshness of their rhetoric. "We saw very clearly that the emergent power of the Republican party is the Religious Right," contended the television producer Norman Lear, who had founded People for the American Way, to challenge Christian conservatives and turn their ties to the Republicans against the GOP. "So strong was their grip on the convention that even the party's nominee, a sitting President, was forced to accept platform planks he didn't particularly want."

"Instead of political debate, we had religious warfare," charged Susan Estrich, who had managed 1988 Democratic standard-bearer Michael Dukakis's losing presidential campaign. "God was invoked. The opposition was damned. In this atmosphere, gay men and lesbian women have become the Willie Hortons of 1992." And so on and so forth. In the days after the convention, with Bush's poll ratings sinking and condemnation of the Houston convention mounting, one Christian Right organizer later complained, "If there was a cat that died in Houston that week, we were blamed for it."

But after the first bitter pangs of defeat had eased, Christian activists found solace in a closer scrutiny of the election returns. A team of four scholars, led by James L. Guth and John C. Green, produced a series of analyses of voting results that contravened the conventional wisdom. Critics of the Houston convention had contended that the hard right rhetoric that dominated that conclave hurt Bush by chasing away moderate voters. But the research by Guth and Green concluded that this rhetoric spoke to the concerns of Christian activists, without whose wholehearted support Bush might have done worse. Indeed, in the 1992 election, white evangelicals made up Bush's strongest constituency, and among those who did not vote for Bush in 1988 but did support him in 1992, social issues seemed to have been a major reason for their support. Even more important for the future, their research showed that as the campaign wore on, more and more white evangelicals identified with the Republican Party. Bush did not on balance lose votes because of his social issue appeals, according to this study. He did lose moderates compared to 1988, but most of these voters had deserted him because they were troubled by the slumping economy—and not because of the harsh rhetoric of the convention.

At the end of the day, the fact that their community had stuck together and supported Bush, even in a losing cause, gave leaders of the Christian Right reason for confidence as they looked forward to the first major electoral test of the Clinton presidency, the 1994 midterm elections. Even though the president himself would not be on the ballot, the elections offered a way to demonstrate their disapproval of him and all his works.

Clinton had started off his presidency wooing religious leaders in general. His first official act as president was to attend an ecumenical prayer service attended by an army of clerics. Nearly every Sunday the television news shows depicted him leaving services at Washington's Foundry United Methodist Church, the choice of First Lady Hillary Rodham Clinton, clutching his Bible. Not only did Clinton cultivate mainline religious leaders, he tried to reach out to conservative Christians by prevailing upon prominent evangelical clergy to provide him spiritual guidance—contacts he made certain were well publicized.

Yet all this was of little avail with the Christian Right, whose resentment of the Southern Baptist president mounted as his tenure lengthened. Not only did his public professions of religiosity not mollify them, it added to their fury at what they viewed as Clinton's blatant hypocrisy—his attempts to exploit the values that were at the heart of Christian belief for his own political advantage.

"Clinton very much wants to be a leader in moral terms," pointed out William Bennett, author of the best-selling *The Book of Virtues* and one of the heroes of the Christian Right. "He thinks of the pantheon of great

American Presidents and wants to be in their company and knows that moral leadership is part of that. As he is drawn to it he speaks of it," Bennett told me. "As he speaks of it, he will be judged."

Evangelicals found reason to judge him harshly. They noted that despite his occasional gestures in their direction, when it came to religion Clinton leaned toward the camp of the Protestant establishment, with its progressive views on cultural issues. Evangelicals found few kindred spirits among Clinton's appointees, whose ranks were studded with figures from the cultural Left, members of ethnic and religious minorities, and a sprinkling of gays.

A particular object of conservative indignation was Clinton's surgeon general Joycelyn Elders, who in addition to advocating abortion rights, sex education, and condom distribution argued that decriminalization should be considered a possible solution to the problem of drug abuse. Also stirring suspicion was the frequent consorting of both Clintons with Hollywood celebrities, many of whom were viewed by conservative Christians as corruptors of the culture.

The president's policy initiatives added to their indignation—his advocacy of gays in the military, even though he had retreated from his original proposal; his steadfast support for a woman's untrammeled right to abortion; along with his liberal positions on other social issues such as feminism and sex education.

In their resentment of Clinton, the Christian conservative attack sometimes seemed to lack any restraint. Pat Robertson seized upon the unanswered questions surrounding the suicide of former White House deputy counsel Vincent Foster to suggest that Foster had really been murdered, implying that Clinton himself had something to do with it. Jerry Falwell's Liberty Alliance, the successor group to his Moral Majority, sponsored a video called *Circle of Power* that included footage of news conferences by Gennifer Flowers supporting her claim that Clinton had been her lover, and of Paula C. Jones, the former Arkansas employee who had charged him with sexual harassment. Also featured were charges by Larry Nichols, one of Clinton's longtime Arkansas adversaries, that Clinton had somehow been connected with the fates of "countless and countless people" who had been foolhardy enough to oppose the then governor and then had "mysteriously died."

The excessiveness of these attacks gave the Democrats an opportunity to make political capital by embarrassing the Republicans, playing on the fears of the Christian Right by their own constituents. First, Representative Vic Fazio of California, chairman of the Democratic Congressional Campaign Committee, assailed "the aggressive political tactics of the religious right" and contended in a talk to a party gathering that Republicans had to choose between "accepting or denouncing the radical right's strategies." Then, in a speech to a lesbian and gay conference in New York, Dr. Joycelyn Elders, the U.S. Surgeon General, herself a frequent target of Christian Right barbs, attacked what she called the "un-Christian religious right."

But the biggest blast of all came from the top—Bill Clinton himself. Dialing into a radio call-in program from Air Force One, Clinton said he respected the religious convictions of all Americans and had strong religious beliefs himself. But he denounced those who "come into the political system" and say "that anybody that doesn't agree with them is godless, anyone who doesn't agree with them is not a good Christian, anyone who doesn't agree with them is fair game for any wild charge, no matter how false, for any kind of personal, demeaning attack." Sounding an all-too-characteristic note of self-pity, Clinton claimed:

> I don't suppose there's any public figure that's ever been subject to any more violent personal attacks than I have, at least in modern history, anybody who's been President. And that's fine, I deal with them, but I don't believe that it's the work of God.
>
> I think that evangelical Christians should be good citizens, should be involved in our politics. They can be Republicans or Democrats. They can do whatever they want. But remember that Jesus threw the money changers out of the temple; he didn't try to take over the job of the money changers.

Such impassioned Democratic protests against the Christian Right's rhetoric brought equally passionate responses from Republican leaders, notably William Bennett, who cast the battle as raising the fundamental issues in the Culture War. "The attempt to discredit the conservative Christian movement is an attempt by some to discredit its underlying philosophy," Bennett charged. "Christianity makes normative claims; stands against moral relativism; is the antithesis of the modern age's worship of the self; and does not endorse unfettered freedom. Christianity is about right and wrong. And politics is, too." The exchange, Bennett concluded, was further evidence that "a cultural divide exists in this nation."

All this served to further energize the Christian Right as Election Day approached. By that fall Ralph Reed's computers in a nondescript office building just off Interstate 64 in Chesapeake, Virginia, counted 1.5 million supporters in the Christian Coalition's data bank, most of whom had been giving at least $15 a month since spring. Backing up the effort directed from this headquarters were 48 state units and 1,400 local chapters. At ground level some 17,000 neighborhood coordinators and 23,000 "church liaisons" distributed 33 million voter guides for congressional state and local contests, mostly to evangelical churchgoers. Nominally nonpartisan, to avoid the snares of the Federal Election Commission and the Internal Revenue Service, the guides left little doubt as to which candidates were friends and which were foes, based on their stands on such issues as abortion, education, pornography, and gay rights. The magazine *Campaign and Elections* reckoned that the Coalition's state affiliates dominated the GOP in eighteen states and wielded significant clout in at least a dozen more.

And the Coalition was just one cog in the alliance of Christian activist groups. Striving to become "the ACLU of the Right," the American Center for Law and Justice, another Pat Robertson offspring, used $6 million and some 200 affiliated attorneys across the country to litigate on behalf of such causes as public school prayer and antiabortion protests. Beverly LaHaye's Concerned Women for America claimed more members than the liberal National Organization for Women. James Dobson dispensed conservative child-rearing advice seasoned with morsels of political philosophy on his radio program, "Focus on the Family," carried by more than 1,600 radio stations.

At a two-day gathering in September 1994, with nearly every top Republican prospect for the party's 1996 presidential nomination in attendance, Reed rallied the Christian Coalition for the midterm vote in

November. "We stand on the threshold of one of the most important elections in post–World War II political history," he told the 3,000-plus cheering Christian activists in the ballroom of the Washington Hilton. "Our message is that we are fed up with Clinton-style liberalism." Pat Robertson predicted the election would serve as evidence of the rise of the Christian Coalition "to where God intends it to be in this nation, as one of the most powerful political forces that have ever been in the history of America."

Clinton's surgeon general, Joycelyn Elders, served as the symbol of the moral turpitude the president represented. "Any administration which has Joycelyn Elders in it has forfeited its right to moral seriousness," said William J. Bennett. And with its passion against Clinton fueling its efforts the Christian Right swept to victory in November.

From the beginning of the campaign the 1994 midterm election had loomed as an uphill march for Democrats and a golden opportunity for Republicans and their conservative Christian allies. The Democratic capture of the White House in 1992 meant that the 1994 campaign was the first midterm election since 1978 in which one party had full responsibility for both the presidency and the Congress. And strategists for both parties were well aware that not since 1934, when a grateful electorate rewarded Franklin D. Roosevelt and his Democrats for checking the ravages of the Great Depression, had the party controlling the White House failed to lose ground in a midterm election.

Moreover, polls indicated that the negative outlook of the electorate was far more pronounced than the normal midterm restiveness. One reason for this pervasive disgruntlement was the economy, the very issue that had carried Clinton and his party to victory in 1992. Despite the indicators suggesting a relatively strong recovery from the recession that had contributed to President Bush's defeat, wages, benefits, and living standards for the average worker continued to decline. And the lion's share of the rewards the economy was providing was going to a relatively narrow segment of the electorate—highly educated, affluent households—widening the sharp economic gulfs between different groups of Americans that Clinton had pledged to bridge during his campaign against Bush.

But the uneven economic progress was not all that was bothering the voters—and threatening Democrats. Pollsters and political scientists saw evidence of a national angst over social change and the erosion of traditional values. "This is the culmination of some very long term trends in American life which are just now finding their expression in electoral politics," said Ross Baker, Rutgers University specialist in congressional politics. Among the reasons for the sense of anomie, Baker cited "the introduction of drugs in American society on a massive scale, the spread of sexual permissiveness, the vulgarity of the media and the debasement of public language as we see it in this campaign."

Many Americans shared this distress, but the negative feelings ran particularly strong among conservative Christians. And they had no trouble tracing the root cause to the occupant of the highest office in the land. The combination of economic disappointment with cultural distress brought the GOP victory on a scale far beyond the wildest dreams of all but a few of its strategists. Before the vote, Democrats contended that the resentful mood of the electorate was really directed against incumbents in general, not just Democrats. But the GOP tide ran so strong that not a single Republican incumbent for major office—House, Senate, or governorship—was defeated, while Democratic incumbents were swept out of office on a wholesale basis.

As striking as was the Republican seizure of Senate control, the GOP's most dramatic success was in the House of Representatives. There Republicans gained 52 seats and took command of that branch for the first time since 1954 with a majority of 230, compared to 204 Democrats and one independent. The Republican gain was the biggest in an off-year election since the first postwar election of 1946, when resentment at the difficulties of converting the economy from a war footing helped the GOP capture 55 Democratic seats.

The role of conservative Christians in the downfall of the Democrats was hard to overstate. White evangelicals cast about one-third of all votes for Republican House candidates, and the overall community of religious conservatives (including conservative Roman Catholics) provided two of every five GOP votes. But the contribution of the Christian conservatives went beyond the votes they themselves cast to the organizing effort they mounted. By one informed estimate the Christian Right probably mobilized 4 million activists and reached 50 million voters—a performance that rivaled such traditional electoral powerhouses as gun owners and labor unions.

Entering at least 120 House races, one-third of all contested elections, the Christian Right saw the candidates it backed win 55 percent of these races. Of the races where the Christian Right–supported candidates won, 30 were settled by margins of 5 percent or less—small enough for Reed and his allies to claim they had helped make a difference. These 30 marginal winners were more than double the 13-seat majority by which the Republicans controlled the House. More than a score of the new Republican representatives had close ties to the Christian Right, and a good many were affiliated with evangelical churches and denominations.

Although most of his cohorts exulted in the victory, Reed, ever the realist, reacted with "foreboding," as he later recalled. "In the days after the 1994 campaign ebullient talk of 'our turn' and 'payback time,' filled the air," he said. Reed worried that the conquering conservatives "could walk into the booby trap of soaring expectations and negative press coverage before the new Congress had a chance to find its sea legs."

Reed's concerns turned out to be well founded. The conservative revolution proclaimed by Newt Gingrich in the wake of the election would die in infancy because the new Republican majorities on Capitol Hill would grossly overplay their hand. But the election did produce a revolution of sorts in the Clinton White House. The president moved drastically to the Right, more concerned with placating conservatives than with carrying out the activist promises of his 1992 campaign. Rejecting the populist rhetoric of the past, he launched no more bold initiatives like the health care reform proposal, which had died of its own weight in the summer before the election. Instead, as the 1996 presidential election approached, he signed into law a drastic welfare reform law which had strong support from religious conservatives but had been opposed by virtually all liberal religious organizations and many constituencies in his own party.

And on the cultural front the president dwelled more than ever on spiritual concerns. Less than three months after his party's midterm calamity, he summoned a group of reporters covering religion to the White House to inform them that he had just read the entire Book of Psalms, 150 hymns that praise God and often ask divine relief from sufferings inflicted by enemies. Friends, he said, had faxed him passages from Scripture on a daily basis as gestures of support.

"During this difficult period, a lot of people were giving me different Psalms to read," Clinton said. "It was amazing, and so I did." That same day, in a speech to the annual National Prayer Breakfast, the president criticized the use of harshly negative language in political discourse, a trend that he said had reached extreme levels. "The communications revolution gives words the power not only to lift up and liberate but the power to divide and destroy as never before—just words—to darken our spirits and weaken our resolve and divide our hearts," he said. Quoting from St. Paul's Letter to the Romans, Clinton said: "Repay no one evil for evil, but take thought for what is noble in the sight of all." Yet as Clinton himself ruefully conceded, no matter how many Psalms he read and quoted, he was unlikely to placate his foes among the Christian Right. "I think the truth is that there are people who don't believe it's genuine because they disagree with me politically," he said.

Clinton was about half right. His critics on the Christian Right did not believe him in part because they disagreed with him politically, but also because he had given them every good reason to doubt his sincerity. He was preaching Scripture out of one side of his mouth and liberalism out of the other.

The Christian conservatives remained just as intense in their opposition to Bill Clinton as they had always been. Indeed he provided his foes more ammunition by his steadfast opposition to a ban on late-term abortions, a proposal with overwhelming support in both houses of Congress. The National Conference of Catholic bishops, including all the cardinals, publicly appealed to Clinton to sign the bill. But Clinton vetoed it, an action that was attacked by conservatives from all the major religious traditions.

It was true that Clinton offered some conservative cultural initiatives. He promoted the "V-chip" that would permit parents to control TV viewing by their children. And he signed the Defense of Marriage Act, aimed at preventing the legalization of homosexual unions. But none of this came even close to healing the breach with the Christian Right.

With the approach of the 1996 election Ralph Reed conceded that Clinton had adopted, or co-opted, some portions of the conservative agenda. "I think you can make a strong case that Bill Clinton is running the most culturally conservative campaign since Ronald Reagan," Reed said. "So even while we have issue differences, Clinton has hammered away on those culture and values issues, and it has paid off for him."

But such a concession was mainly a thinly veiled ploy by Reed to seem fair minded toward the president and at the same time take the credit for Clinton's newfound cultural conservatism. For on Election Day in 1996, when push came to shove, Reed made plain how he thought any right-thinking Christian conservative should choose between Clinton and the Republican standard-bearer, Bob Dole. Addressing the Christian Coalition's annual conference, Reed attacked the Clinton administration on "matters of the soul." He cited the selection of Joycelyn Elders, a surgeon general willing to consider the legalization of marijuana; the appointment of "ACLU/Clinton-style judges"; and the fact that reports of drug use by presidential aides had forced "the first random drug testing of White House employees in American history." In denouncing Clinton for failing to set a proper moral climate for the nation, Reed could not resist needling the president about the scandal involving Clinton's chief political adviser, Dick Morris. The consultant had been forced to quit in the midst of the Democratic convention following the disclosure that he had consorted with a high-priced Washington prostitute and had shared with her sensitive conversations. "Now I ask you: Is that the kind of moral leadership we need in the White House?" Reed asked, to a ringing chorus of "No's" from the estimated 4,800 activists gathered at a Washington hotel.

As the 1996 election turned out, with the U.S. economy roaring along in high gear and the Republican standard-bearer running a brain-dead campaign, not even the righteous wrath of the Christian Right was enough to unseat Bill Clinton. But if Clinton remained in the White House, the Republicans still held the reins of power on Capitol Hill. And the Republican majorities there, particularly the contingent in the House of Representatives, remembered the voters who had sent them there in 1994. And so they served as the voice of Ralph Reed and his Christian conservative minions.

The GOP's control of the House of Representatives held particular significance. For although that chamber is often considered junior in prestige and importance to the Senate, it has certain powers arrogated to it that reflect its populist makeup. Concerned as they were about the powers of taxation, having just fought a revolution to rid themselves of a sovereign who abused that power, the Founders of the Republic saw to it that only the House, whose members were answerable directly to the people every two years, had the power to initiate revenue bills. And they also reserved to the peoples' representatives another equally significant authority—the power to bring charges of impeachment against the chief executive for high crimes and misdemeanors. And it was the control of this impeachment power, bestowed on the Republican Party in good measure because of the efforts of Ralph Reed and the Christian Right in the 1994 election, which would loom ever larger over the Clinton presidency as the inquiry that had commanded the attention of Eric Holder steadily gained force and significance in the months ahead.

CHAPTER

3

THE MINISTER'S SON

Just as Bill Clinton symbolized to his enemies the embodiment of all they despised in the culture of the Sixties, at the other pole in the cultural conflict, in the view of *his* enemies, stood the president's chief inquisitor, the head of the Office of Independent Counsel, Kenneth Winston Starr. Starr was of course a man of the law first and foremost, just as the president was a political man. But in his role as independent counsel Starr had broad authority to interpret the law as he saw it. And inevitably those judgments reflected his background and training.

Both Clinton and Starr were bright and ambitious men who had risen from humble circumstances to the heights of public affairs. Both were trained as lawyers. But Starr and Clinton in their fundamental natures and approaches to their respective vocations were as opposite as any two men could be. Clinton was a politician who never saw a corner he could not cut, a dilemma he could not compromise. Starr was a lawyer whose devotion to the rule of law and what he perceived to be the truth was absolute.

It was while he was solicitor general of the United States, a post to which he had been appointed by President George H. W. Bush, that Starr gained an insight into Clinton that would serve to dramatize the contrast between the two men. Called on to address an Arkansas Bar Association meeting in Hot Springs in 1992, Starr struck up a conversation with the state trooper who served as his driver. The trooper, part of whose duties included chauffeuring then-governor Clinton around the state, with very little prompting filled Starr in on details of Clinton's philandering, much of which the state police expedited. Before too long such stories would be widely publicized. But at the time of Starr's visit during the height of Clinton's first presidential campaign, little was known of Clinton's womanizing outside of Arkansas. Starr was genuinely shocked by what the trooper told him, all the more so because of Clinton's recent indignant denials of the allegations made by Gennifer Flowers. Starr toyed with the idea of passing on what he had learned to the Bush presidential campaign, which no doubt would have made good use of it. But he had pledged to the trooper that he would keep the information confidential at least until the election was over. Starr kept his word.

In the cut-and-thrust world of Washington lawyers Ken Starr was a shining example of civility. As solicitor general his manner was so courteous and amenable, and he went so far out of his way to avoid giving offense, that clerks at the Supreme Court referred to him as the "solicitous general." When he left that post for private practice, he had earned a reputation for solid judgment and discretion. Reflecting the widespread confidence in Starr's sense of fairness, the congressional panel probing sexual harassment charges against Senator Bob Packwood put him in charge of reviewing the intimate secrets in Packwood's diaries before turning them over to his prosecutors.

Later, when Starr took the post of independent counsel, Abner Mikva, his former colleague on the Circuit Court of Appeals bench, who was then White House counsel, used words such as "ethical," "fair," and "decent" to describe him to his clients, Bill and Hillary Clinton. And when Starr had occasion to question the Clintons in 1995 about Whitewater, he handled the interviews with utmost discretion, so much so that Mikva thanked him for his courtesy. "I realize it was not done for this President. I appreciate your concern for the presidency," Mikva said. "I would not have it any other way," Starr replied. "The Republicans will elect a president again and I want the presidency to be there."

Consistent with Mikva's experience was Starr's determination as independent counsel to avoid what he himself had called the "monomaniacal" qualities that many of his critics ascribed to the controversial Lawrence Walsh, who had spent seven years and nearly $40 million pursuing the

Iran Contra scandal during the Reagan and Bush years. To steer clear of that trap, Starr maintained his law practice and his adjunct professorship at New York University, functioning only as a part-time independent counsel. This was the same Kenneth Starr who in the months to come, because of his aggressiveness and seeming obsession with the prosecution of President Clinton, would become a whipping boy for Clinton's defenders, a target of criticism by the leaders of his profession, and, judging by the polls, one of the most detested men in the country. And who, as a result of this reputation, lost whatever hope he had of fulfilling a lifelong dream that had once seemed very plausible, succeeding to the Supreme Court of the United States.

How did this gracious and courtly Starr allow himself to be transformed into an effigy of Torquemada? Circumstances beyond his control accounted for some of this metamorphosis. But the best explanation is rooted in the kind of person Starr was brought up to be. "Part of what I think annoys people today about Ken, and annoys me too as a former prosecutor, is the sense of moral certainty that he brings to his work," Sam Millsap, boyhood friend of Starr's, who later became the top prosecutor in his hometown of San Antonio, told reporters. "That certainty is a result of two things: the fact is that he's smarter than everybody else, and he has his faith."

Starr's faith in God was the cornerstone of his life from the day he was born July 21, 1946, in Vernon, a dusty one-filling-station town in the heart of the Texas Bible Belt. His parents, Willie and Vannie, struggled to get by. Willie Douglas Starr, the boy's father, was a barber, and he was also a fundamentalist minister, adhering to the Church of Christ. The Starrs lived a frugal and simple existence governed by the very strict doctrines of their church. Young Ken had no store-bought toys, used clothespins to play soldier, and had no books, except for the Bible and religious tracts.

From the beginning, religion was central to the boy's life. "He's gone to church ever since he was 2 weeks old and never known any different," said his mother, Vannie. "We just started him from babyhood to know right from wrong."

"The Church of Christ in which we were raised was a very fundamentalist church," Sam Millsap recalled.

> The message from the pulpit was very fatalistic. It was we were all sinners. And we were going to hell because we were sinners. We were told—Sunday morning, Sunday night, Wednesday night—almost everything fun was wrong. We weren't permitted to dance, we weren't permitted to go to movies, anything that would cause you to brush up against a girl, a woman was dangerous.

As the baby of the family, the youngest of three children, Kenneth was somewhat spoiled and given to temper tantrums, which ultimately led to spankings. But he struggled through most of his early years to control his temper.

As he reached his teens, what struck his contemporaries about Starr was that he was smart, and he knew it. Millsap's earliest impression of Starr was that "he was 13 or 14, but going on 40, mature, goal oriented and ambitious beyond his years." Although some of his peers thought him to be stuck-up and aloof, Starr made friends, because he worked at it, as he did everything else.

"He had a quick, warm way of getting to know people," Gary Smith, another schoolboy chum, recalled. The friends helped him get to the top because Starr was bursting with ambition. He went out for just about every extracurricular activity that was available, except for sports. And he excelled at almost everything. At Sam Houston High, he was elected class president both his junior and senior years, besides being a member of the drama club and the yearbook and newspaper staffs. His achievements earned him a nickname: "Heap Big Boss Man." Driving ambition was coupled with an unbending commitment to morality. Though some of his classmates strayed from the narrow path of the Bible Belt, Starr never rebelled against the strict mold imposed upon him by his family and church. "He was a straight arrow and unfailingly polite," recalled Gary Smith. "He lived by a code of right and wrong that seemed etched in his heart. He was always a person who was very certain, very sure, a person guided by moral compass, for better or worse," another schoolmate remembered. "He was following his own light—he didn't give a hoot about the group. When we were in church as kids, we knew we were out of step with the mainstream in high school, because we believed what others didn't and we understood we could be subject to persecution—it was part of the yoke that made us special."

School politics was not the only kind that interested Starr. And just as his family's strong religious faith made clear what was right and wrong, his upbringing left little room for doubt about the good and bad in politics. His father despised Lyndon Johnson, who dominated Texas politics when Starr was growing up. As a ninth grader, in the 1960 election campaign, Starr did his bit for Richard Nixon, passing out leaflets in the neighborhood.

But his support for Nixon did not stop him from admiring the man who defeated him, John F. Kennedy. And when JFK spoke in San Antonio on November 21, 1963, the seventeen-year-old Starr went to hear him. It was the next day that Kennedy was assassinated in Dallas. Starr would later tell friends that seeing the president just before his tragic end had inspired him to make his way in the political world.

Starr's quest for higher education followed a path that might have been expected of him, considering his upbringing. From high school he entered Harding College, a Church of Christ school in Arkansas, where he sold Bibles door to door to help pay his tuition. He also wrote a column for the campus paper offering his views of the world on and off campus, called "Starrdust." But Starr had too much ambition and too much imagination to settle for the life that a Harding College education would have brought him.

He chafed at some of the church strictures, notably its prohibition of alcohol, not because he wanted to indulge in spirits but because to his logical mind it seemed inconsistent with the profuse references to wine in the Gospels. Then, too, he resented it when the college president made a point of disapproving of one of his "Starrdust" articles as too free thinking.

In his junior year the young man made a huge leap from the confines of Texas and the dictates of the Church of Christ. He transferred to

George Washington University in the nation's capital. Like most other campuses outside the South, GW in the mid-Sixties was a hotbed of permissiveness and protest. But while his classmates marched against the war in Vietnam in scruffy jeans and T-shirts, Starr sat out the protests and wore a jacket and tie to class.

In a way he was fortunate. He supported the war in Vietnam but did not have to serve. A bad case of psoriasis exempted him from the draft. After graduating he took a summer course in Spanish at Harvard. There he met the proverbial "nice Jewish girl" from Mamaroneck, New York, a sophomore at Skidmore named Alice Mandel. Their backgrounds could not have been more different, but the contrast evidently added to the attraction they felt for each other. In two years she would become his wife, married by a Church of Christ minister at her home.

His bride taught Starr to dance but the young man still had more serious subjects on his mind. After Georgetown he earned a master's degree in political science at Brown and then, as Richard Nixon was serving his first term in the White House, Starr entered Duke Law School, where Nixon himself had prepared for the bar. His performance at Duke— Order of the Coif, notes and comments editor of the law journal, Hughes Inn Graduate of the Year—earned him much coveted judicial clerkships, first at the U.S. Court of Appeals, then at the Supreme Court with Chief Justice Warren Burger. And that experience led to a job at the prestigious Los Angeles firm of Gibson, Dunn & Crutcher, where Starr caught the eye of one of the firm's senior partners, William French Smith. He happened to be legal adviser to Ronald Reagan, who soon thereafter won the presidency and made French Smith his attorney general. French Smith immediately sent for Starr, who served him as a sort of aide de camp in his fifth-floor office at the Justice Department.

One of Starr's first tasks was to help in the drafting of the new administration's position paper opposing reauthorization of the independent-counsel statute, to which Congress turned a deaf ear. The law was reenacted in 1982. Starr was more successful on another front—he extracted the new attorney general from a series of potentially embarrassing ethical questions—convincing him in one case to return a $50,000 severance payment he had received from a steel company that had been a former client.

His stands on two other issues were more revealing of his beliefs and helped to stamp him as a moderate among conservatives. His was one of the few political voices raised in opposition to the Reagan administration's decision to defend tax exemptions for religious schools discriminating against blacks in the 1983 Supreme Court case involving Bob Jones University. And he steered Sandra Day O'Connor's Supreme Court nomination through the Senate, managing to obscure her sympathy for abortion rights, a gambit which angered pro-life conservatives when they found out about it.

Remarkably, though, only two years after his arrival at Justice and ten years after his graduation from law school, French Smith persuaded Reagan to name Starr to the U.S. Circuit Court of Appeals in the District of Columbia at the ultra-tender age of thirty-seven. To most court watchers it seemed like a clear case of too much, too soon. But Starr proved his critics wrong. With his eye on what had now become the ultimate goal of his life, a seat on the Supreme Court, he turned in a polished performance at the Court of Appeals that belied his years and his lack of judicial experience.

Though his reputation as a conservative preceded him to the bench, he took care to avoid the fierce ideological feuds that sometimes divided the court. On one occasion, Abner Mikva, a liberal former congressman appointed by Carter, and Lawrence Silberman, a conservative former Justice Department official named to the bench by Reagan, nearly came to blows in the conference room over a case they had decided as part of a three-judge panel that also included Starr.

"If you were 10 years younger, I'd punch you out!" Silberman snarled at Mikva. Mikva looked over at Starr but saw that neither help nor hindrance would come from that quarter. Maintaining a studious silence, Judge Starr stared fixedly at the ceiling while, it seemed to Mikva, ardently wishing he were somewhere else. To Mikva, Starr was every inch "the gentle son of a minister who didn't like controversy."

Though he was a reliable member of the conservative bloc of the court, in certain areas of the law, such as press and religious freedoms, Starr showed a willingness to join his liberal or more moderate colleagues. Professor Richard Pierce, Jr., of Columbia University School of Law, a specialist in the decision-making patterns on the D.C. Circuit Court, called Starr a "moderate and impressive jurist" who provided a contrast to a number of his colleagues whose judgments seemed colored by the sharp ideological cleavages of the Reagan years. "They were frankly having difficulty forgetting they were Democrats or Republicans, and it was too easy to predict outcomes," Pierce recalled. "Judge Starr distinguished himself in that he was frequently able to stand back, look at issues in a more detached manner and write on the facts."

Starr also showed a sensitivity to civil liberties concerns not typical of conservative jurists. In one case he overturned a libel judgment against the *Washington Post,* while in another he held that an Orthodox Jew should be allowed to wear a yarmulke while on military duty.

Six years after he was appointed to the bench, Starr was given another offer he could not refuse—the solicitor generalship of the United States. He knew that taking the post might jeopardize his prospects for reaching the Supreme Court. As solicitor general he would be obliged to argue controversial cases that might make him enemies. But since the man who would pick him for the Supreme Court, President Bush, was the same man who had picked him to be solicitor, Starr was not in much of a position to turn him down.

Starr had an easy time gaining Senate confirmation, in part because his predecessor, Harvard Law School Professor Charles Fried, who served in the post under President Reagan, was considered an irascible right winger by Senate Democrats, making him an easy act to follow. Instead of probing into Starr's beliefs during his nomination hearings, Senate Judiciary Committee Democrats spent most of their time complaining about Fried's bias. This was of course a subtle way of driving home to Starr the notion that they expected something different from him.

But in fact, it was clear from the outset that, based on his record on the Court of Appeals, Democrats did not believe they had much to fear from Starr. Indeed, in his opening comments on Starr, Committee Chairman Joseph R. Biden, Jr., of Delaware, who had presided over the stormy hearings that doomed the Supreme Court nomination in 1987 of Robert Bork because of his conservative beliefs, likened Starr to former Supreme

Court Justice Lewis F. Powell, Jr.—a comparison roughly equivalent to elevating him to sainthood.

When the Democrats did ask specific questions, Starr provided answers that reassured them. Would Starr sign a brief that was "unduly political or legally improper?" Biden wanted to know. He was alluding, of course, to the Reagan administration's brief support for tax credits for racially discriminatory Bob Jones University. Starr did not mention that he had opposed that position within the Justice Department; he saw no point in advertising internal disputes. But of course he had no need to do that, since it was safe to assume that Biden, and any other senator who cared about the issue, would already know what Starr had done. Now, he simply told Biden: "I would not sign a brief which I found to be legally indefensible."

Asked about his views on *stare decisis,* the legal doctrine that the court should stand by its prior rulings, Starr, calling himself a "traditionalist," said a solicitor general should be especially "mindful and respectful" of the doctrine. "But if he thinks a decision is wrong," he added, "he has an obligation" to ask the court to reverse it. He cited the 1954 *Brown v. Board of Education* case as an appropriate instance for a solicitor general to ask the court to reverse the "separate-but-equal" doctrine. Starr said he found himself in accord with many of the high court's liberal rulings on privacy. And he made a point of setting himself apart from the controversial Bork's views in that sensitive area of the law, saying he agreed with the 1965 *Griswold v. Connecticut* ruling overturning a state ban on contraceptives, a judgment to which Bork objected. But lest anyone think he was craven in siding with liberals, Starr said he also agreed with the Supreme Court's 1986 ruling saying there was no constitutionally protected privacy right for homosexuals.

On a more personal note, Republican Arlen Specter of Pennsylvania asked Starr why he would leave his appeals court seat, with its lifetime tenure, to take a job that could be over in less than four years. "I was asked," Starr responded, adding that he considered the offer a high honor and "a great privilege."

As solicitor general, the lawyer who most often represents the government before the justices, Starr, as might have been expected, took up the cudgels of the Bush administration in arguing for the reversal of *Roe v. Wade*, the landmark 1973 case establishing a woman's right to abortion. But Starr also showed that he was still his own man, backing up his assurances to Biden, when early in his tenure he defied the White House by siding with a group of whistle-blowers against defense contractors. He also retained his personal reputation for moderation. Nan Aron, president of the Alliance for Justice, a liberal lobbying group that tries to protect the rights of minorities and women, testified against Starr's nomination for solicitor general because she believed that Starr, with his opposition to judicial activism, was reluctant for judges to take an aggressive role in protecting minority rights. Nevertheless, even after her testimony, Starr greeted her warmly and introduced her to friends when their paths crossed at legal conferences. "I take this at face value," she said, calling Starr "a very nice man whenever I've talked to him."

But for all the satisfactions that the solicitor generalship brought Starr, he had to accept one major disappointment. The call to the Supreme Court that he had hoped for and many expected he would get never came. Bush had two chances to fill vacancies to the high court. Early in his presidency Bush used the first to pick David Souter, about whom so little was known that, as Bush must have expected, he caused almost no controversy, though later, conservatives outraged by Souter's support for abortion rights and other liberal positions had reason to regret that Bush did not pick Starr. With Bush's second choice, the president himself would have reason to second-guess his own decision. His decision to pick a black led him to Clarence Thomas, whose selection triggered charges of sexual harassment from a former aide, Anita Hill, provoking one of the bitterest nomination fights in Supreme Court history.

It may have softened the sting of disappointment for Starr that after Bush's defeat in 1992 the outgoing solicitor general became the focus of one of Washington's most active bidding wars as several major law firms competed for his services. He eventually chose Chicago-based Kirkland & Ellis, where his earnings reportedly ran about $1.2 million a year and his clients included some of the nation's biggest tobacco companies.

Starr was making money hand over fist, enough to provide amply for his own security and his children. But it was not long before he began to get restless. With Democrat Bill Clinton in the Oval Office, Starr's dream of a Supreme Court seat had been put on hold, certainly at least until another Republican president sat in the White House. And he missed the spark that politics brought into his life. Starr involved himself in local Republican politics in suburban McLean, Virginia, where he and his family lived, and thought seriously about running for the Senate in 1994 against incumbent Democrat Charles Robb. He snatched eagerly at the offer of the Senate Ethics Committee to oversee the vetting of Packwood's diary. And he looked for other openings that would permit him to reinvolve himself in public affairs. When President Clinton made a claim of legal immunity to shield himself from the sexual harassment suit filed by Paula Jones, Starr made no secret of his disapproval and talked to other lawyers about filing a friend of the court brief in opposition.

But it was a freakish situation not of Starr's making that opened the door for his return to the public arena. The opportunity presented itself because the Independent Counsel Act, first passed in 1978 in response to Watergate, had been allowed to expire in 1992 when Republican opponents managed to prevent its reenactment. In 1994, with no such law on the books, and with congressional Republicans clamoring for an investigation of the Whitewater affair, Clinton asked Attorney General Reno to name an independent counsel to look into the controversial real-estate deal. She picked New York lawyer Robert B. Fiske, Jr., a Republican, to conduct a wide-ranging criminal investigation.

Meanwhile, though, Congress reenacted the statute into law in the summer of 1994. And a three-judge federal panel set up to implement the law decided that to assure the independence of the inquiry, Fiske needed to be replaced because he had originally been chosen by the Clinton administration. Their choice: Kenneth W. Starr.

The White House, which had expected Fiske's reappointment, was stunned and immediately protested. Clinton's aides claimed that Starr was overly partisan, citing his interest in the Virginia Senate race and in the Paula Jones case. And Democratic Senator Carl Levin of Michigan, leading Senate sponsor of the independent counsel law, urged the judicial panel to ask Starr for "a complete accounting" of his recent Republican political activities and to ask him either to resign or explain why the activities would not impair his "appearance of independence." But the judges turned Levin down flat. And Starr himself rejected the protest. "I accept this assignment with a firm commitment to fairness, thoroughness, dispatch and professionalism," Starr said.

If the White House was surprised at Starr's appointment so were most of his close friends, who could not understand why he had taken the post. It had been Starr's custom before making major decisions in his professional life to bounce the proposition off several colleagues. The ones he normally consulted were people whom he had known for more than a decade, since they had worked together at the Justice Department under William French Smith.

This time Starr talked to none of them. One reason he did not do so may have been that he probably guessed they would be opposed to the idea. After all, nearly every one of them, like Starr himself, had been united in their contempt for the Independent Counsel Act itself, which they felt gave too much power to one person. Another reason for their opposition was that they believed the job was a self-defeating proposition, that no matter what Starr did he was bound to be condemned either for being too lax or too harsh.

Starr himself must have perceived these obstacles. Why then did he take the job? For one thing he was bored with corporate law. For another he missed the drama and significance of public life. But perhaps most important, some believed, was the religious faith that was the main driving force in Starr's life. "I think Ken believed that since God had put him in all these lofty posts, he had a duty to use his experience when a public-service challenge arose," said one longtime colleague.

What everyone agreed on, both then and later, was that Starr did not have a full appreciation of the burden he was taking on. "He thought he could parachute in, do it in a year or two, not consume his whole life and get out," said Rusty Hardin, a lawyer who had served in the Independent Counsel's Office under Fiske at the start of the Whitewater investigation.

Indeed, Starr tried to make the job fit his own misperception, by keeping on with his work at the law firm and his teaching slot at New York University. As a result, he came under fire from critics who charged that he had a conflict of interest because he still represented tobacco companies. Who had good reason to hope for the crippling of a president who was leading a crusade against smoking.

To be sure, Starr had been able to nail some coonskins to the wall, as Lyndon Johnson would have put it, notably the conviction on fraud and conspiracy charges of Arkansas Governor Jim Guy Tucker and James McDougal and his ex-wife Susan, business partners of Bill and Hillary Clinton in the Whitewater venture. But for the most part his tenure was marked by frustration, his probe stymied by the refusal of Webster Hubbell, Hillary Clinton's former law partner and later associate attorney general, and Susan McDougal to provide information that Starr needed to advance his investigation.

All this makes it easy to understand why in February 1997 Starr decided to resign as independent counsel and accept two deanships at Pepperdine University in Malibu, California. The storm of indignation the announcement of his intended departure created taught him that as thankless as his job was, the public nevertheless expected him to work at it full time until the task was completed. "My vision of the function of the independent counsel was not a sufficiently complete vision of what that role is," Starr explained in announcing that he would stay on, after all.

This episode—his abortive decision to quit, the public protest, and his reversal—would have fateful consequences for Starr, for the Clinton presidency, and for the country. Once having made this full-scale commitment, Starr seemed determined to discharge this obligation to the utmost of his energy and ability. He became increasingly aggressive and more and more began to act as a prosecutor, a job he had never had before.

Hardening Starr's determination was his growing realization that the Clinton White House would do everything possible to delay and obstruct his investigation. This presidential strategy had been dramatized soon after Starr had changed his plans to go to Pepperdine by what Joseph E. DiGenova, himself an independent counsel in 1992, called the "immaculate conception" of Hillary Clinton's billing records from her days as a Little Rock lawyer. These records suddenly materialized in the White House living quarters nearly two years after they had been subpoenaed.

More and more Starr talked publicly and privately about the fundamental purpose of his job being the search for truth. "There's no room for white lies," Starr proclaimed with his customary fervor. "There's no room for shading. You cannot defile the temple of justice." Time and again he repeated, "Our job is to search for the truth." And yet every step of the way, it seemed to him, Clinton and his defenders did all they could to block that search, to twist the truth, to dishonor justice.

And so it was that this amiable and scholarly appellate lawyer, who had originally seen the independent counsel's position as nothing more than a part-time job, had become a full-time prosecutor. Thus when the chance came to delve into the president's affairs, public and private, Starr reacted not like an appellate lawyer, but like a prosecutor. This opportunity presented itself in the form of a disgruntled former White House secretary whose name, as Starr would ultimately learn, was Linda Tripp. She claimed to have evidence, not merely hearsay evidence but tape-recorded evidence, that Bill Clinton had conducted an affair with a friend of Tripp's, a White House intern named Monica Lewinsky, and was now bending every effort to get Lewinsky to conceal their relationship. More than mere gossip was involved. Lewinsky was being called as a witness in the Paula Jones sexual harassment suit. To protect Clinton, and his presidency, by Linda Tripp's account, Lewinsky was being asked by the nation's highest official, the guardian of every citizen's rights and liberties, to lie under oath.

When Starr's aide Jackie Bennett heard about Linda Tripp and her tape records, he decided he wanted to follow the trail of that evidence. But first he had to clear things with Starr. On the morning of Monday, January 12, 1998, Starr heard what Bennett had to say and agreed that Bennett's instincts were right. This was a lead worth pursing. It was this green light from Starr that led Jackie Bennett to call the deputy attorney general, Eric Holder, two days later to ask for a meeting. And it was this meeting that would touch off a constitutional crisis and open a new front in the Culture War.

CHAPTER 4

DAY OF JUDGMENT

The Office of the Independent Counsel of the United States is at 1001 Pennsylvania Avenue on the north side of that thoroughfare, just a few blocks east of the White House. The Department of Justice is directly across the street, on the south side of Pennsylvania Avenue. That gulf had never seemed wider than it did on the evening of January 15, 1998, a Thursday, the day after Bennett's late-night phone call to Eric Holder, when Bennett and three of his deputies crossed the street to keep their date with Holder in his office.

Bennett treated the occasion with the solemnity he figured it deserved. His manner was serious and sober as he related to Holder information that the Independent Counsel's Office had "unhappily" come across. "There is inchoate criminality involved," he said. "It goes to the White House and very likely to the president." There was reason to believe, Bennett said, that Clinton's close friend, Vernon Jordan, was involved. Evidence suggested, he explained, that Jordan, the supremely well-connected Washington lawyer, had been enlisted in an effort to find Monica Lewinsky a job, presumably to prevent her from providing testimony that would damage the president in the Paula Jones case.

This was a matter that would always demand high priority. But there was a need for extra urgency in this case, Bennett explained, because the press was hotly following the same leads pursued by Starr's office, raising the possibility of an imminent news break that could wreck the chances of investigating evidence of a grave violation of the laws.

Then Bennett got to the point. The investigation needed to go forward, but that would mean pushing into territory beyond Starr's initial mandate. His authority had been broadened twice before, to take in Travelgate—the cognomen applied to the ill-conceived firing of the White House travel office staff—and Filegate—the rubric used to describe the mysterious presence in the offices of White House political aides of sensitive FBI files containing personal data on hundreds of prominent persons, including many Republicans. These expansions had been ordered on the initiative of the Justice Department, and Starr had accepted the added responsibility, though not without reluctance. This time it was Starr himself who was at least indirectly asking for extra authority by raising the issue with Holder. "We welcome DOJ participation at this point," was the way Bennett's colleague, Bruce Udolf, put it to Holder. "We don't have strong feelings who, but someone needs to work the case."

But it was pretty clear from the beginning who that "someone" would turn out to be. As soon as the meeting was over, Holder paged Reno. But the attorney general was at the Kennedy Center and did not return his call until early the next morning. Holder reviewed the situation in his mind. If Clinton was involved, the Justice Department, headed by his appointee Janet Reno, could not investigate. On the other hand, the idea of getting a new independent counsel appointed and functioning in a timely fashion seemed out of the question. Holder sent an investigator to Starr's office to listen to the tape of a conversation between Linda Tripp and Monica Lewinsky that had been arranged by the FBI. By the time Holder met with Reno the next morning it was clear to both of them that they had no choice. One of Reno's aides called U.S. Judge David Sentelle, chief of the three-judge panel that had initially appointed Starr, and asked for his jurisdiction to be broadened to look into these new "specific and credible" charges.

Despite Bennett's warnings to Holder about the danger of the new information from Linda Tripp becoming public, not a word was heard on Saturday, January 17. But that date provided the first indication of the impact Starr's new information would have on the Clinton presidency. For this was the day that Clinton was scheduled to give his deposition in the Paula Jones case.

That episode had been plaguing the president since the beginning of his second year in the White House in 1994. Clinton had managed to survive allegations of womanizing during his first presidential campaign, despite the publication of a taped phone conversation between him and Little Rock nightclub singer Gennifer Flowers. Clinton had denied Flowers's story of a long-term affair and eventually it had been all but forgotten.

He had denied Jones's claim of sexual harassment as well. But Jones's charge was not so easily swept aside, because Paula Jones had filed a sexual harassment suit against the President of the United States. When the federal district court refused to postpone action on Jones's suit until Clinton left the White House, his lawyers appealed to the Supreme Court, and lost there, too. For Clinton, Jones's allegations and the other charges swirling around his presidency were not just a legal and political problem but a financial burden, too. In 1994 the president had established a legal defense fund, the first ever set up by a sitting president, to help cover the legal expenses of the Whitewater probe and the Paula Jones case, costs that would ultimately exceed $10 million.

But all of the controversy over Clinton's behavior that had raged for his first five years in the White House would soon be overshadowed by the damning new information that Linda Tripp had given to Starr's investigators. Clinton would get his first inkling of what was to come on January 17, when he gave his deposition.

Clinton had always known this would be an unpleasant experience and had used every weapon at his command to delay it as long as he could. The circus-like atmosphere was as bad as he could have expected. Throngs of photographers, reporters, and tourists stationed themselves on the streets outside his lawyer's office, waiting to glimpse the president and his accuser, who arrived with her own spokeswoman and her own hairdresser. "I feel so proud to be an American to know that this judicial system works, to know that a little girl from Arkansas is equal to the President of the United States," Jones said through her spokeswoman, adopting just the sort of tone Clinton himself would have used had their positions been reversed.

Clinton had expected all of this hullabaloo at the scene of the deposition, and he had also anticipated that once the deposition began, he would be grilled about his past escapades with women. He knew that Jones's lawyers had cast a wide net seeking evidence that his encounter with Jones was part of a pattern of behavior. And he had good reason to believe that he would be asked about his relationship with one particular young woman, a concupiscent former White House intern named Monica Lewinsky, since she had previously been subpoenaed by Jones's lawyers. What he did not anticipate was the number and specific nature of the questions he would be asked about Lewinksy—not only had he ever had sex with her, but had he ever given her gifts, had his conversations with her been tape recorded, and so forth. Under oath, Clinton denied any sexual relationship with Lewinsky but gave carefully worded answers to the other questions. He acted like a man who feared he had walked into a trap. And he was right.

It was a trap of his own creation: One jaw of the trap was the Paula Jones case, the other was Whitewater. Paula Jones's lawsuit allowed her lawyers to ask Monica Lewinsky, and also her friend and onetime coworker Linda Tripp, questions about his sex life. It was Tripp's answers to their questions that had given them a basis for asking Clinton such specific questions about Lewinsky in the deposition. Tripp had subsequently become an agent of Starr's and under direction from his aides had tape recorded her conversations with Lewinsky, providing evidence that belied Clinton's denial of a sexual relationship with the intern.

Whitewater had led to the appointment as independent counsel of Starr, who then found in Tripp's tapes evidence of what in his view verged on the obstruction of justice by the President of the United States. In particular, what sent Starr and his bloodhounds into high gear was learning of the involvement of Vernon Jordan, Clinton's crony and adviser, a man renowned both for his charm and his deftness as a fixer, behind the scenes and under the table. From the time Monica Lewinsky became a subpoena target for Paula Jones's lawyers, Jordan had talked to her on the phone and in person nearly a dozen times in an ultimately successful effort to find her a job. Jordan's efforts were a signal of how sensitive and urgent Lewinsky's job hunt was to the president. There was no one Clinton trusted more. "Vernon knows a lot of stuff about the President and his personal life, but he'll never trade on it," said Dee Dee Myers, Clinton's former press secretary. "Vernon understands how power works better than anybody I know. He talks to the President about everything, I think, but it would diminish his power if he talked about it. He protects the President, his friend." And protecting the president was just what Jordan was doing, or so Starr's investigators concluded.

While Starr pressed his probe Clinton and his defenders mounted a vigorous defense. First the president denied the charges, which had leaked to the press a few days after his deposition. "I did not have sexual relations with that woman, Miss Lewinsky," Clinton told startled Americans in a televised appearance carefully arranged to seem spontaneous. "I never told anybody to lie, not a single time. Never. These allegations are false." Then, while Clinton himself stonewalled the investigators, his allies, led by the First Lady, denounced his accusers.

"The great story here is this vast right-wing conspiracy that has been conspiring against my husband since the day he announced for president," Hillary Clinton had famously declared. Starr she branded as "a politically motivated prosecutor who is allied with the right-wing opponents of my husband."

And so the battle lines in this latest struggle in the Culture War were set, with the future of the Clinton presidency at stake. Some of the terrain and rhetoric recalled previous furors over Clinton's behavior that seemed to challenge the middle-class cultural values he claimed to champion. Clinton had so far always fought back successfully. "The people whose character is really an issue are those who would divert the attention of the people and divide the country we love," candidate Clinton had declared six years earlier campaigning in New Hampshire in 1992 when his behavior first came under attack on the national political stage. And ever since, Clinton has used much the same argument—that the violations of middle-class standards he was accused of were irrelevant to the nation's serious concerns.

But the Lewinsky case amounted to the most serious character charge of his career—and the cumulative toll taken on his credibility by all these previous controversies escalated the peril to his presidency. As a result of his past transgressions Clinton's rating for integrity and trust had been notably low among politicians. In a 1997 Gallup Poll Americans asked to compare Clinton's ethical standards to other recent presidents rated Presidents Reagan, Bush, and Carter ahead of Clinton by margins of about two to one or better. Indeed, only Richard Nixon, forced to resign in disgrace because of Watergate, trailed Clinton in this regard.

Yet Clinton had won two presidential elections. One reason was that while the public did not necessarily believe his denials they accepted his argument that the charges about his personal conduct had nothing to do with his presidency. "Americans for some reason believe that the distinction between a president's personal conduct on one side and things that are pertinent to his public performance is one that should be taken seriously," the opinion analyst Everett Carl Ladd acknowledged in an interview.

But there was another, perhaps more important, advantage that Clinton had in his battle for survival; simply put, he was more determined to stay in office than any of the other actors on the political stage were to get him out. The irresolution among Clinton's opponents was evident at the annual Conservative Political Action Conference in suburban Arlington, Virginia, which convened a few days after Hillary Clinton's outburst at the right wing. Assembled there were the chief movers and shakers of American conservatism, topped off by House Speaker Newt Gingrich. They seemed to be just the sort that the First Lady had in mind when she decried the conspiracy against her husband. But the only kind of conspiracy in evidence at this gathering was a conspiracy of silence.

Fear of backlash tied the tongues of the most prominent among the speakers. And their references to Clinton's predicament were cryptic and oblique. Asked about "family values," Gingrich talked about curbing drug use, improving schools, and cutting taxes. "Every family I know wants a drug free country," he said. "Every family I know wants to make sure their children really learn. Every family I know wants more money they can spend on their own needs." But if Gingrich saw any connection between the charges against Clinton and family values, it did not occur to him to mention it.

For a few speakers at the gathering this restraint seemed excessive. "Leaders who suggest they can separate their private lives and their public actions are wrong," cried Republican Senator John Ashcroft of Missouri, who was trying to base a prospective candidacy for his party's presidential nomination in the year 2000 on the support of Christian conservatives, who presumably would be most offended by the president's behavior. "Morality is not divisible," Ashcroft insisted, in rebuttal to the claim of Clinton's supporters that the excesses of his personal life should not count against his presidency.

But as the days wore on it became increasingly clear that Ashcroft was in a distinct minority among Republicans. Most of the leaders stood aside from the controversy raging around the presidency and offered various rationalizations for their behavior. Perhaps most striking of all was the attitude of Ralph Reed, who as the leader of the Christian Coalition had been one of the firebrands of cultural conservatism. But following the 1996 election Reed had left the Coalition to set himself up as a political consultant. And in that role the strategist who had once seemed eager to stake his future and his party's on the cause of family values now sang a more pragmatic tune. "The overarching strategy for the Republican Party needs to be to not appear as if they are trying to make political capital," Reed told reporters. "All that does is further energize the Democratic base."

Some conservatives, however, feared the GOP risked alienating its own base in an election year if it was not more openly critical of Clinton's alleged behavior. "There is deep frustration and disappointment that there's not more moral leadership," said Gary Bauer, a conservative activist who founded the Family Research Council and mounted an unsuccessful campaign for the Republican presidential nomination in 2000. "The reluctance to speak on this by politicians is a reflection of their fear to not look judgmental in an age that has elevated tolerance above all other values."

Then, too, for a good many the silent treatment for Clinton was inspired by the desire to avoid retaliation from Clinton supporters, who, Republicans justifiably feared, might try to probe for skeletons in their closets. Allegations of sexual misconduct have long been a staple of U.S. politics, even derailing the careers of lawmakers from Bob Packwood to John Tower. House Speaker Newt Gingrich himself was no stranger to such controversy: Charges that he was involved in extramarital affairs in the 1970s had surfaced in various publications over the years. "There are a lot of folks in this town whose own lives will not stand up under scrutiny," Bauer said.

While Republicans were cautious in responding to Clinton's plight, Democrats, with few exceptions, were downright craven. Remarkably, at this stage of the scandal, not a single Democratic leader of note had come forward to call for the president to abandon his silence and give an honest account of himself and his behavior to the voters he was elected to serve. Instead, the Democrats monitored the polls. And when these dubious barometers of public opinion showed the president's approval rating soaring, despite, or it seemed almost because of, the charges against him, his Democratic brethren needed no further cue to embrace him fully. "I told him for all of us that we support him and more importantly the American people support him," said Michigan Congressman John D. Dingell, dean of the Democratic House caucus, at a gathering with Clinton soon after the Lewinsky charges had become public. And Congressman Charles Rangell of New York, claiming that there had not been "one scintilla of evidence to contradict the president's denial," said he would like to "see more outrage" directed against Starr.

Outrage was just what the White House was trying to whip up as the president's staff deployed an assault force on the television talk shows dedicated to turning the focus of the scandal away from Clinton and onto the independent counsel, whose insensitivity to appearances made him all the more vulnerable. Apart from his strong religious faith, which helped Clinton's allies depict him as some type of fanatic, Starr, more than most people, had trouble grasping how his actions and behavior would strike other people. After his confirmation hearing for the solicitor general's job, Starr called Robert McConnell, a former Justice Department colleague, to ask how he had come across.

"I watched myself on CNN and I must tell you, I thought I sounded pedantic," Starr said.

"Ken, you are pedantic," McConnell told him.

What was particularly striking about the defense of Clinton and the attack on Starr was that it was joined by leading Democratic feminists, many of whom had been unrelenting and unforgiving in their attack on Clarence Thomas, when that Republican Supreme Court nominee was accused of sexual harassment by Anita Hill, and on Republican Senator Bob Packwood of Oregon, who was drummed out of the Senate for sexual misconduct. "I don't know what the facts are of the charges against the president," said California Congresswoman Nancy Pelosi on "Meet the Press." "But what I do know is that Kenneth Starr went well beyond the constraints of ethics in his investigation of the president." As far as the rights of women were concerned, Pelosi contended that the real suspect was not Clinton, accused of seducing his intern, but rather Starr and "how he's investigating, exploiting, Monica Lewinsky, how he used Linda Tripp to do that."

But like the Republican consensus in favor of silence, the feminist consensus against criticizing Clinton was not unanimous. Clinton's staunchest feminist defender, Hillary Rodham Clinton, got short shrift from the feminist writer Barbara Ehrenreich in *Time:* "Someone needs to tell this woman that the first time a wife stands up for an allegedly adulterous husband, everyone thinks she's a saint," Ehrenreich contended. "The second or third time, though, she begins to look disturbingly complicit." As for Monica Lewinsky herself, even if she had not been harassed, "feminists have plenty of reason to be concerned about a workplace where any young woman with sufficiently tartlike demeanor could reportedly enjoy the President's precious attentions, along with the career-counseling services of his closest friends. Meanwhile, who pays attention to all the other, harder working and no doubt more productive interns whose hair is short and necklines are high."

To fend off such misgivings about the First Couple, the Clinton forces stepped up their assault on the independent counsel via the television talk shows, seeking to portray him as alien to the mainstream culture. "Mr. Starr wants to indict everybody for everything," declared James Carville, who had dedicated himself to destroying Starr's reputation. "They have to keep him in check. We have an out-of-control, sex-crazed person running this thing. He has spent $40 million of the taxpayers' money investigating people's sex lives."

Along with the frontal assault by Clinton's supporters, Starr had to guard his back against more subtle attacks from within the Justice

Department spearheaded by Eric Holder. At the White House, Clinton's aides found it hard to understand how it was that Holder had not talked Reno out of extending Starr's jurisdiction to include the Lewinsky affair, a reaction that had clouded Holder's prospects for advancement. Now Holder seemed to have found a way to make at least partial amends.

When Clinton's lawyers publicly accused Starr of leaking grand jury information, an indignant Starr vowed to conduct an internal investigation to disprove the charges. But when he went to Holder asking for FBI help to conduct the probe, Holder talked him out of it, giving Starr the impression that he, Holder, did not think much of the accusation. Starr breathed easier, until he learned that Holder had quietly called the presiding judge in the case and offered the Justice Department's help in looking into the charges against Starr.

Meanwhile, Starr's own heavy-handedness gave ammunition to his enemies. "Starr is politically tone-deaf," said conservative icon and Clinton critic William Bennett. "It's too bad, because everybody knows the central issue here should be the president."

Starr's obtuseness led to his getting what was probably even worse press than Clinton, some suspected in part due to the desire of journalists to make up for whatever injustices their trade might have done to Clinton. Thus the *Washington Post,* one of a handful of papers that are influential in coloring the attitudes and judgments of other journalists, on March 2, 1998, headlined its front-page lead story: "Starr Is Urged to Curtail Inquiry," a recommendation that, emanating as it did from Rahm Emanuel, one of Clinton's most energetic propagandists, seemed about as surprising and newsworthy as if the *Post* had discovered a man who had been bitten by a dog.

The unsteadiness that marked the coverage of the Lewinsky affair demonstrated that journalists, too, were caught up in the cultural upheaval that began in the Sixties. History records a few notable exceptions, such as the expose of Thomas Jefferson's affair with Sally Hemings, and the furor over Grover Cleveland's illegitimate child, but for the most part reporters in bygone days had looked the other way whenever philandering reared its head. This had been true whether the supposed culprit was a

Republican, like Warren Harding, or a Democrat, such as Franklin D. Roosevelt. A. H. Raskin of the *New York Times* used to tell of overhearing presidential candidate Estes Kefauver instructing a hotel clerk back in the 1950s: "Send up whiskey and women in that order," but never printing a word about Kefauver's well-known proclivity for boozing and philandering. Similarly, another *Times* man, R. W. Apple, recalls staking out the lobby of Manhattan's Carlyle Hotel, where President Kennedy was spending the night, to observe the comings and goings of politicians. Kennedy's only visitor was a stunning woman, whom Apple later realized was actress Angie Dickinson. "No story there," Apple's editor told him.

Kennedy was the last president to enjoy this journalistic double standard of personal behavior. He was able to put his personal assets and virtues on public display to his political advantage while remaining confident that his personal shortcomings would be cloaked in privacy. That state of affairs began to change soon after JFK's tenure in the White House ended as profound changes in sexual attitudes and behavior swept through American society and engulfed the media. The children of the middle class began living in what used to be called sin. Premarital "tryouts" and extramarital relationships became commonplace. Homosexuals asserted their identities. And journalists, too, abandoned previous restraints, publishing more of what they saw and knew of the private lives of political leaders.

In a way, it seemed paradoxical that when American sexual mores relaxed, the new freedom of the press led to politicians' being held to a stricter standard of conduct. Some journalists may have been influenced by the "Personal Is Political" credo of the burgeoning feminist movement. But the main reason for the change was that the media began to see more relevance in the personal behavior of presidents, including their sexual behavior, and for this presidents had themselves largely to blame. By focusing attention on themselves as cultural icons, not just political leaders, following the pattern established by JFK, presidents have opened the way to scrutiny of their weaknesses.

Some presidents have benefited by their skill in manipulating the cultural issues. Among the Democrats, Jimmy Carter's presentation of himself as a born-again Christian, who promised never to tell a lie, helped to vault him from obscurity to the White House. From Republican ranks, Ronald Reagan used the media to present himself as the embodiment of middle-class values, alerting Clinton and his strategists to the power of cultural issues and leading to the middle-class paradigm as the foundation of Clinton's candidacy, and his presidency.

All Clinton's efforts at cultural imagery seemed undermined when, after months of delay and denial, he finally submitted himself to questioning by Starr before the grand jury. Faced with the evidence of Monica Lewinsky's semen-stained dress, Clinton was forced to admit in testimony guarded with legalisms that he had indeed had a sexual relationship with the intern. "It depends what the definition of *is* is," Clinton remarked at one point in his interrogation, giving birth to one of the most memorable utterances of his presidency. It was from such tortured constructions that the country learned that the president had lied to his fellow citizens on television and lied under oath.

The president's supporters were stunned. Democratic Senator Joseph Lieberman of Connecticut, head of the Democratic Leadership Council, the same centrist group that had helped launch Clinton's presidential candidacy in 1992, denounced Clinton's behavior as not just "inappropriate," the term favored by the president, but "immoral." In a Senate speech that would turn out to be the launching pad for his own career in national politics, Lieberman contended that by stressing middle-class cultural values in his rhetoric and in his policy proposals Clinton had "reconnected the Democratic Party to the mainstream of American values. This misconduct, behavior that is both immoral and untruthful, undercuts that."

Something drastic needed to be done in the view of White House aide Harold Ickes. This Clinton troubleshooter was known to be as curmudgeonly as his namesake father, who, as FDR's interior secretary, had mocked the populist pretensions of Wendell Willkie by calling him "a simple barefoot Wall Street lawyer." Now the old curmudgeon's heir scurried around Capitol Hill, suggesting to Democratic elders that they consider asking Clinton to resign for the good of the party.

But Clinton had no intention of doing any such thing and no senior Democrat had the kidney to try to persuade him otherwise. When Starr submitted to Congress a 445-page summary of his investigation containing "substantial and credible information . . . that may constitute grounds for impeachment," the die was cast. Despite polls showing most Americans opposed the idea, in October 1998 House Republicans pushed through a resolution calling for an impeachment inquiry. A month later the Republican losses of House seats in the midterm elections gave Democrats hope the impeachment might be avoided. But the Democrats did not look closely enough at the election returns, or at the mindset of the Republican leadership.

Though the Republicans did lose five seats in the 1998 midterm election, they actually *won* the election by maintaining control of the House. The 1998 returns meant that the House had stayed Republican for three successive elections, the first time this had happened since Herbert Hoover's time. Moreover, a study of the returns showed that the Republicans still had powerful support from conservative Christians. Indeed, evangelicals, devout Protestants who viewed old-fashioned fundamentalism as too extreme but the liberalism of the modernists as too wishy washy, made up the largest single portion of the GOP vote, and a majority of these voters believed that Clinton should be impeached.

So it was that when the Republican leaders in the House, spearheaded by Majority Whip Tom DeLay of Texas and Judiciary Committee Chairman Henry Hyde of Illinois, decided to press on with the impeachment inquiry, they were in the fortunate position of being able to fulfill their constitutional responsibility of holding the president accountable and at the same time staying on the good side of the voters who mattered most to them. Brushing aside Democratic proposals for censure as a substitute, the House Judiciary Committee voted along party lines to send to the House floor four impeachment articles—charging Clinton with perjury, both before the federal grand jury and in his Jones case deposition, obstruction of justice, and abuse of power. It was the first such action by the Judiciary Committee since 1974 when charges were brought against Richard Nixon as a result of the Watergate scandal.

The House debate over the impeachment of William Jefferson Clinton demonstrated the potential perils that accompany the hoped-for rewards of cultural politics. Members on both sides of the aisle found the going awkward. For Democrats, the problem was to separate themselves from the president and his behavior and at the same time oppose impeachment. A convenient way to accomplish this feat was to distinguish morality from the law and to attack Ken Starr, the course chosen by Edward Markey of Massachusetts. "Yes, the President made a grievous personal error to the detriment of his family," he conceded. "But, no, it is not an offense against the state or our Constitution. We are now on the threshold of overturning the people's choice for President through a perversion of the independent counsel law, a runaway, partisan investigation of the most intimate private activity."

Some of the Republicans, the so-called moderates, those who had to answer more to voters with mainstream religious beliefs than to evangelicals, seemed at least as much on the defensive as the Democrats. Just as the Democrats tried to put distance between themselves and Clinton, so did many of the GOP's moderate Republicans strive to set their support for impeachment apart from its cultural overtones. "The case against the President is not about sex or the privacy of the President and the first family," contended Marge Roukema of New Jersey. "It's about the very public legal action of perjury in a civil deposition and before a Federal criminal grand jury. These are matters of public policy and the law along with the questions of obstruction of justice and abuse of power."

Yet for many of the Republicans the concepts of law and morality were intertwined, as they were for Kenneth Starr, and at the moment of truth on the floor of the House they could not disavow this connection. South Dakota's John Thune targeted the contention by Clinton's supporters that the president genuinely believed he was telling the truth in refusing to acknowledge his affair with Lewinsky. "If the President's claim was to be taken at face value," Thune declared, "we are left with one of two equally miserable realities: either the President chooses contempt and complete disregard for the truth, or his conscience is so diminished as to leave him unable to discern the truth from his lies. Both conclusions are ruinous to a constitutional republic whose leaders must command the trust of those they lead."

Truth and trust were the core principles that the two leaders of the impeachment drive, Tom DeLay and Henry Hyde, claimed impelled their efforts. Whether these two were driven by conscience, as their admirers maintained, or sheer malice and political ambition, as their Democratic detractors charged, no one could question their determination.

DeLay, a steely-eyed Texan who had once operated an exterminating business in his hometown, had, in his seven terms in the House, come to be known as a shrewd, ruthless, and heavy-handed operator, a reputation testified to by his sobriquet, "The Hammer." To throttle the Democrats' efforts to convince Republicans to offer censure of Clinton as a substitute for impeachment, an idea that had gained some sympathy, DeLay relied upon his grasp of the technicalities of House procedures, which seemed to stem from an inherent gift. Even as a child, the fifty-one-year-old DeLay had such a head for detail that his parents woke him early on Christmas morning so he could help assemble the toys for his siblings. "I read the instructions," he recalled years later. "I've always been a rules person."

DeLay's devotion to rules went hand in hand with his commitment to traditional values—he was a born-again Christian and a champion of the Religious Right—and all this made him a formidable cultural warrior. "Rules are rules, right is right," DeLay liked to say. As for the political consequences, as DeLay saw it, those who claimed the Republicans would suffer from the push to impeach were probably Democrats at heart. Far from damaging the GOP leadership in the impeachment crusade against Clinton, DeLay claimed, the efforts would serve to solidify the party.

In manner and style Judiciary Committee Chairman Henry Hyde was just about as different from chief collaborator DeLay as he could be. The contrast between them reflected the cultural and geographic distance between Hyde's suburban Chicago constituents and the voters in the outlying precincts of Houston who sent DeLay to Congress. In contrast to the blunt, hard-nosed DeLay, who often abraded Republicans as well as Democrats, Hyde's courtly manners and intellectual flair had won him admirers in both parties and also in the media.

Yet not a great deal separated the two architects of impeachment on political issues. Long before the impeachment challenge arose, Hyde had made his mark on the Congress, and earned the undying hatred of feminists, by his successful advocacy of the eponymous amendment banning federal funding for abortions.

And when it came to impeachment, Hyde was as committed to the cause as DeLay or anyone else on the Hill. It was no easy task for him. At seventy-four, though his intellect seemed as keen as ever, the lingering effects of prostate surgery made the long public-hearing sessions an ordeal, and his ponderous, six-foot-five-inch figure shuffled along the Capitol corridors at a pace a tortoise could easily have matched. Threats on his life were numerous enough and serious enough to compel him to accept being chauffeured back and forth from his home to his duty station at the Judiciary Committee by the Capitol Hill police. "I haven't driven my car in about a month and a half now," he remarked. "I hope it will start."

As the leader of the assault on the president he had learned to ignore the abuse of wild-eyed Clinton defenders—and he had been forced to own up to the all-too-accurate findings of investigative journalists. In September, the Internet magazine *Salon* disclosed an adulterous affair Hyde had had in the 1960s with a married woman. At the time, her husband had come forward to accuse him of breaking up his family. His attempt to dismiss the affair as "a youthful indiscretion" only stirred more hoots and jeers from his critics. "But he's 74 years old. He was 41 then. It's all relative," a sympathetic friend sought to explain.

In the 1998 midterm election Hyde had easily regained his own seat. But his party's losses had given new energy to his task as coxswain of the impeachment drive. Before the election Hyde had talked about concluding the committee's probe before year's end. Now that possibility had become a necessity. Hyde could not let impeachment drag on into the next Congress, when the Democratic minority would be bigger and bolder as a result of the midterm vote. The impeachment clock was ticking and Henry Hyde had less than two months to deliver the goods. "Let's just lay it out," he told his aides.

Over the next few weeks, Hyde would nurture and protect the impeachment effort like a fragile plant. Not only had Clinton broken the

law, Hyde believed, but he had violated the moral underpinning of the
political system. The moral concepts expressed by the president's actions
and his utterances—"this idea that everything is relative, that stretching
the truth is acceptable because everyone does it"—had defamed the cultural values that Hyde had pledged himself to serve.

It was this connection between the commandments of morality
and the rule of law that Clinton's defenders sought to deny, not only
on the floor of the House, but even more vehemently in the world outside the beltway. Supporting a president who was more of an antihero
than a champion, as the debate rose to a climax on Capitol Hill the
Left took to the streets displaying a passion not exhibited since the
Vietnam War.

In the cultural debate conservatives were widely accused of being ex-
cessively strident. When William Bennett addressed a meeting of religious
broadcasters, he was booed because his audience felt he did not exhibit
forgiveness for the president's sins. And writing in the *New Republic,* John
B. Judis deplored the "extreme" language used by the proponents of impeachment who were "waging a cultural or religious crusade against the
president, one in which he figures as a symbol of moral relativism and ir-
religion." Conservatives, he claimed, were like the Salem witch hunters
and Joe McCarthy, driven by their "fear of the cultural netherworld associated with the Sixties—feminism, free love, Unitarianism, bilingualism,
drugs, abortion, and rock 'n' roll."

Yet when it came to ferocity Clinton's defenders seemed at least a
match for their foes. Notable among the president's champions for his
unrestrained fury was the film actor Alec Baldwin, who on a late-night
television show suggested that if Clinton's supporters lived in some "other
countries," they would be able to take out their wrath on House Judiciary
Committee Chairman Henry Hyde of Illinois in some sort of mass lynch-
ing. "We would stone Henry Hyde to death and we would go to their
homes and we'd kill their wives and their children," said Baldwin. A
spokesman for NBC, which aired the show, dismissed Baldwin's tirade as
"obviously a joke and meant to be taken as such," but added, "In retrospect, there are sensitivities, given the climate in Washington, and we
won't re-air it." Baldwin himself wrote a letter of apology to Hyde.

Though Clinton was scarcely representative of the entire Sixties generation, he had become, as Austen Furse, former Bush White House speechwriter, put it, "like the Weather Underground or the Black Panthers in the Sixties. He's not entirely representative of his generation, but he's a super-concentrated distillation of its worst disabilities," which would include "sanctimony, moral hauteur, the presumption that all of your enemies are bad people, a moral relativism and an exaggerated sense of ethical mission."

Clinton thus was a figure whom the inheritors of the Sixties found hard to condemn without confessing that some of their own values were ill founded. But if they could not condemn him, and found it awkward to defend him, their only recourse was to attack his foes, which they did with great gusto.

Their demonstrations stretched coast to coast, from Charlotte, North Carolina, where hundreds gathered in a church for a prayer vigil in support of Clinton, to San Francisco, Sacramento, and Los Angeles. In the City of Angels, at an event sponsored by People for the American Way and Jackson's Rainbow Coalition, the United Farm Workers Union, the National Organization for Women, and the American Civil Liberties Union, more than 1,000 anti-impeachment demonstrators gathered on a typically Californian balmy December day to hear from Barbra Streisand and Jack Nicholson while they waved placards reading, "Watergate, Iran-Contra and Monica?" and "He lied about sex. So what?"

Backers of impeachment staged scattered efforts of their own. In Newport Beach, California, the Reverend Steven Gooden held a vigil to pray for Clinton to resign. "The only way of getting this man out of office at this point is divine intervention," said Gooden, chairman of No Compromise Inc., a conservative group dealing with moral issues confronting youth. As biblical precedent for praying for the president's resignation, Gooden cited a passage from the Book of Samuel: "Fall down on your sword, for those who walk in pride will be brought down." And in San Diego, debates broke out in Balboa Park among 300 demonstrators—almost evenly divided between Clinton supporters and opponents. The former carried signs reading, "The Right is wrong"; the latter held placards that said, "Impeach the perjurer" and "It's the felonies, stupid." Both sides waved American flags.

But Clinton's defenders had the biggest numbers and the biggest names. At the forefront of this Culture War counteroffensive were the stars of the no-longer-so-new New Left's cultural firmament, famed figures from Hollywood, such as the vituperative Alec Baldwin, as well as from literary and academic circles. Some of the same celebrities who had once condemned the immorality of war and racism now contended that immorality, or at least the instances of Clinton's behavior that had been adduced as immoral, was irrelevant to politics and government.

"Who could have imagined that we would be living in a time when those we elected to office would turn their backs on the public and ignore the voices of the American people?" Barbra Streisand asked at the Los Angeles rally. "While we believe the president's behavior may deserve censure, in no way do these charges rise to the standard for impeachment."

As for Nicholson, his remarks illustrated the internal contradictions of his position and his own difficulties in working without a script. The master impersonator of countless ruthless and cynical protagonists cautioned that the impeachment crisis was not to be considered entertainment, even though the rally was covered by TV's "Entertainment Tonight." "But," he added, "we live in a television age. We're going to always live in a television age. These things regrettably sell a lot of soap," he said. "We can't confuse these issues." If there was anyone in earshot who was not confused by this time, Nicholson offered another conundrum: "We're kind of a strange country," he said. "We're Puritan-formed about sexuality."

The Clinton supporters who met in New York that same week were less troubled by ambiguity, moral or otherwise. Since the Big Apple's outdoor weather in December was no match for Los Angeles, the crowd of 500 found shelter in an auditorium of New York University in downtown Manhattan. The feminist leader Gloria Steinem, who once masqueraded as a Playboy bunny in the course of a journalistic exposé, cut to the chase in explaining the root cause of the controversy. Impeachment, she said, was not about what the president had done but rather about conservatives' "desire to win the culture war at last. To get rid of a president they hate." The feminist icon also called for an "end to the public humiliation of Monica Lewinsky," who "could be us and our daughters." Whatever the sins of Clinton, Steinem claimed, they were surpassed by the wrong his foes were trying to commit in threatening the stability of the nation.

Novelist E. L. Doctorow, who declared the impeachment proceedings to be a "conflation of church and state," placed the blame squarely on the independent counsel. "Ken Starr," he thundered, "has shown us how a conscienceless and ideologically vindictive use of investigative privilege can undercut the legitimacy of a duly elected American government. More than partisan politics is going on here. This is the unseating of a democratically elected president, with all the legitimacy of a coup d'etat."

The impeachment-as-coup story caught on with the crowd. Feminist scholar Blanche Wiesen Cook took advantage of it when she said that the impeachment proceedings were simply a "coup over a cock," a line that won her the expected laugh. But Cook was in no mood to treat the impeachment threat as a joke. "There is no reason for us to be here unless it is to reignite our Democratic-activist movement. . . . For weeks, for months, the Christian Coalition has gone around to churches and written letters. They're on that phone tree! Where are our phone trees?" Retired Episcopal bishop Paul Moore delivered what amounted to the benediction. "I think of the millions and millions of people who will suffer and die," he declared, "because the Republicans want to get President Clinton for a personal sin."

But the outcry in the streets was drowned out by the roll call in the House, where the majority Republicans had the last word. The GOP lawmakers were unshaken in their determination even by the self-immolation of one of their leaders on the morning of the vote. House Speaker Designate Bob Livingston of Louisiana, after admitting that he was an adulterer in a confession forced out of him by information unearthed by Larry Flynt, publisher of *Hustler* magazine, announced his resignation from his post and his House seat and invited President Clinton to follow his example. In a strange display of the vagaries of Culture War politics, Republicans praised Livingston for his moral courage, while Democrats, fearful that his action might spur more demands for the president's resignation, urged Livingston to stay on. Even as the Democrats rushed to the side of the fallen leader of the opposition to persuade him to renege on his vow, one of their own, Jerrold Nadler of New York, whose squat figure had earned him the nickname of "Congressman Fireplug," sought to recast Livingston's dramatic gesture as an argument against the Republican cause, branding Livingston's resignation "a surrender to a developing sexual McCarthyism." He warned his colleagues: "We are losing sight of the distinction between sins, which ought to be between a person and his family and his god, and crimes, which are the concern of the state and of society as a whole."

Henry Hyde was not about to stomach that. Having endured his own exposure earlier in the year, and unwilling to allow his pain to go to waste, he sought to make clear the difference between private acts of infidelity and public acts. "As a government official," Hyde said, alluding to Clinton's grand jury testimony, "you raise your right hand and you ask God to witness to the truth of what you're saying. That's a public act. Infidelity— adultery," he said, now referring to his own misconduct, "is not a public act, it's a private act, and the government, the Congress, has no business intruding into private acts."

Finally the House got down to its main business, voting almost entirely along party lines to approve two articles of impeachment, accusing Clinton of perjury before the grand jury and obstruction of justice.

After the drama of the House debate, the Senate trial was an anticlimax. Simple arithmetic explained why. In the Senate, Republicans outnumbered Democrats 55 to 45. They could get their way on procedure. But the framers of the Constitution in their wisdom had mandated that conviction on impeachment requires a two-thirds vote of the senators— that would mean 12 more voters than there were Republican senators.

No one imagined that those 12 votes would come from the Democratic side. So the fundamental reality that governed the trial in the Senate was that there would be no conviction—the president would be acquitted. The White House professed to take solace from the failure of the Republicans to get more than 50 votes on either count. But no one on Clinton's side could take much satisfaction from the day's reckoning. In addition to the 50 senators who had voted for conviction on the charge of obstruction of justice, another 32 signed on to a censure resolution. Blocked by a filibuster threat from reaching the floor, this resolution stated that by his conduct the president had "brought shame and dishonor" to himself and to his office and had "violated the trust of the American people." All told, 82 Senators had gone on record, in one form or another, as denouncing the president's conduct.

After the Senate trial concluded with Clinton's acquittal, Chief Justice William Rehnquist, who had presided over the proceedings, told the Senate: "I leave you a wiser, but not a sadder man." But the experience left nearly everyone else concerned on both sides not merely sad, but also confused.

Among conservatives, some called for a withdrawal from the battlefields of the Culture War. Until now, said Paul Weyrich, who as head of the Free Congress Foundation, a right-wing think tank, had for years been in the vanguard of the defenders of traditional values, "We have assumed that a majority of Americans basically agrees with our point of view. I no longer believe that there is a moral majority," a term he himself had helped coin. The mood was scarcely any brighter on the Left. In speaking out on Clinton's behalf, many of the artists and thinkers had had to stifle their own inner qualms about his policies and behavior. Some felt little sympathy for either side in the controversy. Harvard's Alan Dershowitz, for example, who had himself written a scathing critique of Clinton's civil liberties policies, nevertheless opposed the "theocracy" seeking to impeach Clinton. But as for Clinton the man, Dershowitz branded his conduct as "despicable," declining to go along with those who claimed that what the president did was irrelevant politically. "It matters a lot," Dershowitz told me. "I might not vote for him if he was running again. I think it's constitutionally irrelevant, but it's politically relevant. I think people who cheat on their wives and who lie tend to be less trustworthy in other matters."

All that could be adduced from these reactions is that the cultural legacy of the Clinton impeachment would overshadow the remainder of his presidential tenure and help to define the competition for his successor. But to deal with what the future held, it was necessary for the country and its leaders to understand the past. And while the circumstances surrounding Clinton's impeachment crisis were unprecedented, that confrontation did not emerge from a vacuum. Indeed, in defending and attacking the beleaguered president, his friends and adversaries were often echoing arguments that had been reverberating through the corridors of the nation's cultural and political life for most of the past four decades and would roil the nation into the next century.

PART TWO
REVOLUTION

ROOTS OF UPHEAVAL

"I live in Woodstock Nation," Abbie Hoffman memorably responded when asked where he was from. "It is a nation of alienated young people," he explained to the federal court jury during his conspiracy trial in Chicago. "We carry it around with us as a state of mind in the same way the Sioux Indians carried the Sioux nation around with them. It is a nation dedicated to cooperation versus competition, to the idea that people should have better means of exchange than property or money, that there should be some other basis for human interaction."

The cofounder of the Youth International Party, which existed mostly in his imagination, Hoffman was the antiwar movement's mad genius of media events. Of course, neither Hoffman nor any other individual could adequately personify the New Left, as the rising radical movement of the Sixties was called. Having abandoned the structured faith of the Old Left as outmoded, the New Left was too disparate, too determinedly disorganized, too lacking in explicit goals, except for the overturning of the established order, to be represented by any specific individual. Moreover, Hoffman was an unlikely paradigm for the movement because he did not take himself as seriously as some of his comrades in dissent. Considered to be the clown prince of the Sixties revolution, he sometimes referred to himself as a "Groucho Marxist." Nevertheless, friend and foe alike recognized that there was a method to his mirthful madness. And far better than many lengthier and more pretentious efforts in this direction, these few words from Hoffman's courtroom soliloquy explained the origins and the zeitgeist of the upheaval he helped to foster and make memorable.

The Sixties are remembered now, and were witnessed at the time, as an age of protest, a loud and angry era in which conversation was drowned out by cries of outrage and screams of hatred—against racism, against war, against the police, and not least against the protesters themselves. There is certainly a measure of truth in those recollections. Indeed, the trial at which Hoffman testified stemmed from the rioting at the 1968 Democratic Convention. But Hoffman's restrained definition of the revolution's underlying ideology as "a state of mind" provides a striking contrast with the sound and fury that colors most discussions of that momentous decade. Hoffman himself diverged from the stereotype which he and his comrades helped create. "A nation of alienated young people" was the expression he used on the witness stand during the trial that made its defendants, the Chicago Eight, folk heroes of the New Left. But when he uttered those words in Judge Julius Hoffman's courtroom Abbie Hoffman was already two years over thirty, the age which by the standards of the Sixties revolution marked the last frontier of trust. So the alienated young people were not all necessarily that young. Indeed rebels over thirty had an advantage; their age gave them a fuller understanding of what they were rebelling against.

Most revolutions are provoked by outrage with the social and economic order. But the revolt of the Sixties was nurtured by just the opposite conditions—materialistic plenitude and spiritual complacency. It began with the end of World War II, "The Good War," in Studs Terkel's phrase, a war fought for the right reasons that came out right, unconditionally so.

Unlike World War I, the Second World War did not leave a legacy of disillusionment. There seemed to be no reason for sour feelings. Samuel Goldwyn made a movie that captured the bullish national mood in 1946. Called *The Best Years of Our Lives,* it was a box office smash and the big Oscar winner that year. That was how Americans felt about themselves and the postwar world. *The Best Years* was also the title journalist Joseph Goulden chose for his chronicle of the immediate postwar era. Goulden, a thoughtful man and a seasoned muckraker, found the nation caught up in a "general euphoria, possessed of a broad national confidence, both in the future of individuals and in the country's ability to solve any postwar problems that arose."

Nothing that happened in the next few years diminished that optimism. "It was an era of general good will and expanding affluence," another respected journalist, David Halberstam, wrote. "Few Americans doubted the essential goodness of their society." After all, it was reflected back at them, not only by contemporary books and magazines, but even more powerfully and with far broader impact by the new family sitcoms on television. These programs, indirectly, and directly in the case of the commercials that paid for them, proclaimed the prosperity of the Fifties and sought to encourage Americans to make themselves even more comfortable in every material way possible. In truth, most in the viewing audience did not need much encouragement in that direction. Adult Americans entering the postwar era had endured two of the greatest traumas in the nation's history—the Great Depression and the Second World War. Now they were determined to make up for lost time, to prove that the sacrifices they had made had not been in vain. With more jobs than ever before, disposable family income soared by nearly 50 percent during that golden decade between 1950 and 1960. The middle class contemplated a bountiful harvest of goods to provide its members with comforts and pleasures the likes of which they had only been able to dream about in the past, merchandise that they now had the wherewithal to acquire.

But before too long, problems began to arise, even among the white middle-class Americans who seemed to have inherited the earth. Contributing to these various strains of discontent was a lingering sense of economic insecurity. Americans had approached the postwar era filled with trepidation that a new depression would overtake them. Most remembered that despite all its much-heralded achievement, the New Deal had fallen far short of solving the nation's economic woes. It took the war to do that. And now that the war was over, what was to stop these problems from recurring?

Indeed, although the Great Depression did not return, its specter continued to haunt the middle class in the form of more modest downturns called recessions. These slumps were relatively short but nevertheless bitter and disturbing blows to the general sense of well-being. They caused some tangible pain themselves, and they also served to reinforce the less tangible sense of anxiety. It was this gnawing nervousness, though normally concealed under a facade of confidence, combined with the simple lust to take advantage of the copious rewards that the economy offered, that created the pressure for conformity and for subordination of the individual spirit that left its mark on the period.

A best-selling novel, *The Man in the Grey Flannel Suit*, by Sloan Wilson, and a number of influential nonfiction critiques—notably *The Organization Man*, by William H. Whyte; *The Lonely Crowd*, by David Riesman; and *White Collar*, by C. Wright Mills—all from somewhat different perspectives called attention to the submersion of individuality by the demands of a society dominated by the goal of acquisitiveness. And the strains reflected by these books contributed to a new tension that ultimately helped generate a revolution.

This phenomenon was called the generation gap. Of course differences between parents and their offspring had always caused some antagonism. It was part of the American way of life, something that had easily been laughed off in radio shows like *The Aldrich Family* and *Junior Miss*. Because whatever the problems were, the kids always grew out of them. Parents of that time liked to reassure themselves with the old joke about the son who recalled that when he was a teenager he thought his father to be a foolish man. "But by the time I got to be twenty-five," the proverbial son would say, "I was surprised at how smart the old man had gotten."

But such humor gravely underestimated the new cleavage between the generations and failed to take into account the reasons for it. Economics had something to do with it. Young Americans, having no direct experience of the Depression, took the material abundance that surrounded them for granted. They did not share the anxiety of their parents nor did they feel, in the judgment of their progenitors, sufficient gratitude for what had been provided to them. Indeed, members of the younger generation wearied of being reminded of how much better off they were now than their parents had been in the Thirties and early Forties. And that impatience encouraged a skepticism about the failure of parents to live by the idealistic standards they had set for their children.

Instead of being duly appreciative of the long hours their fathers worked, the younger generation found hypocrisy in the contradiction between the values espoused by their fathers and mothers and the narrow materialism that seemed to govern their lives in reality. As Abbie Hoffman's family moved up the economic ladder in the 1950s, like most other American Jews they sought to blend into the Protestant middle class, an attitude that their oldest son regarded as a cop-out. "Having opted for a life in mainstream America, it became very difficult, even hypocritical, for them to try to push any strict code down our throats," Hoffman later wrote. On their way to vacation at a resort hotel the Hoffmans discovered the hotel had a policy of rejecting Jews. Instead of demanding that their reservation be honored, the Hoffmans headed for another hotel. "My parents wanted desperately to avoid a scene," Hoffman later recalled. "I was angry enough to muster up an asthma attack."

But there was another and more disturbing reason for the unease that afflicted adults even in this good-times era and strained their relationships with their children. This was a danger that transcended family relationships and had its roots in a world that had never gone back to normal after the havoc of World War II. This threat had been brewing since the closing days of that war as tensions built between the United States and its Western allies, on one hand, and the Soviet Union, on the other. This new challenge to peace came to be known as the Cold War. The nation's response was institutionalized by President Harry S Truman in February 1947 when he proclaimed the Truman Doctrine, a broad initiative intended to arrest the threat of Soviet aggression. The still-fresh memories of the victory over the Axis helped Democrat Truman bolster his case with the Republican-controlled Congress. "The United States contributed $341 billion toward winning World War II," Truman reminded the lawmakers and the nation. Now, the president said, the United States must pledge to stand by countries imperiled by the might of the Kremlin. "It is only common sense that we should safeguard this investment and make sure that it was not in vain."

And so it was that United States committed itself to the Cold War. Truman's language cast his new policy as an investment, a business deal, a time-honored element of the American cultural tradition that the patriotic Republican leaders of the Congress, all staunch defenders of the free-enterprise system, could readily join with their Democratic colleagues in supporting. What would become, as John F. Kennedy later called it, the "long twilight struggle," dominating the second half of the American Century, had been launched in the name of protecting an investment. But no one, not even Truman, could have imagined the ultimate cost of this commitment.

The greatest toll, both economic and psychological, was levied by the defining artifact of the Cold War, the atom bomb. The danger of nuclear annihilation lingered through the years as a specter that chilled the human heart. Psychologists found that even children as young as five could give remarkably accurate descriptions of how atomic bombs could obliterate life. Among some youngsters fear of the bomb seemed to have entwined itself with innate fears of losing their parents.

The bomb emerged as a major protagonist in the science fiction films of the period. In 1951's *The Day the Earth Stood Still,* a well-intentioned visitor from outer space tried to warn Americans against unleashing their nuclear fury into the other galaxies but was shot dead by panicky U.S. troops before he could get his message across. *Them,* made in 1954 in Japan, the only nation to have yet absorbed the fury of the bomb, featured rampaging monsters who were spawned by the fallout from nuclear blasts. *On the Beach,* starring, oddly enough, the debonair song-and-dance man Fred Astaire, depicted for 1959 audiences a world laid waste by nuclear war, making the point that the prospect of such a catastrophe was being overlooked.

But for all the political significance and cultural impact of the nuclear menace, those most worried about it had a hard time getting a hearing in political campaigns. Democratic standard-bearer Adlai Stevenson called for the suspension of hydrogen bomb testing in his 1956 bid for the White House. But his arguments were drowned out by a chorus of catcalls from the steadfastly anti-Soviet press and from supporters of incumbent President Dwight D. Eisenhower, whose prestige as leader of the crusade in Europe against Hitler made him hard to assail on any military issue.

Still, dread of the bomb remained a potentially powerful political force. In 1962, Abbie Hoffman, then fresh out of Brandeis University, broke into politics as an organizer for the Massachusetts Senate campaign of Harvard political scientist H. Stuart Hughes, a leader of the Committee for a Sane Nuclear Policy, or SANE as it came to be known. Hughes was running as an independent for the seat that had been held by John Kennedy, his candidacy built mainly around proposals for cuts in defense spending and curbs on nuclear weaponry.

From all over the United States organizers poured in to help bolster the Hughes campaign, Hoffman later recalled. By October polls showed Hughes with nearly 20 percent of the electorate; since most Hughes supporters were Democrats this was enough to threaten the candidacy of the party's own nominee, Edward M. Kennedy, who was running for the seat once held by his brother, the president. Then came the Cuban Missile Crisis, when President Kennedy ordered a blockade of Cuba to stop Soviet missile shipments and brought the world to the brink of nuclear war. Hughes accused President Kennedy of recklessness. That remark would have been damaging to whoever made it anywhere in the country, given the mood of the times. In Massachusetts Hughes's statement amounted to a suicide note for his candidacy.

But if the Left was having hard going against the bomb, where it ran up against the shibboleths of patriotism and the fear of communism, another issue emerged to generate the energy and inspiration that would give birth to the Sixties protest movement. This was the American dilemma, the tensions between blacks and whites living in a society dedicated to the proposition of equality but pervaded by racism and discrimination.

Many tributaries emptied into the flood tide that overflowed the barriers of segregation in America. But the one episode that probably more than any other single incident set these great events in motion started to unfold in the fall of 1957 in Little Rock, Arkansas. There the state's Democratic governor, Orval Faubus, in defiance of a federal court order, mobilized the Arkansas National Guard to block the admission of a handful of black students to the city's all-white Central High School. President Eisenhower, who had succeeded Truman in the White House, was sympathetic to the white South and resentful of the 1954 Supreme Court decision in *Brown v. Board of Education,* which had proclaimed the end of "separate but equal" education in Dixie. While tension mounted in Little

Rock and around the country, Ike temporized. Ultimately mob violence erupted in Little Rock. Eisenhower dispatched to Little Rock 1,000 men of the 101st Airborne Division, which had stormed Hitler's *Festung Europa* on D-Day. Central High was integrated at bayonet point. Eisenhower stressed that he was sending in the troops only to enforce the law, not because he favored desegregation. He lamented that "our enemies," presumably the Soviet Union and its allies, were "gloating over this incident and using it everywhere to misrepresent our nation." But he made no mention of the indignities and the terror inflicted on the Negro schoolchildren in Little Rock, nor of their right to an equal education.

Foes of integration were outraged. Georgia Senator Richard Russell predicted that the use of troops "would have a calamitous effect on race relations and the cause of national unity." But for their part, supporters of integration found little to cheer about. Adlai Stevenson, twice defeated by Eisenhower for the presidency, who had criticized Ike's failure to exercise moral leadership, called the outcome "a national disaster." And the *Arkansas Gazette,* though it had vigorously backed the school board's integration plan, said as the paratroopers took up their duty stations: "This is a tragic day in the history of the Republic." Little Rock was a watershed for racial relations in America, polarizing the issue of civil rights, locking U.S. politics and society on a divisive and often violent course, and helping to trigger the prolonged cultural conflict that rages on in the new millennium.

The struggle for civil rights had begun before Little Rock. The initial Negro protesters did not count on white support. Whatever they got they viewed as gravy. But the backing of whites would turn out to be more important than they could have imagined. Not only did whites join in their cause; they would seize upon the civil rights protests as inspiration for causes of their own. For the whites saw that the significance of the movement went beyond the issue of race. The black civil rights fighters of the Fifties were the first modern Americans who challenged the centuries-old notion that practically all power belonged in the hands of Protestant white men, and that challenge opened a wide gate.

The black revolt had begun slowly, quietly, and patiently. Rosa Parks helped lead the way. A forty-two-year-old tailor's assistant in Montgomery,

Alabama, she had been an active member of the National Association for the Advancement of Colored People (NAACP) since 1943. On December 1, 1955, with "no previous resolution until it happened," she refused to give up her seat on a city bus to another passenger who enjoyed the privilege of being white. Her impulsive act of conscience sparked a black boycott of the bus system that turned out to astound the white establishment because of its persistence.

Helping to sustain Parks and the other blacks of Montgomery in their struggle was the emergence of a powerful champion, a hitherto unknown clergyman named Martin Luther King, Jr. Though only twenty-six, he was a Harvard-educated Ph.D. who often cited the likes of Socrates, Aristotle, and Mahatma Gandhi in his sermons. "This is not a tension between the Negroes and whites," King said of the bus boycott. "This is a conflict between justice and injustice." To inspire the boycotters, King taught them new words to an old Baptist hymn whose unadorned lyrics and melody would echo through the century.

Deep in my heart
I do believe
We shall overcome
One day.

It took 382 days of boycotting for the city of Montgomery to give up the fight. King became the first black passenger to sit in one of the first ten rows of a Montgomery bus. The boycott established King as a national figure, made Rosa Parks a heroine to many, and gave black people everywhere reason to rejoice.

But blacks in the South had long ago learned to be realists in a way white folks never had to be. And after the victory over the buses, what else had changed? Not much. So it was not surprising that their patience was near exhaustion as they wondered what they might gain from the courts, and the good will, of white people.

Then came Little Rock, and many blacks no longer were willing to wait. The episode had dashed their fragile hopes but given them a new sense of desperate urgency. Their leaders became more aggressive. It was more than coincidence that it was 1957, the year of Little Rock, when the first lunch counter sit-ins were staged in the South, all told reaching at least sixteen cities in the next couple of years.

They were largely ignored by the media. But word of mouth carried the news through the black communities of the South, the churches, the NAACP, and a new organization called the Congress for Racial Equality, and slowly but surely the idea spread. On the first day of February 1960, in the textile city of Greensboro, North Carolina, four black freshmen from the state Agricultural and Technical College walked into the F. W. Woolworth store on South Elm Street and quietly sat down at the lunch counter. The white waitress ignored their studiously polite requests for service, just as the students ignored the hostile stares of the white customers. They got nothing to eat or drink for their pains but sat stubbornly until closing time. And the next morning they reappeared, reinforced by twenty-five fellow students. The scenario was the same, the students sitting quietly, politely, and very nonviolently while they were rudely, but again nonviolently, ignored.

It seemed as if nothing was happening. But it turned out to be a moment of great drama for the South and for the culture of race. By the Ides of March sit-in demonstrations at segregated lunch counters had spread from North Carolina to South Carolina, Virginia, Florida, Tennessee, and even Alabama, the heart of the Deep South. Nor were the sit-ins the only manifestations of the civil rights movement's new-found assertiveness. In Montgomery, Alabama, cradle of the confederacy, after a white man beat a black woman with a baseball bat in a sidewalk incident, 1,000 blacks silently marched to the white-columned first capitol of the Confederacy to pray and sing the "Star-Spangled Banner."

The white South was angry now and fighting back. In 1961, the year after the sit-in drive was launched, the Freedom Riders campaign to desegregate bus terminals led to violent retaliation. Setting off from the Greyhound depot in downtown Washington, the biracial force of protesters followed a zigzag course, south through Virginia and the Carolinas, veering to the west through Alabama, and then across Mississippi and down to New Orleans. Though some southerners blamed the Kennedy administration for instigating the expedition, that suspicion could not be further from the truth. John Kennedy had entered the White House determined to do as little as possible about civil rights. He was far more concerned with waging the Cold War against Nikita Khrushchev and the Soviet Union. What Kennedy certainly did not want was what the Freedom Riders provided—another reminder of America's racism, which was bound to create an international embarrassment. And this was not to mention the damage within his own Democratic Party, deeply split over the issue of race.

The Freedom Riders could not have cared less. White and black alike they were determined to end racial prejudice at whatever the political cost to Kennedy or the physical cost to themselves. And they paid a heavy price. At first the police greeted them simply with arrests. But as they penetrated deeper into the heart of Dixie the cops assaulted and beat them unmercifully.

Ultimately the Freedom Rides were counted a triumph for civil rights. By their sacrifice, the riders forced the Kennedy administration to finally bring an end to Jim Crow in all interstate bus terminals. More than that, they provided a demonstration of will and determination that meant even pragmatic politicians like Kennedy had to take the civil rights revolution seriously. And the Northerners who joined in the protest against segregation created a bond between the protest cultures of North and South, between the young students of both regions and of both races, that would help define the decade.

Much of the bond was forged by music. Years before the civil rights revolution caught fire, rock and roll began to make its way onto radio stations across the country. This music—whether it was performed by Little Richard or Elvis Presley—owed its largest artistic debt to American blacks and their forebears from Africa. "The first crashing intimation" of what the Sixties would be like, George Will observed, came in 1955 with the opening chords of the soundtrack of the movie *The Blackboard Jungle,* with Bill Haley and the Comets playing "Rock Around the Clock." The film dramatized the problem of juvenile delinquency, a Fifties preoccupation that, as Will wrote, would come to seem "quaint" compared with the disorders of the next decade. More enduring was the music, a blend not only of rhythm and blues but of black and white. The white performers appropriated the beat of the blacks, which had been done before. Yet by contrast with the rigidly racial lines that had previously divided the pop music industry, this new relationship was porous and flexible. Southern white boys like Presley, Buddy Holly, and Jerry Lee Lewis shared the airwaves and the record charts amicably with black stars like Little Richard, Chuck Berry, and Fats Domino in what amounted to, as one commentator, Todd Gitlin, put it, "cultural miscegenation."

In 1956 another discordant note in another medium, poetry, challenged the prevailing complacency with the publication of "Howl" by Allen Ginsberg. "I saw the best minds of my generation destroyed by madness, starving, hysterical, naked," cried the poet laureate of what came to be called the Beat Generation. Actually the Beats were never large in number, scarcely more than a few thousand, and in their early years they were mostly scorned and reviled by the mainstream press and culture.

But by their rejection of conventional mores the Beats had an almost subliminal influence on members of the Baby Boom generation, then still in early adolescence. The antimaterialism that was one of the major themes of the Beats was reflected in one of the early defining manifestos of the decade, the so-called Port Huron statement. Issued in 1962 by young, white students who had established a new organization, Students for a Democratic Society, and billed as nothing less than a blueprint for a new "participatory democracy," the Port Huron statement established the credo that would guide the as-yet-undeclared cultural and political revolution:

> The goal of man and society should be human independence: a concern not with image or popularity but with finding a meaning in life that is personally authentic. We would replace power rooted in possession, privilege, or circumstance by power and uniqueness rooted in love, reflectiveness, reason and creativity.

It was this same spirit of estrangement from traditional lines of authority, born with the Beats, that Abbie Hoffman expressed in the

Chicago courtroom when he talked of "alienated young people" dedicated to "cooperation versus competition." Further afield, the example of
the Beats inspired a struggling young quartet from Liverpool, England, to
name themselves "The Beatles" and, with their high-heeled boots and
overabundant hair, change the nature of popular music on both sides of
the Atlantic. When they appeared on the "Ed Sullivan Show" in February
1964, 68 million people, one of the largest TV audiences in history,
tuned in.

Plenty of home-grown voices also reflected and influenced the times,
among the most prominent being the folk singer Bob Dylan. With his
hard-lick guitar, whooping harmonica, thin voice, and shaggy sideburns,
at twenty-two Dylan looked barely fourteen. His accent made some listeners think of a Brooklyn hillbilly. But he helped American folk singers,
including Joan Baez, rediscover a long forgotten truth—the political
power of folk music. Not since the Civil War era had folk singers, now led
by Dylan among the men and Joan Baez among the women, sung about
the nation's traumas in such numbers or with such intensity. "Instead of
keening over the poor old cowpoke who died in the streets of Laredo or
chronicling the life cycle of the blue-tailed fly (the sort of thing that fired
the great postwar revival of folk song), they are singing with hot-eyed fervor about police dogs and racial murder," *Time* reported.

These were the myriad paths of protests in the early years of the Sixties—the picketing and the sit-ins, the passive resistance and the marches,
the ballads and the verse. Many of these trails seemed to head in different
directions, in keeping with the diversity and freedom that they celebrated.
But as the decade lengthened a new cause loomed larger than all the rest.
And this was the war in Vietnam.

Truman had begun the U.S. involvement in Indochina in 1949, giving
military and economic aid to the French colonial government as part of
America's worldwide struggle against communism. Weary of the drain of
blood and treasure, the French left Indochina in the Fifties. But the United
States under Eisenhower continued to pour in support, with the help now
going to the anti-Communist regime that governed South Vietnam. President Kennedy ordered the creation of an elite military unit, the Green

Berets, and found the first use for these shock troops in Vietnam, where they were part of an expansion of U.S. involvement there.

No one will ever know what Kennedy would have done in Indochina had he lived. What his successor Lyndon Johnson did was escalate the war, a decision that would change America more than any event since World War II. In the process, Johnson created a cause that over the years would pull the diverse strands of the Sixties unrest and protest together and give them unity and purpose. And ultimately, the bloodshed in Southeast Asia touched off another war on the streets of America.

6

EVE OF DESTRUCTION

In the fall of 1965 Abbie Hoffman organized the first antiwar march in the history of his hometown, Worcester, Massachusetts. The resentful townspeople did not just sit back and watch. They threatened the marchers with violence when they first got wind of the idea, and Hoffman, who for the past two years had been active in civil rights protests in the South, used that experience to coach his marchers in nonviolent defense.

As Hoffman led 250 demonstrators through the heart of town, a mob shouting "traitors" broke through police lines and charged the demonstrators. They defrocked a priest and threw him to the ground and beat others with brass knuckles and their fists. But the marchers made it to City Hall and mounted their picket line. "Aside from a few slashed tires and broken windows, we survived our initiation," Hoffman recalled.

The Worcester march, duplicated in cities across the land that autumn, was an important signpost along the tumultuous path the New Left had already traveled pointing to the even more strife-torn road ahead. For 1965 was a watershed year for Hoffman and for the uprisings spawned by the Sixties. It was a year of broken promises, crushed expectations, and sundered alliances. It was the year that dashed the hopes stirred first by John Kennedy's election and then by Lyndon Johnson's promise to carry on what Kennedy had started. It was the year that the civil rights revolution, hamstrung by violence and divisiveness, ground to a halt. Its leaders would now be forced to do battle to hold on to the gains they had already made, even as they fought among themselves.

Most of their erstwhile white comrades in the assault on the barricades of racism channeled their energies and passions elsewhere, into the protest against the escalating U.S. involvement in Vietnam. But in that struggle against the war abroad they carried with them the lessons they had learned and the disappointments they had suffered in the struggle against racial injustice at home.

Hoffman's experience was typical of many. He had gotten his baptism in the civil rights movement in his hometown in 1963, following H. Stuart Hughes's failed political crusade against the bomb in 1962. Taking over Worcester's long-dormant NAACP chapter, Hoffman had turned it into the most militant branch in the country. His success there led him to become embroiled in the passions of Mississippi's bloody Freedom Summer of 1964 that claimed the lives of three young men—two whites and one black—all organizers for the Student Nonviolent Coordinating Committee, known as the SNCC or simply "Snick."

For a time Johnson's landslide victory in 1964 over Barry Goldwater seemed to represent a great victory for the civil rights forces. The following year, as blacks pushed for voting rights, Johnson not only backed their efforts, he made their cause and their stirring battle cry his own. "We *shall* overcome," he declared in a memorable address to both houses of Congress. The voting rights bill became the law of the land and ultimately changed the political face of the South.

But well before that victory, signs of the trouble facing the civil rights movement were not hard to find. Though the gains against segregation had left many blacks unsatisfied, they had been enough to stir rancor among whites. "Backlash" became a new buzzword among white politicians, who used it as an excuse to go even slower than before in yielding to black demands. In the 1964 presidential campaign Alabama Governor George Wallace, having made himself a hero to diehards in the South as a result of his defense of segregation, had ventured outside of Dixie to enter Democratic primaries in Wisconsin, Maryland, and Indiana. Running against favorite son stand-ins for the incumbent president, Lyndon Johnson, Wallace got enough votes to shock Northern liberals and to demonstrate the political potency of the white backlash.

A more immediate problem for Johnson was the burgeoning resistance to the war, because it represented a broad attack on his policy in Southeast Asia. Johnson had buried Barry Goldwater in the 1964 campaign by pronouncing him a warmonger and promising that for his part, he would not send American boys to Vietnam "to do what Asian boys ought to be doing." But in the months after the election, frustrated by the tenacity of the Communist forces in Vietnam and fearful that defeat there would jeopardize his plans for a Great Society at home, Johnson decided to escalate the war, sending tens of thousands of young Americans to Vietnam.

Hoffman and the other youthful rebels who had gained confidence and experience from the civil rights battle now turned their attention to this new cause—the war in Indochina. Resistance to the war had been building for some time, since the Tonkin Gulf resolution, which gave Johnson a blank check for fighting communism in Indochina, had passed Congress against the nay votes of only two senators. But the antiwar forces were slow to grasp the seriousness of the threat and their early efforts were muffled by uncertainty. Some who objected to the war were fearful of being branded as Communists and un-American. And at the same time they worried that if they did not act they would lose the initiative on the issue to radical forces then taking root on the nation's campuses. Ambivalence reigned.

So in December 1964 when Students for a Democratic Society (SDS), emerging as the most important and aggressive of the student groups, met to discuss staging a national protest against the war, Todd Gitlin, one of its leaders, was more interested in mounting a sit-in at the Chase Manhattan Bank to protest its loans to South Africa. And the SDS meeting tabled a resolution that declared: "I will not be drafted until the U.S. gets out of Vietnam," as too controversial. Ultimately SDS agreed on a grab bag of antiwar slogans, including "War on Poverty—Not People" and "Ballots Not Bombs for Vietnam," and went ahead with a rally in Washington attended by more than 20,000 demonstrators, the largest peace protest in the nation's history.

The protest movement had to contend with Lyndon Johnson's Department of Justice. Dr. Benjamin Spock, the man who literally wrote the book used to rear millions of baby boomers, and Dr. William Sloan Coffin, the Yale University chaplain, were indicted for conspiracy to encourage violations of the draft in 1965. But such actions seemed only to spur resistance to the war, particularly on the nation's campuses. Antiwar students and sympathetic faculty combined to organize "teach-ins" at schools around the country. At the University of Michigan, for example, some 3,000 students attended all-night colloquia in which their professors made the case against the war and debated government policy with State Department officials dispatched from Washington.

Nevertheless, the war ground on. With more troops pouring into Vietnam and the white backlash against civil rights heightened, the threat of violence in the nation's cities increased. An ominous mood spread among the once hopeful and confident student movement. This darkening zeitgeist was capsulized by a jarring folk rock melody called "Eve of Destruction," which in the summer of 1965 became the fastest selling rock song ever recorded—even though many stations refused to air its apocalyptic message. Chanted in the sullen tenor of Barry McGuire as guitar chords rasped, the lyrics described a world under constant nuclear threat "explodin'" and with "bullets loadin'" and "bodies floatin'" even in the River Jordan.

The difference between these somber 1965 lyrics, better suited to a dirge, and the upbeat spirit of the music of 1964, typified by the Beatles' "A Hard Day's Night" and the Beach Boys' "California Girls," pointed up the changing attitude of young people toward American society. The mood shift was reflected in the perceptions transmitted by the media, as illustrated by the differing tones of two major stories in *Time* magazine on young Americans. In its issue of January 7, 1966, *Time* accorded "The Young Generation"—men, and yes, by some androgynous stretch even women, under the age of twenty-five—its ultimate accolade, "Man of the Year." Rarely the first to sniff out a new social trend, *Time* was still dewy-eyed and gushy about young people the world over, even as the generation's mood darkened. "What makes the Man of the Year unique?" the magazine asked rhetorically:

> Cushioned by unprecedented affluence and the welfare state, he has a
> sense of economic security unmatched in history. Granted an ever-

lengthening adolescence and life-span, he no longer feels the cold pressures of hunger and mortality that drove Mozart to compose an entire canon before death at 35; yet he, too, can be creative. Reared in a prolonged period of world peace, he has a unique sense of control over his own destiny—barring the prospect of a year's combat in a brush-fire war.

But a year later, as the evidence of severe social stress and strain reached even the high-rise offices in Rockefeller Center where *Time's* editors toiled, the magazine took a more stringent view of the under–twenty-five set. "The young seem curiously unappreciative of the society that supports them," the magazine complained. "'Don't trust anyone over 30,' is one of their rallying cries. Another, 'Tell it like it is,' conveys an abiding mistrust of what they consider adult deviousness." Though seeking to dismiss liberal activism as passé, *Time* could not ignore Vietnam, and it acknowledged that the young Americans had become "increasingly perturbed by the war."

To say the least.

As the protest against the war burgeoned, and as frustration with racial conditions intensified, these political attitudes were simultaneously reinforced and reflected by what came to be known as the counterculture, producing a joint cultural-political revolution that defied comparison in the annals of American history. Clothes and appearance became a badge of rebellion. Long hair, usually supplemented by beards among males, was the most conspicuous and pervasive totem of countercultural appearance. But it was only part of an effort to achieve an overall effect of slovenliness and disreputability that included such garments as torn jeans, beaded headbands, and ragged T-shirts. This outlandish garb became identified with a new breed within the younger generation whose members called themselves "hippies," a term once used disparagingly by Beats for those who were only half hip, or plugged into the latest trend. The hippie objective was to gently undermine the traditional values of society by "flower power," a conceit inspired in part by the mod fashions of London's Carnaby Street and in part by force of example. Besides decking themselves with love beads made of shells and eucalyptus balls some also painted their faces and torsos in psychedelic shades. They were also fascinated with strobe lights, ear-shattering music, exotic clothing, and erotic slogans.

Underpinning their beliefs and their lifestyle was the use of hallucinogenic drugs. Those who took the "trip" glided beyond middle-class reality into a glittering but cacophonous universe in which perceptions were heightened and senses distorted, the imagination dazzled with visions of teleological verity. The hippies and their hallucinogens were only one dimension of the new drug culture that enthralled the young even as it alarmed their parents. Marijuana, variously dubbed "pot," "grass," or "Mary Jane," which had once had only a limited use among the fastest set of teenagers, now found a vastly expanded market, reaching not only college and high-school students but in some places even their young siblings in elementary school. All of young America seemed caught up with drugs. One group of protesters told Todd Gitlin of driving through Michigan and being honked at by a car in the next lane. As the two autos sped along the highway, the driver who had sounded his horn rolled down his window and with a grin handed a joint across to the total strangers in the next car.

Musical idols of the youth culture promoted the use of drugs, none too subtly, with such songs as "Lucy in the Sky with Diamonds" and "I'll Get By with a Little Help from My Friends" by the Beatles and "Mother's Little Helpers" from the Rolling Stones. But probably the most active booster of drugs was former Harvard professor Timothy Leary, who, after being fired from Harvard for conducting LSD experiments with students, founded the League for Spiritual Discovery to "introduce the sense of psychedelic celebration." His slogan for many captured the spirit of the times: "Turn on, tune in, drop out." "Laws are made by old people who don't want young people to do exactly those things young people were meant to do," Leary told an interviewer. "Make love, turn on and have a good time," he urged.

As time wore on the counterculture and the war resistance, the hippies and the SDS, began to find more in common. Some bonds were mainly symbolic. At a rally in Berkeley in 1966, someone started singing the old union anthem "Solidarity Forever." But Ralph Chaplin's melodramatic lyrics—"We can break their haughty power, gain our freedom when we learn, that the union makes us strong"—were rooted in another decade of upheaval—the 1930s—and few of those well-nourished youngsters knew those words or comprehended the economic inequities of that era. As an alternative some began to chant "The Yellow Submarine," the title song of the Beatles' latest hit film, and soon it was taken up by the whole room. Later a hardened Berkeley activist put out a leaflet hailing the song, which he claimed helped celebrate "the growing fusion of head, heart and hands of hippies and activists; and our joy and confidence in our ability to care for and take care of ourselves and what is ours. We adopt for today this unexpected symbol of our trust in our future, and of our longing for a place fit for us all to live in. Please post, especially where prohibited. We love you."

All the while, the war in Vietnam raged with no letup. Seeking a rationale for the killing, the Pentagon placed great stress on the "body count," the numbers of Communist soldiers killed each day, and promised in a phrase already achieving a self-mocking connotation that there was "light at the end of the tunnel." But whatever the claimed body count in the Indochina jungles, it could not offset the impact of the body bags carrying the remains of U.S. troops back to the parents of America. It was the weight of those body bags that began to turn even some fixtures of the political establishment against the war, among them, surprisingly enough in view of later events, Mayor Richard Daley of Chicago, one of the most puissant leaders of the Democratic Party.

During a visit to the White House in 1966 to talk to the president about the needs of Chicago and domestic politics in general, Daley was surprised when Johnson brought up another subject—Vietnam.

"Look, Dick, I've got a lot of trouble over there in Vietnam," Johnson began. "What do you think about it?"

Daley waited for a moment and then replied: "Well Mr. President, when you've got a losing hand in poker you just throw in your cards."

"But what about American prestige?" Johnson wanted to know.

"You just put your prestige in your back pocket and walk away," Daley retorted.

Yet Lyndon Johnson turned aside Daley's advice, just as he rejected the counsel of others who urged him to find a way out of the quagmire.

Convinced he had no other choice, Johnson stayed the course. A lyric by Pete Seeger captured the resentment of the opposition to the war. "We're waist deep in the Big Muddy," went the refrain, "and the big fool says, 'Push on!'"

As Johnson escalated the war, the opposition escalated its demonstrations. In the spring of 1967, a broad coalition of liberals, radicals, and cultural revolutionaries calling itself the National Mobilization to End the War in Vietnam, known as the MOBE, sponsored marches in San Francisco and New York. In New York, Martin Luther King, Jr., led several hundred thousand marchers across Manhattan from Central Park to the United Nations to demand an immediate U.S. pullout. Some carried signs declaring "Burn draft cards, not people." Others joined into the by now familiar chants: "Hey, hey LBJ, how many kids did you kill today?" And "Hell no! We won't go!"

But not everyone in New York was in tune with the protest, and the Culture War turned nastier and violent. Some New Yorkers were so angered by what they viewed as this display of un-Americanism that they climbed on top of cars to shout: "Bomb Hanoi." Construction workers from their vantage points on buildings dumped wet concrete and paint on the demonstrators.

Undeterred by the protest against their protest, antiwar forces mapped demonstrations around the country for the fall designed to signal the transformation of their stance from mere protest to outright resistance. But before their autumn effort could get under way, the summer of 1967 turned into the longest and hottest season of this decade of urban unrest.

In began in July in Newark where long-festering black resentment against the police erupted when white cops were seen beating a black cab driver as they dragged him into a police station. The rioting in New Jersey's biggest city that followed claimed 26 lives. A week later Detroit was engulfed by violence that was not only worse than in Newark but bloodier than the Motor City's infamous riot of 1943, which had claimed 34 lives. In the 1967 outburst 43 died, 2,000 were hurt, and 5,000 left homeless by the flames that ravaged the black neighborhoods. Ultimately, 4,700 U.S. Army airborne troops occupied the ghetto as if it were a conquered city. The riots cast a pall over the nation and increased the sense of alienation and desperation among the leaders of the antiwar movement. "We live in the space between the end of the movement and the beginning of revolution," Todd Gitlin wrote to a friend that bloody summer.

Nevertheless the war resistance soldiered on, finding new schemes to dramatize the cause. In late October the protesters kicked off "Stop the Draft Week" with demonstrations from coast to coast. The main event was a march on the Pentagon that turned into the capstone of the year's efforts. The success of this demonstration was due to its two experienced organizers with complementary talents, Abbie Hoffman and Jerry Rubin. "Just as Che needed Fidel and Costello needed Abbott, Jerry Rubin and I were destined to join forces," Hoffman wrote later. Rubin and Hoffman both considered themselves populists who scorned intellectual pretension and depended instead on direct action in the streets.

But they relied on different strengths. Though Rubin was familiar with the protest theater of the absurd, his style lacked what Hoffman called "a silly element and the appeal to the spirit," which Hoffman was fully prepared to provide. Rubin had a keener understanding of how to combine the two streams of protest—cultural and political. "Jerry's forte was political timing, mine dramatic," was the way Hoffman put it.

As the appointed day neared, the Pentagon girded for action. Defense Secretary Robert McNamara decided to ring the building with troops armed with rifles and to station U.S. marshals as a buffer between the troops and the protesters. Reinforcements were helicoptered into the Pentagon's center courtyard at night, in case the demonstrators broke through the first line of defense.

Encouraged by abundant ballyhoo, some 30,000 showed up to confront the military establishment in its five-sided lair on October 21, 1967. Most remained outside the cordon of armed guards defending the bastion. But a few thousand of the bolder demonstrators broke through that outer defense to the side building where the U.S. Army troops were posted and expressed their feelings against the war in ways that demonstrated the heterodoxy—and heterogeneity—of the peace movement.

A few carried Viet Cong flags. Some, in the most poignant and indelible gesture of the demonstration, placed flowers in the gun barrels of the soldiers who confronted them and then shouted: "Join us" at the troops. Others urinated on the walls. Some young women, according to Defense Secretary McNamara, who was watching from the Pentagon roof, "rubbed their breasts against the soldiers standing at attention with rifles at their sides, and even unzipped their flies; the soldiers did not move." Later McNamara would confess that the protesters scared him. "An uncontrolled mob is a frightening thing," he explained. "Luckily in this case, frightening but ineffective."

On the last day of 1967, looking forward to the presidential election year, Hoffman and Rubin staged what was probably their most successful put on—they created a new political party, the Yippies, an acronym later defined as standing for Youth International Party. "The YIP is a party— like the last word says—not a political movement," claimed Hoffman, battling for legitimacy, but mostly for attention.

But events were now in train that would make it no longer necessary for the opposition to resort to stuntsmanship to get the public's attention. As 1968 began, and the war continued with no letup and no sign of progress, Johnson's Vietnam policy came under fire from a voice far removed from the disreputable looking crowd that had massed outside the Pentagon and flocked to Yippie rallies. Columnist Walter Lippman, by then regarded by many as the reigning seer of the American establishment, sounded a stark warning for Lyndon Johnson and the party he led. "No one should ignore the depth of the revulsion which a large number of Americans—who are essential to a successful Democratic Party—feel at the spectacle of Vietnam," Lippman wrote.

But few in the Democratic Party or elsewhere in the political world shared Lippman's view. Johnson's renomination seemed inevitable. Only a few weeks after Lippman's warning, though, the political world turned. As January 1968 ended with the Vietnamese Tet New Year, the Viet Cong staged their boldest stroke of the war, a remarkably well-coordinated guerrilla assault against South Vietnamese cities that had been depicted as secure bastions for the Saigon government. Before their attacks were finally repelled, the Viet Cong had even penetrated the compound of the U.S. embassy in Saigon.

Tet was the first milestone of the 1968 presidential campaign. Its weight on public opinion, magnified by the overwhelming media coverage of the fighting, prefigured the heightened influence of the new electronic mass media in politics. In covering Tet, television led the charge. Even before the surprise Vietcong offensive, television news had made the Vietnam War its own, giving Americans at home an unprecedented, wrenching linkage with their sons in combat. It was this compelling intimacy that led the *New Yorker* to label the fighting in Indochina "the living room war." But until Tet the war had consisted mainly of skirmishes and firefights scattered around the lush countryside, seemingly lacking pattern or direction. Now the Communist offense defined the conflict in stark outline. The story dominated the network news shows, most notably NBC's *Huntley-Brinkley Report,* whose vivid portrayal of the action was climaxed by the on-camera execution in a battle-torn Saigon street of a Viet Cong prisoner by General Nguyen Ngoc Loan of the army of South Vietnam, America's ally in the fight to save Asia from communism.

The print media did not lag far behind. Editors splashed the stunning Pulitzer Prize–winning photo of General Loan, pistol in hand, and his human target on front pages around the country. Despite Johnson's claims that the Viet Cong had been turned back, the president was hoist with his own petard. Americans were shaken by what they read and especially by what they saw of the Tet Offensive because of its variance from the reassuring impression the administration had presented.

The political fallout was soon evident in public opinion polls. Public opposition to Johnson's Vietnam policy mounted sharply, and the antiwar movement benefited greatly. In the New Hampshire Democratic presidential primary, insurgent candidate Eugene McCarthy got 42 percent of the Democratic vote compared to 50 percent for Johnson, hitherto regarded as invincible.

Events in early 1968 then moved swiftly. Robert Kennedy, heir to his slain brother's political legacy, who had previously rejected entreaties of Vietnam protest leaders to run, announced his own candidacy for the Democratic nomination. "I do not run for the presidency merely to oppose any man," said Kennedy. "I run because I am convinced that this country is on a perilous course." Before the month of March was out, Lyndon Johnson dropped out of the race. "With America's sons in the fields far away," Johnson told an amazed nation, "with our hopes and the world's hopes for peace in the balance every day, I do not believe that I should devote an hour or a day of my life to any personal partisan causes."

Though the ferment on the political scene seemed to offer hope to opponents of the war, some in that restless generation were not placated. In April, long-simmering resentment of Columbia University student activists against the administration for its high-handed treatment of blacks in nearby Harlem and its involvement in Pentagon research programs exploded. Hundreds of students took over five university buildings, including the campus landmark, Low Library, and barricaded themselves inside. Protesters made themselves at home in the office of President Grayson Kirk, whose cavalier treatment of previous student grievances had particularly outraged them. After eight days Kirk summoned the police, 1,000 strong, who clubbed and beat the students, arresting more than 500 of them as they took back the campus. The police violence seemed to unite the students and build support for the goals of the insurgents, if not their tactics. Kirk was forced to resign. Protest leaders congratulated themselves that they had succeeded in accomplishing an important short-term objective—forcing Columbia to expose its ruthless side, a stratagem that was to become increasingly common for the New Left in the turbulent months ahead.

At any rate, similar insurgencies soon flared at campuses around the country. In California, the state's new governor and Republican presidential prospect, Ronald Reagan, fired the head of San Francisco State University because he agreed to meet with student activists to discuss their complaints. When his successor, an English professor named S. I. Hayakawa, called in police to break up a student rally, the students and faculty called a strike and Hayakawa had to shut the university down.

The bitter end to the Columbia uprising and the further campus disruptions it triggered were part of a pattern of polarizing events that dominated that spring, devastating the once bright hopes of the New Left and rending the fabric of society itself. In April, about three weeks before the student rebellion at Columbia, Martin Luther King, Jr., was assassinated in Memphis, where he had gone to lend his support to a strike of garbage workers. In the wake of his death, rioting swept more than 100 cities, including the nation's capital, as blacks expressed their long pent-up fury.

Soon after this tragedy Johnson's vice president, Hubert Humphrey, entered the race, clearly as Johnson's surrogate, and incongruously dedicated his candidacy to a restoration of "the politics of happiness and the politics of joy." While Kennedy and McCarthy fought it out in the primaries, Humphrey stayed out of the fray, counting on the backing of the bosses. They were committed to supporting him regardless of the outcome of the primaries, which then selected only a minority of the delegates.

Antiwar leaders knew the cards were stacked in favor of Humphrey; still, they clung to the hope that Robert Kennedy might prevail. His assassination in June crushed those dreams and stunned the nation, which had yet to recover from the loss of King. But it had a powerful catalytic impact on the New Left and its plans for the Democratic Convention. Leaders of the Vietnam protest had first discussed arranging some sort of militant nonviolence at the convention the previous fall when their frustration with Johnson's war policies was at its height. They had shelved the idea after Johnson's withdrawal from the presidential campaign. But with Kennedy's death, and the crushing of the antiwar forces in the contest for the Democratic nomination, the idea of a protest at the Democratic convention in Chicago in August 1968 took on new life.

No one was more enthusiastic about antiwar activity in Chicago than Abbie Hoffman. If the Democrats and Republicans were holding nominating conventions, Hoffman announced, then his own Youth International Party surely must have a conclave of its own. In contrast with the Democrats and their convention of death, the Yippies, Hoffman said, would hold a convention of life. And their nominee was all set: it would be a pig. "They nominate a president and he eats the people," Hoffman explained. "We nominate a president and the people eat him." It was a good laugh at the expense of the Democrats, and most of the antiwar leaders laughed along with Hoffman. It was just as well that they did. Because once they got to Chicago in August, they found the laughs were few and far between.

THE GUARDIAN

The view from the Conrad Hilton, the headquarters hotel for the 1968 Democratic Convention, provided a peaceful contrast with the rest of Chicago's habitual din and clangor. The windows opened onto the broad expanse of Michigan Avenue, the verdant space of Grant Park, and beyond that, the sparkling waters of Lake Michigan. The park, which runs parallel to one of Chicago's major thoroughfares, Lake Shore Drive, was ordinarily a gathering place for Loop workers, many of whom liked to sprawl out on the lawn to relax during their lunch hour.

But on this particular afternoon, Wednesday August 28, 1968, no such peaceful vista presented itself. Grant Park teemed with 15,000 angry demonstrators, surrounded by a cordon of belligerent police officers. About six miles to the south in the Chicago amphitheater, on the edge of the city's celebrated and odoriferous stockyards, in a whitewashed structure where Richard Nixon had first been nominated for the presidency in 1960, the Democratic National Convention was in the process of rejecting a plank to the party's national platform that called for speeding the end of the Vietnam War. In the park the demonstrators had met to vent their resentment of the vote, and indeed of everything for which the convention and the Democratic Party stood.

In a few hours their anger would boil over. The revolution that had been building for the better part of the decade would declare itself and burst forth amid clouds of tear gas, a rain of clubs, and cries of hatred and terror. In this outburst, cultural strife was so intertwined with political struggle that the two could scarcely be distinguished. The uprising had roots around the country, from the Jim Crow towns in Dixie, where demonstrators had been beaten at lunch counters and assaulted by police dogs, to the teeming cities of the North, where tear gas and clubs had turned back massive demonstrations against the war.

On a smaller scale, the upheaval, which was truly national in origin, could have erupted almost anywhere and at any time in the past few years. Yet Chicago in the summer of 1968 was the manifestly logical place for the cultural and political conflict of the Sixties to reach its violent climax. The assemblage of the Democratic Convention delegates brought to this city the representatives of the political establishment against which the rage of the protest movement had been steadily rising. Moreover, just as Washington was the nation's political capital and New York its financial capital, Chicago, Carl Sandburg's "City of the Big Shoulders," was the quintessential American city, the capital of Middle America, the stronghold of the cultural values that the protesters had been assaulting for years.

The final reason why Chicago would become the battleground supreme was that if the protesters were looking for a fight, there was a man in that city who would not flinch from one. Indeed, the mayor of Chicago, Richard Daley, would do everything he could to make sure there was a fight—and that he would come out on top. Viewing himself as the guardian of middle-class values, Daley considered a good fight the best way to preserve and define what he believed. Not that there was much question about Daley's beliefs. In his own person he combined the political power and cultural stance that was exactly what the demonstrators were against. That, after all, was the way he had been brought up.

The Irish families in Bridgeport, the South-side neighborhood where Dick Daley first saw the light of day in 1902, had little time or patience for protests or public demonstrations of any sort, except, of course, for the annual St. Patrick's Day parade. They were too busy raising their families and earning a living. Bridgeport was a place of few pretensions. Its citizens drank out of the beer pail and ate out of the lunch bucket. The men worked in the nearby stockyards, of whose proximity their noses always reminded them, or in nearby factories, or on construction jobs.

And a good many, like the Irish in Al Smith's New York and James Curley's Boston, found room on the public payroll and in the world of politics. For the Irish, as Daniel Moynihan observed, the hierarchial urban political machine was comfortably similar to the structure of the Irish village, "a place of stable, predictable social relations in which almost everyone had a role to play, under the surveillance of a stern oligarchy of elders, and in which on the whole, a person's position was likely to improve with time. Transferred to Manhattan, these were the essentials of Tammany Hall." Or, Moynihan might have added, of the Chicago Democratic Party.

By the time Daley came of age, the Irish of Bridgeport were already famous for generating politicians—including Daley's two predecessors— and for the strength of their voter turnout, extending, some cynics contended, even into the graveyards. But the political life was not for Richard Daley's father. A short, wiry man, Michael Daley, who had come from County Waterford, made an honest living as a sheet metal worker.

Michael Daley's wife, Lillian Dunne Daley, whose parents had come from Limerick before she was born, had more to do with shaping young Richard's mind and soul. A strong-willed woman, she ran the household and still found time for volunteer work at the Church of the Nativity. For all her traditional beliefs, Lillian Daley did not shy away from change or tumult. She fought for a woman's right to vote, and her son's first political memories were of the suffrage marches to which his mother took him.

Just as his mother dominated young Richard's home, his church dominated his community, its walls towering over the small one-family homes and its rigorous standards and strict demands controlling the way its parishioners lived their lives. From childhood on Daley attended daily mass, and he would do so every day of his life. But if the Church asked a good deal from the faithful, it also gave them much of what they needed. Dick Daley learned his numbers and his alphabet under the stern tutelage of the Church of the Nativity's nuns. And together with the local Democratic machine, the priests looked out for those in need of a job, a loan, or sometimes enough groceries to get through the week. Chicago offered no other welfare program.

Though the Chicago of Daley's birth was the nation's second-largest city, in a way, as his most acute biographer, Chicago journalist Mike Royko, pointed out, Daley was raised as a small-town boy, in a tradition that the small-town politicians who mobilized against Al Smith would not have found entirely alien. Daley's real hometown was Bridgeport, not Chicago. And Bridgeport's Irish, like Chicago's other ethnic communities—the Germans to the north of the Loop, the Poles to the northwest, the Jews and Italians to the west, and to the east, the blacks—made up what was essentially a small town, with all the cultural markings of the small towns in rural America. Each had its own saloon, funeral home, bakery, grocery store, churches, schools, police station, and fire house and its own Main Street where mom could buy a new dress and get shoes for the children. Within the complex of these ethnically homogeneous neighborhoods old hatreds flourished and new ones took root. The Irish who came to Bridgeport from the Old Sod would arrive there hating the English from the very start. Before long they learned to despise the Poles, the Italians, and the blacks, and the animosities were cordially reciprocated.

As a boy, Dick Daley was painfully shy, a trait that persisted into adulthood, along with a difficulty in expressing himself. "I think the reason he's always had trouble talking," said one old family friend, "was there weren't any other children in his home and his parents were quiet people."

But Daley's reticence did not keep him from hustling for extra money. Nearly every spare hour he put to use at odd jobs, selling newspapers at streetcar stops and delivering vegetables from a horse-drawn wagon. Such industry deserved to be cultivated. Somehow Michael and Lillian Daley scrimped enough to raise the $50 tuition, plus $10 for typewriter rental, plus trolley fare, to send him to the De La Salle Institute, a commercial school, where the Christian Brothers taught their son the white-collar skills that would mean he would not have to work with his hands.

Upon graduation in 1919 Daley got what he and his classmates had worked and paid for—a job. His was in the stockyards, but he got no blood on his hands. Putting his training under the Christian Brothers to good use, he worked as a clerk and a bookkeeper and saved his money. But he had broader interests—in politics. In 1922, while the Republicans were in charge in Washington and Al Smith was getting ready to run for president for the first time, Daley, then just turned twenty, took a big step toward making his way in public life by enrolling at DePaul University's law school at night. It was a hard, slow way to get a legal education, and Daley had to put in eleven years, but he ultimately earned his degree.

More directly, he signed himself up as a precinct captain in the local Democratic organization. Shrewd, tough, and ambitious, Daley made the most of this entry-level position. Nobody ever had to ask where Dick Daley was when it was time to muster out the precinct on primary day. He was clearly a man determined to make the most of his opportunities. But he was not greedy. He kept his nose clean.

Just as important, he kept it out of other people's business. If some of his colleagues found a way to have a little extra something come their way from saloon keepers and merchants eager for their good will, Daley did not take notice. Or if he did notice, he kept things to himself. Daley was a faithful Catholic. But Holy Mother Church commanded him to confess only his own sins—not the transgressions of others.

Daley was astute enough to find himself a mentor in politics, a fellow Irishman known as Big Joe McDonough, alderman of the eleventh ward and one of the most potent Democrats in the Cook County Democratic machine. McDonough put the young man and his De La Salle Institute skills to work as his personal secretary, a position that provided a postgraduate education in practical politics, Chicago style: the rewarding of the faithful with jobs and the dismissal from the payroll of the disloyal, the greasing of bureaucratic wheels for friends, the pressuring of enemies through the exertions of city inspectors, and last but certainly not least in importance, the tabulation of votes so that the home team won. Daley performed these tasks so faithfully and efficiently that the grateful McDonough helped to make him city clerk.

For Daley, life was by no means easy. After putting in his eight hours a day clerking at City Hall he spent four nights a week in law classes at DePaul. A fellow classmate, Louis Wexler, remembered Daley as "a nice fellow, very quiet, a hard worker. He never missed a class. There was nothing about him that would make him stand out, as far as becoming special in life."

Nevertheless, for all his lack of flair, Daley's drive and discipline would indeed make him something special. In 1931, with the nation mired in the Depression, Daley took another step up. His patron, McDonough, was elected treasurer of Cook County, and he rewarded Daley for his labors and loyalty by making him his administrative assistant. McDonough did not care much for numbers, but his assistant Dick Daley loved nothing better than to dabble in figures all day long. It was experience he knew would pay off for him later on.

For patience was one of Daley's greatest strengths. Slow and steady was his pace, not only in politics but in his personal life. The charm and ease for which Irish politicians are justly famous somehow escaped Daley. Withdrawn around men, he became downright backward and tongue-tied in the presence of women. Not until he reached twenty-eight did he have a steady girlfriend, a nineteen-year-old secretary named Eleanor Guilfoyle, generally known as Sis. It took until 1936, five years after they were introduced at a softball game, before Daley worked up the courage to ask for "Sis" Guilfoyle's hand in marriage. Their first child, a girl, was born on St. Patrick's Day in 1937, and over the next twelve years Daley and Sis would have two more daughters and four sons, the eldest of whom, Richard M. Daley, would follow his father into Chicago's mayoral office.

In 1936, the year of his marriage and one year before the birth of his first child, Daley won his first election for public office, as a representative to the state legislature. The same election that sent Daley to Springfield also returned Franklin Roosevelt to the White House after having won every state but Maine and Vermont. Though Daley was a novice in the legislature, a lawmaker did not need a profound understanding of politics to figure out how to vote in 1937. He compiled a record as a reliable New Dealer who backed every bill that purported to offer succor to the stricken working people of Illinois.

Being separated from hearth and home did not alter Daley's adherence to the straight and narrow. He still went to church every morning. Evenings he stayed in his hotel room and worked hard, boning up on the revenue issues that had become his forte.

After ten years in Springfield, Daley wangled an appointment to the Cook County Democratic Central Committee, the politburo of the Illinois Democratic Party, then riven by a postwar battle for power between reformers and the old guard. Daley adroitly kept one foot in each camp. His connection to McDonough earned him the acceptance of the party veterans, and his reputation for honesty and his grasp of public finance won him respect among the reformers. So it was that Daley, for all his machine ties, was able to fit in with the new breed of reform politicians who were moving to the forefront in Illinois politics. It was 1948 when the reformers came into their own, sending Princeton-trained Adlai Stevenson, scion of a distinguished Illinois family, whose grandfather and namesake had been Grover Cleveland's second vice president, to the governor's mansion. Stevenson needed someone who could serve as a liaison with the Old Guard, who still wielded substantial power in the legislature, but who also could pass muster with reformers. Daley filled the bill, and Stevenson promptly named him state director of revenue.

All those years spent drilling himself with the account books of government now paid off. Given a prominent position in the state's power structure, Daley made the most of the opportunity, strengthening his hand in Chicago and enlarging his reach downstate, consolidating old alliances and forging new ones. Anyone who was paying the slightest attention to Illinois politics could hardly have been surprised when in 1953 the Cook County Democratic Committee made him its chairman. At age fifty-one, thirty years after he broke into Chicago politics, he had worked his way up to the command post of the machine.

One more rung remained to climb, but that would not take long. In 1955, with the backing of 48 of the 50 ward committeemen—he never forgave the two who supported Thomas Kennelly, the reform candidate who opposed him—Daley breezed to victory in the Democratic primary and then trounced his Republican foe in the general election for mayor of Chicago.

The new mayor wasted no time in consolidating his power, hiring more police officers and firefighters, installing more streetlights, paving more streets, doubling the construction crews on the city's new expressway, all with attendant public fanfare. He saw to it that the Loop was revitalized along with the rest of the downtown area. As for the neighborhoods, if they missed out on the fancy refurbishing, Daley took care that they were maintained sufficiently to avoid complaints from the people who lived there. Daley's showy performance built a contrast between Chicago and most of the nation's other urban centers, which, bogged down in deficits, red tape, and political infighting, were beginning to fall apart in the late 1950s. Chicago became known as "the city that works."

Daley made sure that it worked the way he wanted it to. On his way to making the City Council little more than a rubber stamp, he arrogated the power it once had to make the budget. He shrank the civil service and expanded the legion of patronage workers. He did so many favors for the city's one Republican congressman that when Daley ran for reelection in 1959 his GOP opponent had a hard time finding prominent Republicans who would campaign for him. On Election Day Daley's unfortunate challenger won only one ward in the entire city, his own.

By now Daley had achieved a nationwide reputation, and his control of the Illinois Democratic Party made him a figure with power on a national scale. His first opportunity to demonstrate that power, and by demonstrating it reinforce it, came during the 1960 presidential campaign, when he did as much as anyone outside John F. Kennedy's immediate family to make the handsome young Massachusetts senator president. Spurring Daley's efforts was the influence of Joseph P. Kennedy, father of the candidate and the owner of Chicago's 24-story Merchandise Mart, then the world's largest commercial building with 93 acres of rentable space valued at $75 million. The Merchandise Mart gave FDR's former ambassador to the Court of St. James a huge stake in the future of downtown Chicago, the crown jewel of Daley's city. And consequently this piece of real estate made the elder Kennedy's voice one to be heeded when it came to Daley's decisionmaking about the 1960 presidential contest, assuring that the bulk of Illinois's 69 convention delegates, votes that Daley controlled as firmly as if they made up a hand of cards, went for Kennedy.

But Daley's greatest contribution to JFK's political career was yet to come. On election night Kennedy's early lead, produced by the big cities of the East, seemed to fade away as Republican Richard Nixon crept closer to the man Daley had helped nominate. But in Illinois Daley somehow found the ballots in Cook County to offset Nixon's strength downstate. In all, 4,750,000 votes were cast for Kennedy in Illinois. With 27 electoral votes at stake, Kennedy edged out Nixon by fewer than 10,000 votes and assured himself and Dick Daley's party of victory.[1] With that achievement and the debt of gratitude accrued from it, Richard Daley moved to a new level. He was no longer just a politician, or even a powerful politician. He was now accorded the status of a political and cultural institution.

Daley had won power and maintained it by manipulating the machinery of American politics. But he had done all this in such a way as to cast himself as a champion of middle-class culture—the solid citizenry who lived in all the Bridgeports of Chicago, went to work every weekday, maybe got a little drunk on Saturday night, and fulfilled their obligations to their maker on Sundays. If their neighborhoods lacked the sheen of Daley's Loop, they did not mind because they knew they could rely on Daley to pick up the garbage, clear the snow, and fill the potholes. If Daley did not always obey the Golden Rule, no one had ever been able to prove him guilty of a crime. If his methods were harsh, his goals were concrete and understandable. He was a practical man, always a steady hand on the tiller, a leader Chicagoans could count on to protect their lives from unwelcome change and intrusive strangers.

People who opposed him gave up challenging him directly. Instead they studied him, trying to understand what made him tick, so they could circumvent him, or perhaps catch him off guard. Daley was not easy to comprehend at first because, although he seemed a very modern

---

[1] As it turned out, Kennedy did not need the 27 electoral votes of Illinois to win. His running mate Lyndon Johnson's organization in Texas, like Daley's in Illinois, worked overtime to assure him victory in that state with its 24 electoral votes. That gave him a total of 303, or 34 more than the 269 votes he needed for a majority. But in the late hours of election night neither Kennedy nor Daley knew for sure whether they could count on victory in Texas.

figure, he was actually a throwback to another time, to the era of small-town America. He cultivated an air of Puritanical self-righteousness that was part of his small-town cultural heritage. On one occasion, flying back to Chicago from one of his many trips to Washington, Daley ordered a Bloody Mary. His aide, Frank Sullivan, who rarely drank, decided he would have a beer mainly to be sociable.

"Do you drink a lot of beer, Frank?" Daley asked. Sullivan replied that he did not, but Daley seemed oblivious to the answer. For the next twenty minutes he spoke of the Irish and the curse of alcohol and how many families in his neighborhood had been destroyed because of fathers and husbands who took to drink. "During the rest of the flight I never took another sip of beer," Sullivan recalled. But Daley ordered a second Bloody Mary.

While in private he fretted about the morals of his aides, the public man was single-minded in his push for more power. In 1967 Daley won a fourth term and with the city firmly under his thumb sought new ways to enhance his prestige and influence. One path was to arrange for the 1968 Democratic Convention to be held in Chicago. When Daley was first elected mayor, Chicagoans had almost taken Democratic Conventions for granted. The party had met there five times between 1940 and 1956 to choose its standard-bearers.

But the 1956 Democratic conclave in Chicago had been followed by an eight-year hiatus, far too long, it seemed to Daley. Underlying Daley's bid for the convention was the claim that the Democrats were the party of the cities, and that Chicago was the ultimate American city—not a collection of freeways, like Los Angeles, which had hosted the 1960 convention, or a faded spa, like Atlantic City, where the Democrats met in 1964. "I would say that it is an important sign of faith to the American people for this national convention to be held here," Daley declared, "not in some resort center, but in the very heart of a great city, where people live and work and raise their families, and in one of the biggest neighborhoods in Chicago, my neighborhood."

It was a compelling argument. Here was Daley, presenting himself as the legatee to Al Smith and Franklin Roosevelt and the other Democrats who built their party around the urban centers of the nation. But on closer inspection Daley's claim was suspect. For in reality, the mayor and his machine had little contact with the diverse millions who lived and toiled in Chicago beyond getting their votes on Election Day. He was a self-styled champion of the city who had turned his back on the diversity that was the hallmark of urban culture. The real truth in Daley's statement was buried in the last two words, "my neighborhood," which happened to be where the International Amphitheater, the convention hall, was located. Daley professed to be a big city leader. But his loyalty and his cultural values really belonged to the small town of Bridgeport, and, of course, also to the heavy hitters in the Loop.

Daley's idea of using the convention to celebrate the glory of the nation's big cities contravened the facts. Though Democrats did not like to admit it, the cities of America had changed and no longer were the outposts of the future. The future had moved to the suburbs, along with the white middle class. The people who remained in the cities were captives—black and white alike, resenting each other, disliking even themselves. The melting pot of Al Smith's day had produced a bitter brew. The cities were made up of sullen enclaves like Daley's Bridgeport, seething ghettos like Chicago's South side, and the glittering downtown where the suburbanites came to their white-collar jobs during the day, only to desert them after dark. All America's cities were like this, more or less, including Chicago. What made Chicago *seem* different was that Daley, by sheer brute force, kept his city's conflicts under control and out of sight.

Secure in his power, Daley pressed his case for Chicago as convention host in Washington with Lyndon Johnson, and, in a private tête-à-tête, convinced the president. When the choice was announced, someone was rude enough to ask about the possibility of protest demonstrations. Daley seemed almost to welcome the question. "Not in Chicago," he explained. "We have a great city. All the people are playing a positive part," he stressed.

In 1967 when blacks had rioted in Detroit, Newark, and other cities around the country, Chicago had stayed calm. Daley's program—which consisted mainly of opening swimming pools and sprinklers in the ghettos—had helped to keep the peace, or so he claimed. But just in case that offering was not enough in that summer of discontent, Daley had alerted the National Guard and served notice that this was no mere symbolic gesture. "I can assure you that there won't be any blank ammunition," he declared. "The ammunition will be live."

Whether it was the carrot or the stick, the sprinklers or the bullets, or just plain good fortune, Chicago got through 1967 without violence. But as the tumultuous year of 1968 unfolded, Daley knew that he would have a harder time maintaining that record. The mayor was well aware of the unrest afflicting other cities from racial tension and the war in Vietnam. Indeed, the turmoil had shaken the grip on the presidency of the master politician, Daley's friend Lyndon Johnson, forcing him to abandon his hopes of another term in office and leaving his party shaken and in disarray.

Though, as he had revealed to Johnson at their private meeting in 1966, Daley had his own misgivings about U.S. policy in Vietnam, he kept those doubts to himself. Daley believed that it was up to the president to decide what to do about Vietnam. That was not a decision to be made in the streets. That was not the way things were done in Chicago.

For Daley, the activism of the Sixties, first the civil rights revolt, then the protest against the war, all linked to far-reaching cultural upheaval, represented a grave threat. The disruptions threatened not only his political power but the cultural values on which he had built his life and his political empire. Some members of the imperiled establishment argued for compromise with the protesters. But this was not Daley's way. He was not fearful of the turmoil; indeed, he viewed it as an opportunity. By crushing the political and cultural dissenters while others were giving way, Daley saw a chance not only to defeat them but to elevate his own prestige to an even higher level.

The events that followed the announcement that Chicago would host the 1968 convention allowed Daley to demonstrate his style in responding to protests. Late in 1967, Dick Gregory, the black comedian and civil rights activist, warned that unless Daley pushed through an open housing bill and installed blacks in the upper echelons of Chicago's police department, he,

Gregory, would lead a civil rights protest march during the week of the convention. This was just the sort of threat Daley was waiting for. He did not let it go unanswered. "No one is going to take over the city—now, in July, or at any other time," he declared. "We live in an age of spreading hatred and violence. We need respect for law and order, we need a unification of citizens."

The following spring Daley showed Chicago and the world how he intended to foster respect and unification, by ordering city police to "shoot to kill, shoot to maim" during the rioting that followed the assassination of Martin Luther King, Jr. A few weeks later, when the Chicago Peace Council, an amalgam of about 200 peace groups, staged an antiwar demonstration, the 6,000 marchers, mostly middle- and upper-class whites, were driven from the streets by 500 helmeted police swinging billy clubs and spraying mace. As the summer of 1968 wore on, and the August convention drew closer, Mayor Daley and the most radical of the dissenters planning to descend on his city each had the same goal, not reconciliation but confrontation. The radicals hoped through such a clash to demonstrate the tyrannical nature of the established order. Daley sought to prove its supremacy, and his own leadership. Each side would get its chance.

THE WHOLE
WORLD IS WATCHING

As he traveled around the country trying to recruit support for the Chicago protest, the antiwar organizer David Dellinger was often asked two questions. "Is there any chance the police won't create a bloodbath?" and "Are you sure that Tom Hayden and Rennie Davis don't want one?" Dellinger, who was chairman of the National Mobilization Committee to End the War in Vietnam, or MOBE, an umbrella organization for the various groups protesting the war, got Hayden and Davis, his two chief lieutenants, to promise him that they would not advocate violence. He could get no such promise from the police, or from the mayor of the city, Richard Daley. Instead Daley's aggressive resistance to the planned demonstrations made inevitable the Götterdämmerung that rocked Chicago and shocked the nation.

As if his response to the rioting and demonstrations earlier in the year were not a clear enough signal of what convention protesters could expect, Daley had turned Chicago into an armed camp long before the first delegate or protester arrived. Determined to stand firm against what he proclaimed to be a threat against the peace and safety of the city he ruled, he denied nearly all permits for parades or demonstrations, assigned all 12,000 Chicago police to twelve-hour shifts, and mobilized 5,000 Illinois National Guardsmen. Some 6,000 U.S. troops, including units of the 101st Airborne, armed with flame throwers and bazookas, stood by in the suburbs.

Then, on the night the convention opened, in his welcoming speech
to the delegates behind the barbed wire that enclosed the convention hall,
Daley underlined his resistance to protest. Speaking of his pride in welcoming Democrats from all parts of the country and holding all sorts of
beliefs to his city, he nevertheless made clear that his welcome was quali-
fied and limited:

> I do not refer to the extremists, who seek to destroy instead of to build,
> to those who would make a mockery of our institutions and values, nor
> do I refer to those who have been successful in convincing some people
> that theatrical protest is rational dissent. I speak of those who came con-
> scientiously because they know at this political gathering there is hope
> and opportunity. I speak of those who came because the instinct that
> brings them here is right.

But it was just people of this conscientious sort whom Daley's police
had clubbed, maced, and arrested at the Civic Center in April. Faced with
the opportunity to go to Chicago, their operative instinct in most cases
was to survive and stay away. As a consequence, the protesters who did
come into Chicago were the ones most likely to welcome a violent confrontation, if not actually provoke one. And these were just the people
Daley and his police were waiting for, with chips on their shoulders and
clubs in their hands.

Against this tense backdrop, the first demonstrators had arrived in
Chicago the week before the convention, braced for conflict. They did
not have long to wait. Most of the early trouble centered on Lincoln Park,
a strip of greensward off North Shore Drive, opposite a residential and
shopping district near the neighborhood known as Old Town. The Shore
Drive and the El connect the park to the Loop, Chicago's downtown,
about three miles to the south. Normally a haven for strollers and pic-
nickers, the park seemed ideal to the Yippies and other protest groups as a
staging area for their demonstrations. And just as important, they saw it
as an overnight bivouac site for their supporters, few of whom could find
a room in the convention-bound city, let alone afford one.

But Mayor Daley would have none of that and imposed a curfew. On the night of August 25, the Sunday before the convention, at the end of a band concert that drew several thousand of the antiwar visitors to the park, police ordered everyone to leave. When some 1,000 demonstrators ignored the orders and the curfew, police attacked, beating those slow to move on their legs with their with billy clubs, driving the crowd out of the park and into nearby Clark Street. Police formed a skirmish line to move the crowd along. But when some in the crowd began to throw rocks and bottles at the police, shouting "Kill the pigs," some of the cops broke out of the skirmish line and charged the crowd, pinning people to the ground and beating them.

As they gathered on Monday to mull over the events of the first day, the more militant protesters could not have been happier with the police reaction. Tom Hayden, writing in the *Ramparts Wall Poster*, mentioned a reference to the convention on NBC as "an armed camp" and bragged that the melee amounted to a "100 percent victory in propaganda." Hayden, who along with Dellinger and Davis made up the troika that more or less took charge of the demonstrations, was the most volatile and unyielding of the three. A University of Michigan graduate, he had helped to found Students for a Democratic Society, one of the earliest and most militant of the groups that had sprung up in the past few years to make up the New Left. He was only recently returned from Paris where he had consulted with North Vietnamese peace negotiators. In his *Wall Poster* screed, Hayden asserted that the skirmish in Chicago's streets was an important test for those opposed to the fighting in Vietnam: "People have to be faced with the existential question of giving their life, . . . forced into a moral squeeze, asked what they are willing to do to stop the war."

But such teleological issues had to be set aside when Hayden was arrested for his role in the disorders of Sunday night. That news energized the demonstrators already gathering back at Lincoln Park, of whom Rennie Davis now took charge. Dellinger's chief lieutenant, Davis was a political science graduate of Oberlin who had been a community organizer for the SDS since 1965 and joined the MOBE after a trip to Hanoi in 1967.

Under his leadership the Lincoln Park demonstrators marched on central police headquarters, some carrying red banners and Viet Cong flags.

Confronted by a cordon of police prepared to repel any assault, Davis tried to head the crowd to Grant Park, across from the Conrad Hilton. But some broke away and rushed up a knoll in the park where they took over an equestrian statue of Civil War General John Logan and draped it with the banners they had been carrying in their march. Swinging their clubs, police charged into the crowd on the knoll and reclaimed the general and his mount.

Most of the demonstrators avoided the battle of the knoll, instead massing in the park directly across Michigan Avenue, which divides Grant Park from the wall of skyscrapers and hotels, including the Conrad Hilton, that make up the urban facade facing Lake Michigan. There they listened to speeches from their leaders, notably David Dellinger. At fifty-two, the oldest among the protest leaders, and possessor of the most distinguished and longest pedigree—Yale Phi Beta Kappa 1936, two World War II prison terms for refusing to serve in the Army—Dellinger was also generally the calmest and most statesmanlike. But for many in the crowd the time for statesmanship had long passed. They chanted obscenities directed at President Johnson and Mayor Daley in what the U.S. Attorney's office would later call "the vilest conceivable language."

On the following day, Tuesday the 27th, the protest leaders decided to make as much propaganda mileage as they could out of the physical beating they were taking by spelling out their treatment at the hands of the police at a press conference sponsored by the MOBE. Nearly 100 reporters and photographers appeared, and a press aide to the group exulted, "It was like the White House during an international crisis." Rennie Davis sounded the theme: "The whole world is watching" the reaction of Mayor Daley's Chicago to the antiwar protest, he declared, and they would not escape retribution.

Before the Democratic Convention and the protests were over, that battle cry would become a familiar slogan to millions of Americans as demonstrators chanted it in the streets. It was both a promise and a threat, an attempt to convince the protesters of the significance of their cause and to warn their adversaries in Chicago that there was a higher authority, the power of public opinion, to whom the protesters would make their case.

On Tuesday night action shifted back to Lincoln Park. A new element had been added to the mix: A group of neighborhood clergymen sympathetic to the protesters assembled with them in the park for a peace vigil, drawing a crowd of about 1,500 who joined in singing various hymns and folk songs, while a smaller and more militant group also gathered nearby.

Police went ahead with their own plans, disregarding the presence of the clergy. They formed a skirmish line with a sanitation department dump truck in the middle, equipped with a special nozzle for spraying tear gas. Convinced from their overly inflamed intelligence reports that the crowd was armed with sharpened spears and shotguns, the cops became increasingly uneasy, a feeling that was heightened when the crowd stoned squad cars on patrol in the area. After several orders to leave the park were ignored, the police sent the sanitation truck ahead, spraying tear gas. Police lines followed the truck, with riot-helmeted officers tossing tear gas canisters into the crowd.

The writer Studs Terkel, who was roaming the area outside the park with a British journalist, tried to escort some of the protesters to safety. He encountered a cop who contrasted the shift in police tactics from Monday night, when they had clubbed the demonstrators, to Tuesday night, when they hurled tear gas. "Last night we had the hitters," he told Terkel. "Tonight we have the pitchers. It's better isn't it?"

Meanwhile, a few miles south, a new front opened up on familiar ground, in Grant Park. A crowd of about 4,000 gathered to hear speeches from, among others, Rennie Davis, who sounded a note of desperation: "We have found that the primary struggle has not been to expose the Democratic Party, they have done that for themselves," Davis declared. "But our primary struggle is for our survival as a movement. Tomorrow afternoon we are to gather here for that march on the convention that Daley and Johnson have brought out all their military strength to stop."

Even as Davis spoke, following an official birthday salute to LBJ the convention was doing its business in a way that only fired up resentments among the throng in Grant Park. Most people there initially seemed in an unrevolutionary mood. In contrast to the ragtag appearance of the demonstrators at Lincoln Park and elsewhere, many at the Grant Park demonstration were dressed in suits and ties and had their hair cut relatively short. They were part of the establishment, even though they saw themselves as working to change it. Many of them were peace delegates pledged to Robert Kennedy or Eugene McCarthy, according to their convention badges, and others were McCarthy campaign workers.

Inside the convention itself another confrontation was taking place—between the bosses and regulars who had long ruled the party and the insurgents who spearheaded the antiwar movement. The insurgents sought to attack the establishment by challenging the makeup of the state delegations to the convention, which they argued had been unfairly selected. But after prolonged debate, nearly all their challenges failed.

As the votes against insurgency were cast and counted during the night, and as the crowd in Grant Park outside the Hilton got the news, the mood in the park turned angry and sour. Some among the protesters began to throw Pepsi cans filled with urine and beer cans filled with sand at the police stationed in front of the Conrad Hilton. And from inside the Hilton, too, paper bags filled with feces rained down on the police while the air was filled with constant shouts of "Pig! Pig! Pig!"

The crowd became nastier and larger—swelled by an influx of demonstrators who had been attending a mock birthday party for President Johnson at the Colosseum—an all but abandoned structure south of Grant Park, so dilapidated that no one had thought to deny access to the protesters. At the "unbirthday party" at the Colosseum nobody sang happy birthday to the nation's thirty-sixth president. Instead the crowd chanted "Fuck You, LBJ" and "Hell No, We Won't Go." Phil Ochs sang the resistance anthem: "I Ain't Marching Any More":

> Call it peace or call it treason
> Call it honor or call it reason
> I ain't marching any more

The influx of the Colosseum attendees at Grant Park made the police increasingly anxious and jumpy. A *Washington Post* reporter on the scene sensed that the police "had had it" and were showing signs of strain. The crowd sensed this, too, and stepped up their efforts to bait the cops who lined each side of Michigan Avenue, batons at the ready. Trying to ease the tension, folk singers Peter Yarrow and Mary Travers, two-thirds of the popular group billed as Peter, Paul and Mary, came to the speaker's stand and got the crowd to sing along with "Blowin' in the Wind," "If I Had a Hammer," and "This Land Is Your Land." Perhaps more important, a police official told the demonstrators over his bullhorn that they could stay in the park all night—as long as they remained peaceful and remained on the east side of Michigan Avenue, across from the Hilton.

In search of support, police officials called in the National Guard. About 3 A.M. Wednesday, 600 members of the 33rd Military Police Battalion moved into position on Michigan Avenue facing the crowd, rifle barrels pointed skyward, with bayonets fixed. But Brigadier General Richard T. Dunn, their commander, ordered the bayonets removed and, after having difficulty making himself heard over shouts of "Sieg Heil! Sieg Heil!" promised the demonstrators that the Guardsmen would not bother them if they remained peaceful. For the next couple of hours, the crowd heard several speakers, including a priest who denounced the war, and then the demonstrators shouted up at the delegates in the Hilton: "Flick the lights if you agree." In at least ten rooms, the lights switched off and on. The Guard battalion stood by impassively, despite a torrent of verbal abuse that one of the officers later called "unbelievable." Shortly before dawn, Tom Hayden ended the rally and the stand off. "Get some sleep," he told the crowd. "If you go somewhere, go in groups."

Wednesday started off with a heavy mist. By early afternoon, the speeches started and demonstrators began to gather at the bandshell in the park, which was used for summer concerts. Shortly after 2 P.M., the crowd numbered more than 1,000, and it would increase tenfold or more in the next few hours. Conspicuous among them was a handful of poorly disguised police undercover men, whose guns jutted out from under their coats. They seemed to believe that if they did not shave and wore dark glasses and sport shirts, they would be taken for protesters. "They fooled no one," a local attorney who was in the park said.

The uniformed police set up lines along two north-south thorough-fares, Lake Shore Drive, which runs along the east border of the park, and to the west on Columbus Drive, which divides the park. To the south, they also massed along Roosevelt Drive. This lineup boxed the park in on three sides, all except the north. And even on this northern edge, some 100 reserve police were assembled, out of sight.

As the crowd gathered the police handed people leaflets telling them that the rally was legal and would be protected—but warning that no rally would be allowed near the amphitheater and that no march would be permitted outside the park. If there was such a march, the leaflets said: "Each and every participant would be arrested." But those warnings went unheeded at the rally. One by one the speakers from the podium—Dick Gregory, Norman Mailer, William Burroughs—harangued against the war in Vietnam and boosted the idea of the march, legal or not, as a ges-ture of defiance against the government that continued the conflict. As the speakers saw it, the threat of arrest, and even violence, only made the gesture more powerful. Most of the demonstrators needed little encour-agement. They had been waiting all week for this moment. They knew there would be violence, but they were determined to march anyway.

Grant Park was not the only forum in Chicago where the Vietnam War was under discussion. At the convention hall itself the issue had come to a head with the debate over the platform plank on Vietnam. The debate itself was a charade. The issue had been settled before the conven-tion even started. For although hundreds of delegates argued about the is-sue on the convention floor, in hotel corridors, and in the city's restau-rants, on this issue, as with the choice of Chicago as convention city, there was only one person whose opinion counted: the President of the United States, Lyndon B. Johnson.

For weeks before the convention opponents of the war had sought to reach some form of compromise on a Vietnam plank with Hubert Humphrey, the party's presumed nominee. But it soon became clear to them that Humphrey had no real say in these discussions, that the deci-sion remained in the hands of the president. Indeed, desperate to reach agreement with the antiwar forces for his coming struggle against Richard

Nixon, Humphrey had decided he could accept a compromise plank on Vietnam. The plank was supported by the Kennedy and McCarthy delegates; Johnson opposed it. But Humphrey had to overcome the resistance of the chairman of the convention Platform Committee, Hale Boggs, a longtime Louisiana congressman and a Johnson ally and confidante.

Humphrey pleaded with Boggs in vain. "The Congressman's position was clear and also immovable," Humphrey later wrote of his encounter with Boggs. "If the President would not accept the plank, then he, as chairman of the platform committee, would resist it, send out the word that the plank was unacceptable." The compromise died, and along with it Humphrey's chance of winning the presidency. He was forced to spend much of his campaign trying to win the backing of the opponents to the war.

Humphrey was in no position to defy Johnson, or so he believed. For what Humphrey and those about him feared, not without reason in the view of most informed politicians, was that any move on Humphrey's part that might be interpreted as a weakening of his support for the administration's policy would incur Johnson's wrath, conceivably causing him to deny Humphrey the nomination. After all, as Humphrey only too well realized, much of his delegate strength at the convention had come to him because of Lyndon Johnson. What the president giveth, he could also take away.

One crucial demand of the antiwar forces was to call a halt to all bombing of North Vietnam. The president was adamantly opposed and would not give an inch. If Johnson would not move Humphrey was immobilized. So it had come down to a debate on the convention floor on Wednesday afternoon, the twenty-eighth hour before Humphrey was to be nominated. The proposal put forth by the antiwar forces was cautiously worded. It called for "an unconditional end to all bombing of North Vietnam," casting the bombing halt as a first step toward peace and pledging to continue supporting American troops in the South, with all means necessary. But Johnson's plank, as framed by a majority of the Platform Committee, called for a halt to the bombing only "when this action shall not endanger our troops in the field."

When the delegates arrived at the convention hall that afternoon they found a "fact sheet" endorsing the Johnson plank and denouncing the peace plan as "emotional, unreasoning," and "a barely concealed attack on the President." Speakers for the peace plank, which included such luminaries from John Kennedy's Camelot as Ted Sorensen, his closest aide, and Pierre Salinger, the former White House press secretary, argued their case with passion. But they knew they were speaking for history, not to sway the delegates on the other side. The majority plank carried by a vote of 1,567 to 1,041. Defeated but unbowed, some of the antiwar delegates began to sing the civil rights anthem, "We Shall Overcome." But another group, more militant, stood in the convention aisles and chanted: "Stop the War, Stop the War." It was 4:30 P.M. on Wednesday, August 28, the third day of the Democratic Convention. A little earlier, that same chant could have been heard a few miles to the north at the demonstration in Grant Park.

As the crowd at the park heard the news of the defeat of the antiwar force's platform, sentiment mounted for a march on the convention hall six miles away. Still, some among the protesters opposed that idea, arguing that not much could be accomplished even if the marchers reached their destination. Then, events took hold. A teenager with the wild hair of a Yippie scrambled up the flag pole that occupied a prominent place in the park and began to lower the American flag that flew there. Convinced that he threatened harm to Old Glory, police rushed to the pole, seized the youth, and began pounding him with their clubs. That outraged many in the crowd of protesters who then began hurling stones and any other objects at hand at the cops.

Alarmed at what he feared to be the collapse of the rally, Rennie Davis, clambering down from the speaker's platform, rushed to the flag pole seeking to quiet the demonstrators. That would have been a hard task to accomplish under any circumstances. Police immediately set upon him, beat him to the ground, and continued to slug him as he crawled away, finally reaching some degree of safety on the other side of a chain link fence. Unconscious, Davis lay there bleeding from gashes on his head that would later require thirteen stitches to close.

"A split head," was the way the infuriated Tom Hayden described Davis's condition to the crowd when he seized the microphone. "This city and the military machinery it has aimed at us won't permit us to protest," Hayden cried. "Let us make sure that if blood is going to flow, let it flow all over this city. If gas is going to be used, let that gas come down all over Chicago, and not just over us in the park. If we are going to be disrupted and violated, let this whole stinking city be disrupted and violated." The crowd, like some aroused animal, roared back its anger. Hayden paused for a moment and then shouted: "I'll see you in the streets." The crowd thundered its response and surged forward.

Demonstrators began to throw stones, bricks, cans, and bottles at the police. In response, a police officer hurled a smoke bomb into the center of the crowd, and while demonstrators tried to escape the smoke, police charged into their midst, flailing their clubs. Surrounded on three sides by police, the demonstrators struggled to find a way out of the park on a bridge leading to Michigan Avenue.

As if this scene was not outlandish enough, a new and even more bizarre element was added with the arrival on Michigan Avenue of a three-wagon mule train of the Poor People's Campaign, organized by the leaders of the Southern Christian Leadership Conference to keep alive the spirit of their slain founder, Martin Luther King, Jr. The SCLC had gained city approval for a march along Michigan Avenue. The train, with the legend "Jobs & Food for All" painted on its cars, was manned by blacks decked out as field hands who shouted to the protesters, "Join us! Join Us!" This the protesters were only too glad to do. Bearing red banners and Viet Cong flags, they marched along with the train down Michigan Avenue. Thus, for a moment at least, the two separate strands of the protest movement, civil rights and opposition to the war, black and white, were bonded together.

But then the cops, viewing this alliance as a threat to their riot control strategy, stepped in and managed to split the Poor People's Train from its white entourage. With some 7,000 people swarming on Michigan Avenue near the Hilton, chanting "Dump the Hump," "Hell No, We Won't Go," and "Peace Now," the police unleashed the blow they had been aching to deliver all week long. Deputy police superintendent James Rochford, who had called up reinforcements, gave the order: "Clear the streets."

At first some officers proceeded in a disciplined fashion, ordering the demonstrators back on the sidewalk and arresting those who refused. But others, impelled by the pent-up frustration and anger of the past few days, struck out in every direction, beating and Maceing militants, peaceful protesters, and bystanders alike and firing teargas at random.

It was about this time that a faint whiff of the medicine being meted out to the demonstrators wafted its way up through the intake valves of the Hilton's air-conditioning system to the twenty-fifth floor suite of the Democratic Party's presumptive standard-bearer, Hubert Humphrey. At first the vice president did not notice. Then, when his skin and eyes started to burn, he took a shower. But the odor alerted campaign chronicler Theodore White, who had been spending the day with the candidate. Never forgoing his reporter's instincts, despite his fame and wealth, White headed for the streets to "find out what this tear gas means."

He soon got his answer. He jotted down the time, 7:55 P.M., on his notepad as he heard demonstrators chanting, "Fuck You, LBJ, Fuck You LBJ." Then, seconds later, he watched, stunned, as a wedge of police, "like a piston exploding from its chamber," cleaved through the crowd, sending screaming demonstrators fleeing in all directions. After a brief pause, the police charged again, using an overturned barricade to ram the crowd. It was now 8:05 P.M., and White made another note on his pad: "The Democrats are finished." What happened on the streets, given the reach of television, "was to be totally unexpungeable in memory."

The demonstrators knew that, too. At 8:30 P.M., as violence subsided, they no longer chanted obscenities. Instead they chorused their battle cry and the rationale for these days of frustration and pain: "The Whole World Is Watching, the Whole World Is Watching, the Whole World Is Watching." And of course they would be right about that.

But it would take a little time. Because a telephone strike, and the harassment of Daley's police, had combined to make live television transmission impossible. An hour and a half passed before the television crews working Grant Park and the streets in front of the Hilton emptied their cameras and developed their film and tape and the production teams edited them for broadcast. Once the pictures of the violence went on the air they had an impact on the convention, where delegates watched them on their portable TV sets.

It was the televised violence that provoked a memorable confrontation between Connecticut's Abe Ribicoff and Chicago's Dick Daley. The cameras switched back and forth between the two of them. Ribicoff was in the process of nominating George McGovern for president to carry forward the antiwar banner, taking time to denounce "the Gestapo tactics on the streets of Chicago." The embattled Daley, his face a mask of contempt and hatred, mouthed obscenities, the precise nature of which could not be discerned at first. His words, as ultimately detected from television film by lip-reading experts: "Fuck you, you Jew son of a bitch, you lousy mother-fucker, go home."

Looking down on the mayor seated only 20 feet from the podium, Ribicoff said calmly: "How hard it is to accept the truth, how hard it is." Finally the violence stopped on the television screen as it had on the streets. And the cameras returned to the business of the convention, the roll call of the states for the presidential nomination, which resulted just before midnight in Humphrey being chosen as the Democratic standard-bearer.

With Humphrey's victory, and the street violence finally at an end, the leaders of the protest, who had made "The Whole World Is Watching" their battle cry, now confidently awaited the reaction, which they imagined would be a great public relations triumph in Chicago. They could hardly have been more mistaken. The whole world, much of it anyway, *was* watching, but most of it came down on the other side. The miscalculation made by the protesters stemmed from an unrealistic view of national politics and of the forces that motivate its practitioners. Moved by the postnomination candlelight vigil of antiwar delegates at Grant Park, some came to believe that, despite the cultural differences between the New Left and the more traditional liberals, such as the delegates, they might now find common cause. Many demonstrators assumed, as Todd Gitlin put it, "that battered liberals had no choice but to shift left to join us." Beyond that, the demonstrators were still under the influence of the adrenaline surge of Chicago. It seemed obvious to the protesters that, as one of their leaders later put it, the millions who watched the violence on television "were going to see matters the way we did, from the wrong end of a billy club." But they were mistaken.

They did not understand the heavy price they would have to pay for the countercultural traits that defined them. The New Left had drawn on its cultural disagreements with mainstream society for energy, ideas, and allies. The bizarre clothes, the drugs, and the music—especially the music—had bound together the Vietnam protesters and the cultural rebels and informed their politics with an emotion rarely seen in America. Moreover, these cultural talismans had made them seem intriguing to mainstream society, whose members were quick to adapt these cultural strains to their own lifestyles. But the adaptations were watered-down versions which had been co-opted purely for symbolic purposes rather than as a catalyst for substantive change. And where the traditional liberal establishment parted ways with the New Left was in making the cultural revolution part of politics. This they refused to do.

The liberal Democrats—the antiwar delegates and campaign workers in the Democratic Party in 1968—shared with the cultural revolutionaries an abhorrence of the Vietnam War and a resentment of many of the shibboleths of society. But they saw the war as an aberration, not a manifestation of mainstream culture and political society. Their main instinct was to survive, but more than that, as William Faulkner would have put it, to prevail in the culture and the political system. Their intention was to work within the political system, to reform it if they could. But they had no interest in overturning it.

As for the mass of the public, Chicago forced Americans to choose between two values, their belief in freedom and justice, which was an abstraction, and their demand for law and order, which was as real and concrete as the streets outside their homes. In such a choice there was no real contest. And so it was that while Chicago marked the apogee of the cultural revolution, it also turned out to be the launching pad of a remarkably successful counterrevolution.

PART THREE
THUNDER ON THE RIGHT

9

"UNBLACK,
UNYOUNG, AND UNPOOR"

Although it was the Democratic Convention in 1968 that paved the way for the cultural counterrevolution to flourish in American politics, the seeds of this backlash were actually sown four years before in the presidential campaign of Republican standard-bearer Barry Goldwater. This phenomenon was hard to detect at first because it was obscured by Goldwater's repeated blunders during the campaign and by his own incoherence. Even as facile a journalist as Theodore White had difficulty describing the cultural themes Goldwater was sounding and settled for the rubric "the quality issue." Goldwater, more directly and more accurately, lumped these arguments together as the "morality issue."

Undergirding these concerns were a series of developments in American life that seemed to confirm the worst fears of the traditionalists of the 1920s about the evils of the new urbanized polyglot culture that was emerging. Crime was a big part of the problem. It was on the rise everywhere, or so it seemed, especially in the big cities, like Al Smith's New York, the city whose best-known boroughs in the minds of outlanders were no longer Brooklyn and Manhattan but Sodom and Gomorrah.

In 1950, those who mistrusted and feared the cities liked to point out that in New York, there was a murder a day. By 1964, there were fewer New Yorkers, as more and more middle-class whites fled to the suburbs, but significantly more murders—almost two a day. The rise in violence was accompanied by a breakdown in moral standards. Syphilis, once thought to be all but eradicated by penicillin, had now reached epidemic proportions in some cities, the Public Health Service reported, attributing this increase to wantonness among the young. The demon rum loomed as a greater menace than ever. Seven out of ten adults now drank hard liquor, and that percentage was even higher among the better educated and in the professions.

And then there was the Supreme Court, which not only seemed to be taking up the cause of blacks, instead of upholding the traditional privileges of whites, but also had ventured into other areas vital to middle-class interests. It had given new protections to suspected criminals, for example, thus making it harder for the police to protect law-abiding citizens. In 1964 the court threw out the murder conviction of a young Mexican-American named Daniel Escobedo, ruling that his confession was invalid because police had ignored his request to see a lawyer. Not content with ordering an end to segregation in schools the justices in 1967 had thrust themselves into the sacred realm between man and his maker and declared unconstitutional the time-honored custom of praying in school. The frustration and resentment of many Americans was summed up by one southern lawmaker who declared: "They've changed the law to let the niggers in and to keep God out."

All of this deeply disturbed Goldwater and his supporters. In his acceptance speech Goldwater stirred the delegates to the Republican Convention when he cried out against the malevolent forces at work in American society: "Tonight there is violence in our streets," Goldwater declared, "corruption in our highest offices, aimlessness among our youth, anxiety among our elderly, and there is a virtual despair among the many who look beyond material success toward the inner meaning of their lives."

But perhaps because he was traversing strange terrain—no other presidential candidate had ever tried to make cultural values into a major issue—Goldwater had difficulty developing a coherent framework for making his case. "Moral decay of a people begins at the top," he liked to say. But he never made clear the connection between Lyndon Johnson and the pervasive turpitude.

All through the campaign that followed Goldwater demanded in his standard stump speech: "What's happening to us? What's happening to America?" Because he could not answer that question in a way that his listeners could comprehend, Goldwater's alarm on morality, the first salvo in the countercultural revolution, did him little good in the 1964 campaign. But out of that campaign emerged a new spokesman for the counterrevolution, vastly more compelling than Goldwater. And this was Ronald Wilson Reagan, small-town son of the Midwest, radio announcer, movie star, New Dealer, union leader, television performer, corporate spokesman, conservative activist, Goldwater supporter, and suddenly before anyone quite realized what had happened, governor of California.

Reagan burst on the national political landscape late in the campaign with a televised address on Goldwater's behalf called "A Time for Choosing." By the time Reagan spoke it was clear even to loyal Republicans that it was too late to do anything for Goldwater. But the time was exactly right to do something for Ronald Reagan. He built his speech on a foundation of anecdotes—about the duplicity of welfare cheats, the oppressiveness of bureaucrats, and other topics that formed the sort of apocrypha for which he would become famous. For millions of conservatives, his conclusion, which appropriated, with cheerful bipartisanship, celebrated statements from Democrat Franklin Roosevelt, the idol of Reagan's younger days, and all-time Republican hero Abraham Lincoln, established the former movie star as their new champion.

"You and I have a rendezvous with destiny," Reagan declared, borrowing from FDR. "We can preserve for our children this, the last best hope of man on earth," a phrase of Lincoln's, "or we can sentence them to take the first step into a thousand years of darkness. If we fail, at least let our children, and our children's children, say of us we justified our brief moment here." Although this appeal was mainly addressed to the threat of Soviet communism abroad, the wording was broad enough to strike a chord with conservatives also disturbed about the insidious changes in the culture at home, many of which were believed to be linked one way or another to communism. With his peroration, as one rhetorician observed, Reagan "made the sacrifices of the Republican Party in the campaign of

1964 and the willingness of the American people to die rather than to tolerate the evils of Marxist government, into the moral equivalent of Christ's Crucifixion."

With their presidential candidate going down to ignominious defeat, partisans on the Right were in the market for a new paladin. California conservatives began pleading with Reagan to run for the governorship of their state, and they found him a willing listener. Roaming the state to get ready for his bid for the statehouse in Sacramento, Reagan discovered that the public was greatly concerned with unrest on California's campuses. And once the campaign was under way Reagan hit hard at the student demonstrations, making clear that in his view the students should "observe the rules or get out." He also hammered at the rising crime rate and the racial violence in Watts, and the rise of crime everywhere, both manifestations of the cultural revolution.

After only two years in public office, drawing on his remembered glamour as a Hollywood star and the prestige of his position as governor of what was fast becoming the nation's most populated state, Reagan made a bid for the GOP presidential nomination in 1968. He fell short, because he was up against the party's master strategist, Richard Nixon.

Alarmed by the rapid rise in Reagan's popularity as the Republican Convention gathered in Miami Beach that year, Nixon moved to cut off his base of support by stealing some of Reagan's cultural thunder. To head off the Reagan threat Nixon promised delegations from the South, where Reagan's appeal was strongest, that he would not select a running mate who would divide the party, language they correctly took to mean he would not pick a liberal. He also confided that he took a dim view of court-ordered school busing. It was not the role of the federal courts, he said, "to be a local school district and make the decision as your local school board." This was what the southerners wanted to hear, and the tactic was enough to hold the line against Reagan. Once nominated, Nixon kept the first part of his bargain with the South by picking as his running mate Spiro T. Agnew, the governor of Maryland, an erstwhile Rockefeller partisan whose only previous claim to national attention had come when he condemned a group of moderate civil rights leaders for racial violence in Baltimore.

In waging his drive for the presidency, Nixon demonstrated that the same cultural concerns that elected Reagan governor of California could decide the contest for the White House. In effect, Nixon, himself a son of California, intended to extend the campaign Reagan had launched in California in 1966. He was greatly aided by all the cultural eruptions that had occurred since Reagan's gubernatorial victory—the riots in Detroit, Newark, and Washington, the unending series of peace marches in the big cities, the disorder on campuses.

"As we look at America, we see cities enveloped in smoke and flame," Nixon had declared in accepting his party's nomination. "We hear sirens in the night. We see Americans dying on distant battlefields. Did we come all this way for this?" Nixon asked. "Did American boys die in Normandy and Korea and Valley Forge for this?" The answers to these questions, he said, came from "a quiet voice in the tumult of the shouting. It is the voice of the great majority of Americans, the forgotten Americans, the non-shouters, the non-demonstrators. They give drive to the spirit of America. They give lift to the American dream."

"The forgotten Americans," the phrase he used in his acceptance speech, served him well during the campaign. Nixon also had another powerful slogan to burnish his appeal to these forgotten Americans. It was short and punchy: "Law and order." Nixon did not have to explain it. Everybody knew what it meant: putting the unruly blacks and the kid protesters in their places and keeping them there.

Nixon needed powerful code words in appealing to the "forgotten" and frightened middle class. Their votes held the key to his success, and he faced stiff competition for their support, not mainly from Hubert Humphrey—the hapless Democratic nominee who was struggling to reassemble his tattered party—but from another contender for the White House, a southerner, a politician who, along with Goldwater, had been among the first to cry out against the cultural revolution.

This was George Corley Wallace, the governor of Alabama, third-party candidate for president. Wallace's candidacy, as nominee of the American Independent Party, stemmed from his successful showing in the 1964 Democratic primaries against Lyndon Johnson. The votes he got then demonstrated the potential appeal of Wallace's populist rhetoric, heavily tinged with racial overtones. The political environment in 1968 was even better suited for Wallace. Born out of racial hostility, his candidacy broadened as it became an outlet for the more general discontent with demonstrations and street crime, the appurtenances of the cultural revolution.

Though few thought that Wallace had a realistic chance of winning the election, he did represent a serious threat to Richard Nixon's chances of winning. Campaign polls showed Wallace getting support in the suburbs of the North as well as in the South. But it was in the South, and in the border states, that Wallace's initial base was substantial enough for him to possibly carry states that Nixon needed for an electoral majority. And Wallace seemed to be a formidable foe. He had a genius for sensing and voicing the grievances of middle-class voters upset by the cultural revolutionaries and the federal government whom they considered to be in league with each other and against them.

Wallace never ran out of steam. But there was not much more to his candidacy than gas. After he had promised that "When I get to be President I'm gonna call in a bunch of bureaucrats and take their brief cases and throw them in the Potomac River," Wallace had no persuasive remedy to offer the crowds that cheered his outbursts. This serious flaw made it possible for Nixon to dismiss him as a spoiler who could not possibly win the White House. Meanwhile, everywhere Nixon went he reiterated his pledge to restore "law and order," a code phrase well understood to be aimed at the two bulwarks of the cultural revolution—blacks and the New Left.

To strengthen his own claim as a spokesman for middle-class grievances, Nixon finessed the press, which had been critical of him in the past, and which he knew many in the middle class mistrusted. Nixon made the press all but irrelevant, relying on television commercials and other means of communication over which he could maintain complete command to get his message across. A favored gambit was the use of commercials in which Nixon answered questions from groups of local citizens. These were far more significant than the reporters' stories because they were seen by a vastly bigger audience and showed Nixon as attuned to the concerns of the middle class. These events were carefully designed not to seem designed. His advisers had concluded, Nixon said, "that the more spontaneous the situation, the better I come across."

Some spontaneity. Nixon's aides handpicked the exchanges and edited the responses. Sample exchange: A well-dressed, middle-aged black asks Nixon about one of the key slogans of his campaign, law and order, a theme designed to appeal to white fears of black crime and violence. "What does law and order mean to you?" the questioner wants to know.

"To me law and order must be combined with justice," Nixon replies. "Now that's what I want for America. I want the kind of law and order that deserves respect."

There was no follow-up.

As narrow as his victory was in November—his popular vote margin over Humphrey was barely 500,000 votes out of 73 million cast—Nixon nevertheless struck a death blow at traditional liberalism centered in the Democratic Party establishment. But he opened the door for the New Left and the cultural revolutionaries to expand their political influence.

As events turned out, the movement's leaders could blame Daley and Johnson for Humphrey's defeat and exploit Nixon's presidency toward their own ends, which included bolstering their role in the Democratic Party. Like Daley, Nixon offered an opportunity for confrontation, for bringing out the worst in the system—a formula, in theory at least, for triumph through adversity. But Nixon was a supple and resourceful adversary, and the struggle between these two cultural and political enemies, Nixon and the New Left, would be notable mostly for the damage it inflicted on both sides.

Confronted with the most unpopular war in modern American history, Richard Nixon used the protest movement to dramatize and reinforce his appeal to the constituents who had elected him. By depicting his law-and-order administration as a safeguard against the dissonance of the cultural revolutionaries, Nixon built a political base among middle-class voters and gained the freedom to try to settle the war in his own time and on his own terms. His tragedy was that he overestimated the advantage his political support at home would give him in dealing with his adversaries abroad. He prolonged the end of the war to a point where the gains did not justify the cost, either to the country or to his presidency. He pursued his goals so intensely that ultimately he could no longer separate the means from the end: Finally, his strategy subsumed his purpose. Just as the Culture War crippled the Democratic Party, it destroyed the Nixon presidency.

The often unruly protesters against the war made a convenient target, as Nixon fully realized. As he analyzed the wave of protest against the war, and the overall permissiveness that accompanied it, Nixon concluded that he was ready "to take a stand on these social and cultural issues. I was anxious to defend the 'square' virtues." On some issues, such as his opposition to funding abortion and legalizing marijuana and his support for "unabashed patriotism," Nixon claimed that "he would be standing against the prevailing social winds, and that would cause tension." But this assertion only demonstrates how difficult it was for Nixon to be candid, even in his memoirs. As he himself well knew, opposition to legalizing marijuana and to funding abortions on one hand and support for patriotism on the other were hardly unpopular positions, except among the liberal elite and their allies. In taking these stands Nixon could count on the wholehearted backing of most middle-class Americans.

Nixon was fully mindful of the potential power of the protest movement. If the resistance to the war intensified and spread, his freedom of action would be restricted and he would find it even harder to govern than had Lyndon Johnson. If Nixon was to wind down the war in Indochina—achieving "Peace with Honor," in his words, or bringing about the "Vietnamization" of the war—he needed to do it on his own option and at his own pace, not in response to the antiwar movement. But this would require sustaining a delicate balancing act for an indefinite period, until no American soldier remained in Vietnam.

Nixon's goal was to drive a wedge between the middle class and the protest movement. It was a strategy relying on cultural tensions as much as political differences. His efforts culminated in his first showdown with the protest movement and his rallying cry to "the Silent Majority" a year after he was elected. During the first months of Nixon's presidency, the protest movement had been relatively quiescent. But as students returned to campuses in the fall, with the end of the war seeming no closer, a new antiwar coalition, the Vietnam Moratorium Committee, announced a new round of demonstrations—the first on October 15, the next on November 15—to demand speedy withdrawal of U.S. forces. Nixon promptly announced that "under no circumstances" would he be affected by the demonstrations. In his memoirs he claimed that he wanted to show the North Vietnamese he meant business about an "ultimatum" he had privately issued threatening to escalate the war if North Vietnam made no concessions. But when the Moratorium demonstrations around the country on October 15 drew 1 million Americans, half a million in Washington alone, Nixon recognized that they had indeed "undercut the credibility of the ultimatum."

The protesters had achieved their purpose, better than they knew. Facing another demonstration on November 15, Nixon knew he must strike back or lose control over events and be forced to abandon his entire strategy for a dignified retreat from Vietnam. Nixon scheduled an address for November 3, in between the two demonstrations, allowing him to claim that he was not reacting to either one. But in reality the timing gave him the chance to respond to the first demonstration and to undercut the second. The substantive significance of the speech lay in Nixon's pledge to end the American role in the war according to a prearranged timetable. But the key to the success of the speech was in Nixon's cultural appeal to the "Silent Majority" as a counterforce to the cultural revolution.

Speaking from the Oval Office over all three major television networks, Nixon initially referred to the protesters in seemingly positive terms, paying his respects to their "idealism" and sharing their "concern for peace." But then those positive traits are overshadowed in the speech by a grave fault of the protesters—"the bitter hatred" to which their opposition to the war had been transformed.

The president reminded his national television audience that in his campaign he pledged to end the war in a way that *we* could win the peace. It was clear that by "we" he meant both himself and the Silent Majority—though certainly not the hate-ridden protesters—and then he defined the role of the Silent Majority in this cultural partnership: "The more support

I can have from the American people," Nixon said, "the sooner that pledge can be redeemed."

It was a smash hit. By morning the White House had received the biggest response ever to a presidential speech—more than 50,000 wires and 30,000 letters, nearly all of them favorable. A Gallup poll gave the speech a 77 percent approval rating, and the next week Nixon's own approval rating climbed to 68 percent, the highest mark of his presidency. Even Seymour Hersh, arch critic of Nixon and the war, would later concede: "America it seemed supported a President who sounded aggressive and sure."

Nixon's speech deepened and hardened the cultural schism between the middle class and the mostly young rebels of the cultural revolution. The parameters of these differences were adumbrated in two highly influential books published in 1970, the second year of Nixon's presidency. On the Left was *The Greening of America* by a young Yale law professor, Charles Reich, which spoke to the most fervent hopes of the counterculture, thus confirming the worst fears of the middle class. On the Right was *The Real Majority* by two opinion analysts, Richard Scammon and Ben Wattenberg.

Reich proclaimed an imminent revolution of the "new generation" in reaction to two threats: the "betrayal and loss of the American dream" and "the rise of the Corporate state of the 1960s." To respond to these threats, Reich declared, Americans had begun to develop a "new consciousness" based on the advances of technology. Ultimately, he asserted, this awareness would revolutionize the structure of society, not by "direct political means" but "by changing culture and the quality of individual lives, which in turn change politics and ultimately structure." None of this was particularly easy to read or digest. But Reich's generational vision appealed to the narcissism and intellectual pretentiousness that characterized many young people who saw themselves as cultural rebels. His book became a best-seller and a sensation on campuses.

But a very different, much grouchier mood prevailed off campus in the bastions of the middle class, and this attitude was captured by the opinion analysts. Richard Scammon, a former head of the U.S. Census

Bureau, and Ben Wattenberg, a former Lyndon Johnson speechwriter, in *The Real Majority* coined a cognomen of their own to label the cultural conflict in American society: "the social issue," which the authors contended was emerging as a force to rival economics on the political landscape. The world they looked at was the obverse of the world that concerned Reich and the leaders of the counterculture. The American voter, they declared, was not "a 24-year-old political science instructor at Yale University," but rather a 47-year-old wife of a machinist living in suburban Dayton, Ohio. In fact, they announced, in a formulation that was destined to be much repeated in political circles for the next decade, the vast majority of the American electorate was "unblack, unyoung and unpoor."

Like the young, the blacks, and the poor, the middle-class whites in suburban Dayton, and most of the rest of middle-class America, were dissatisfied with the nature of society. "Some say that you can't rationalize the plight of the kids," said Frank Armbruster of the Hudson Institute, a conservative think tank, "you have got to feel it. The same thing is true of Middle America; you have to feel it." Many of the complaints of this majority differed from the faults the young found with the country, and even when members of the two groups shared the same grievances their remedies had little in common.

Both the counterculture and Middle America lamented disorder and purposelessness in society. The former saw the answer in a greater sense of community and cooperation. The latter believed in harsher laws and stricter enforcement. These concerns seemed like echoes of the complaints made by Barry Goldwater only a few years before, with racial unrest and rising crime prominent among them.

But the whole of the distress of the middle class was greater than the sum of its parts, as *Time* suggested when, four years after it had chosen the younger generation as "Man of the Year," it paid the same tribute to Middle Americans:

> The American dream that they were living was no longer the dream as advertised. They feared that they were beginning to lose their grip on the country. Others seemed to be taking over—the liberals, the radicals,

the defiant young, a communications industry that they often believed was lying to them. *The Saturday Evening Post* folded, but the older world of Norman Rockwell icons was long gone anyway. No one celebrated them: intellectuals dismissed their lore as banality. Pornography, dissent and drugs seemed to wash over them in waves, bearing some of their children away.

Looking ahead to the rest of the decade Middle Americans saw the political arena divided in two—one half would be the traditional arena of economic policy, the other would be given over to the Culture War— with crime, drugs, racial tension, and protest demonstrations the main skirmish lines. Truly, for many among the beleaguered Middle Americans, Nixon's Silent Majority, the war was already under way. They did not wait for Election Day to hit back at their enemies. Defying the Supreme Court's ban on prayer, students and their parents gathered in a school in Netcong, New Jersey, to read aloud the morning invocation from the Congressional Record. Around the country, state legislators offered more than 100 drastic measures to suppress campus dissent, and in West Virginia they adopted a statute giving the police immunity from legal action for anything they did to bring rioters to heel. Their constituents plastered their car windows with American-flag decals and wore miniature flags in their buttonholes. To counter "Hell No, We Won't Go" and the other slogans of the demonstrators, they displayed bumper stickers proclaiming "Honor America," and "Spiro Is My Hero" in admiration of Nixon's vice president.

In fact, Agnew had carved out a special place for himself in the hearts of Middle Americans. Early in Nixon's first year of the White House he had countered the protesters with rhetoric so baroque and intemperate it verged on self-parody. Speaking in the wake of the October 15, 1969, Moratorium, Agnew charged that "a spirit of national masochism prevails, encouraged by an effete corps of impudent snobs who characterize themselves as intellectuals." He followed up that blast a few days later by warning that "America cannot afford to write off a whole generation for the decadent thinking of a few. . . . We can however afford to separate them from our society, with no more regret than we should feel over discarding rotten apples from a barrel."

The stridency of Agnew's language disturbed even some Republican leaders. But he was doing exactly what Nixon wanted done and voicing the feelings of millions in the Silent Majority who were infuriated by the protests against the war. And no one was more furious at these challenges to the establishment than immigrants and the children of immigrants who only a few decades earlier had themselves been viewed as outcasts. "The Moratorium was a stab in the back to our boys on the firing lines," declared Paul M. Deac, executive vice president of the National Confederation of American Ethnic Groups, which claimed to represent 18 million foreign-born and first- and second-generation Americans. "Our families don't have long-haired brats—they'd tear the hair off them. Our boys don't smoke pot or raise hell or seek deferments. Our people are too busy making a living and trying to be good Americans."

With Agnew as his decidedly non-silent partner, Nixon steadily sharpened the lines of cultural conflict, intensifying his attacks on the protest movement as a shield for his policies and a sword to rally the Silent Majority. In the spring of 1970, even as he was promising to wind down the war, Nixon abruptly decided to open a new front, sending U.S. troops into neutral Cambodia. This incursion, the president claimed, was intended to wipe out North Vietnamese "sanctuaries" of supplies and communications that had escaped a year of clandestine bombing. A few hours after his announcement, even as protests were building on campuses, Nixon, in talking to a friendly crowd of Pentagon workers, made a point of contrasting the sons of the Silent Majority, in uniform in Vietnam, with the student protesters. "They're the greatest," he said of the soldiers; in contrast, referring to the students, he said, "You see these bums, you know, blowing up the campuses. Listen, the boys that are on the college campuses today are the luckiest people in the world, going to the greatest universities. And here they were burning up the books, storming around about this issue."

Nixon's words touched off a controversy that was still raging a few days later when at Kent State University, the Ohio National Guard, called to quell an antiwar demonstration, gunned down thirteen students, four of whom died. Campuses all over the nation erupted in protest, and at Mississippi's Jackson State University two more students died in a hail of bullets fired by state police. Nixon responded with calculated coldness. Recalling that after the Chicago riots he had praised the police and received kudos for his words, he took a similar stance. "This should remind us all once again that when dissent turns to violence it invites tragedy." William Safire, who at the time was a White House speechwriter for both Nixon and Agnew, later called that response "as ill-conceived as it was well phrased." But there is no reason to believe that Nixon fully understood what he was saying and why.

The Nixon and Agnew rhetoric accomplished its purpose. A *Newsweek* poll showed that 60 percent of the public supported the way authorities had handled the Kent State demonstration. And some in Nixon's Silent Majority plunged into the fray. The week after the Kent State shootings, some 200 hard hats working on a construction project in Manhattan put down their tools and assaulted antiwar demonstrators, chanting, "America, love it or leave it" and "Kill the commie bastards." A few weeks later, thousands more construction workers—who since the New Deal had formed the backbone of the Democratic Party—marched in New York to demonstrate their backing for the war. Summoned to the White House to receive the president's gratitude, their leaders presented him with a hard hat labeled "Commander-in-Chief."

In the face of Nixon's intransigence, continued troop withdrawals from Vietnam, and declining U.S. casualty rates there, much of the steam went out of the protest movement. Scattered demonstrations continued in 1971 but they were unable to convey the urgency or command the attention they had in the past.

A few in the protest movement turned to the darkest kind of violence. A group of radicals calling themselves the Weathermen—after the Bob Dylan lyric from "Blowin' in the Wind"—"You don't need a weatherman to tell which way the wind blows"—sponsored four "Days of Rage" in Chicago, a window-smashing spree that produced 150 arrests and three casualties from police gunfire. Reveling in violence, Weathermen also claimed credit for bombing the New York City Police Department and the Bank of America's Manhattan offices. All told, the police countered some 250 major bombings from the fall of 1969 through the spring of 1970 involving ROTC buildings, draft boards, and induction centers. And that did not include the unplanned destruction in March 1970 of a townhouse in a fashionable lower Manhattan street that was being used as a bomb factory. Police recovered the bodies of three Weathermen and enough dynamite to level a city block.

Of far more significance for the antiwar movement and its counter-culture allies was one consequence of the presidential campaign in 1968 which created the potential for them to exert greater influence in the Democratic Party. Following the bitter campaign, the party, whose leader-ship, notably Chicago Mayor Richard Daley, had fought the protest movement and the New Left with all the weapons at its command, had made itself into a more hospitable environment.

One reason for this change was that Hubert Humphrey's loss was a setback for the entire party establishment. But another, more fundamen-tal, factor was that, in a delayed acknowledgment of the protest move-ment, the party transformed the way it went about nominating its presi-dential standard-bearer. As a peace offering to the frustrated antiwar delegates who had supported Eugene McCarthy and Robert Kennedy, the 1968 convention had passed a resolution calling for a commission to re-form the party's nominating rules.

Under the chairmanship of George McGovern, then a little-known senator from South Dakota, the newly created commission on party struc-ture and delegation selection laid down a new set of laws and standards to govern Democratic parties in every state and territory in time for the 1972 campaign. The new rules, or "guidelines" as they were styled, struck directly at the confusion and arbitrariness of the delegate-selection process that had frustrated the antiwar forces in 1968. They required the selection of dele-gates within the year of the convention and all but eliminated the power of party officials to appoint delegates. In addition, the new guidelines did not merely attempt to end discrimination, as in the past; instead, they called for the inclusion of women, and also of minorities, in rough proportion to their representation in the voting population, a dictate that came close to a quota system. The full significance of this change did not become clear until the party's national convention in 1972. But even before that, party leaders realized the new rules would make a big difference. After his first look at them, Lawrence O'Brien, the former aide to President Kennedy, who had been newly installed as the Democratic National Chairman, hailed them as "the greatest goddam change since the two party system."

Still, no one took much heed except for the reformers and the antiwar contingent. One among them who paid particular attention was former chairman McGovern himself, who, having completed his work on the commission, set out to make the new rules work to his own benefit by running for president. The basis of his campaign was an unconditional pledge to end American involvement in the war, a promise that soon gained him the support of the protesters. With the help of their energy, passion, and not inconsiderable organizing skill, McGovern won the 1972 Democratic presidential nomination and in the process, abetted by the new delegate guidelines, made over the face of his party.

This transformation was evident—all too evident, in the view of some Democrats—at the 1972 Democratic Convention in Miami Beach. At the 1968 convention, with the party still mired in its segregationist past, fewer than 7 percent of the delegates had been black. In 1972 that proportion doubled. The closing of the gender gap had been even more striking—from a mere 13 percent in 1968, the number of women delegates rose to nearly 40 percent in 1967. And the most dramatic change of all, reflecting the influx of the protest movement and its ancillaries, was the greening of the convention. The percentage of delegates under thirty had increased more than eight-fold—from fewer than 3 percent in 1968 to 23 percent. And some states, captured by the enthusiasm of the counterculture, had gone well beyond the guideline requirements. California, now the nation's largest state, led the way in what its delegates proudly hailed as "overcompliance" with the guidelines; though minorities made up only 27 percent of the state's population, they constituted nearly 40 percent of its convention delegation. By contrast with the middle-aged, middle-class white men who had traditionally filled the convention's seats, the appearance of the 1972 delegation seemed exotic to some and downright disturbing to others.

Theodore White, the bard of Middle American politics, found the minorities in California's delegation picturesque: "Tall, high-cheekboned maidens, their black pigtails stiff as Sitting Bull's in old monochromes; Japanese and Chinese youngsters with their delicately sculpted faces; blacks of every type—sturdy responsibles, matrons in housedresses, intense, bespectacled intellectuals." New York's image had also been vastly recast, the machine barons and their apparatchiks, with their dark suits and permanent scowls, having been replaced by a youthful crew, tieless and coatless, exuding conviction and energy.

Not surprisingly, those who had ruled the party in the past were not pleased with the change. "What kind of delegation is this?" grumbled George Meany, the president of the AFL-CIO, Bronx born and bred, about the delegation from his native state. "They've got six open fags, and only three union people."

Just as the appearance of many of the delegates seemed bizarre to much of Middle America, so were the ideas they espoused. And these beliefs were promoted with relentless vigor as the delegates debated the report of the party Platform Committee. Even before the debate started, the committee had given Nixon fresh ammunition for use in his cultural offensive by endorsing the use of court-ordered school busing to speed school integration, an idea abhorrent to millions of white suburbanites. And there were other ideas, at least as controversial and more personal, which the forces of the new culture forced into the convention spotlight. Undismayed by their defeat in the Platform Committee, advocates of a woman's right to abortion, a right the Supreme Court had yet to uphold, fought to gain approval for a minority report on the issue. Speaker after speaker marched to the podium, raising their voices on a controversy rarely before discussed in public, seeking a plank upholding the right of women to control their own bodies. After a long and bitter debate they suffered yet another defeat on a roll call vote.

The rights of homosexuals (the term "gay" not yet having gained common usage) was still another cause whose advocates sought a place on the party platform. Once again a minority plank was introduced, calling for repeal of all laws restricting sexual acts by consenting adults in private. And once again the result was defeat, this time by a voice vote.

Even though these causes failed to find majority support at the convention, just the notion of such matters being discussed in public was enough to disturb many Middle Americans. Whether or not they chose to watch the convention itself, they could not escape being exposed to what took place there because of the media attention it received. Plainly the forces of the counterculture saw the convention not merely as a component in the political process but as a sort of political bazaar in which they could display their wares to a national television audience.

In the long run, the impression they created mattered more than the vote count on platform proposals, adding up to a general perception, as Theodore White put it, "of a movement rushing through and beyond the political and cultural limits all politicians had up to now accepted." In a similar vein, Ben Wattenberg, whose argument in *The Real Majority* had helped convince Washington Senator Henry M. ("Scoop") Jackson to recruit him as an aide for his 1972 presidential campaign, contended that the convention had revealed the true nature of the McGovern candidacy: "What really pulled the mask off was Miami. The McGovern people did it on national television. The whole troupe was going around—the people who were pro-busing and pro-abortion and pro-amnesty and stop-bombing the dikes—and 50 million people watching it on color television. It was then that the election was decided."

Of course, given the magnitude of McGovern's defeat by Nixon—who swept all before him on election night except for the District of Columbia and the state of Massachusetts—it is hard to pinpoint one cause. Some said that McGovern's choice of Tom Eagleton as his running mate without first checking out rumors that he had suffered from mental illness was the nail in the coffin of his candidacy. Others argued that given the seeming health of the economy, and of national Security Adviser Henry Kissinger's pre-election claim, on behalf of Nixon, that "Peace is at hand" in Vietnam, McGovern never had a chance. But what does seem hard to dispute is that watching the Democratic Convention, with all its dissonance from the themes of middle-class values, convinced many Americans that they knew all they wanted to know about George McGovern's candidacy. It was that perception that colored the reaction of both the press and the public to the Eagleton episode and led to the widespread condemnation of McGovern's behavior, rather than a willingness to give him the benefit of the doubt. Without the damage done to his candidacy by the cultural revolution, McGovern would have had a better chance of getting a hearing for his substantive positions, and might have been able to force Nixon into a genuine debate on the issues.

As for Nixon, his waging of the Culture War helped him gain a landslide victory and also to end the U.S. role in Vietnam more or less in his own way and on his own timetable. But in the long run, he turned out to be a victim of the very strategies that yielded this success. Because his will and his middle-class values had made his ideological strategy of polarization pay off, he seemed unwilling or unable to make peace with his enemies for fear he would lose his middle-class supporters. Having gained a majority, he did not try to persuade the minority. Instead he sought to destroy its adherents. In the process he destroyed his own presidency.

Nixon later offered this self-revealing analysis:

> Once I realized that the Vietnam War could not be ended quickly or easily and that I was going to be up against an antiwar movement that was able to dominate the media with its attitudes and values I was sometimes drawn into the very frame of mind I so despised in the leaders of that movement.
>
> They increasingly came to justify almost anything in the name of forcing an immediate end to a war they considered unjustified and immoral. I was similarly driven to preserve the government's ability to conduct foreign policy and to conduct it in the way that I felt would best bring peace.

But it was not only in foreign policy that Nixon adopted this combative stance. In responding to domestic challenges his championship of middle-class values and his cultural polarization strategy combined to produce bitterness and division. His most critical domestic cultural challenge was dealing with the tension between black demands for civil rights expansion and white resistance to those demands, the same problem that in different forms had plagued each of his four most recent predecessors. As Eisenhower's vice president, Nixon, mindful of the potential of the black vote, had suggested that Republican leaders try to rally moderate whites in the South against extremism. But that had been a decade earlier, before racial divisions had hardened along partisan lines, in part because of Eisenhower's policies, creating formidable obstacles to any Republican effort to gain by appealing to moderation.

The votes of southern whites had helped make Nixon president—he had carried seven southern states—and once in office he sought to solidify their support, relying on a strategy similar to the approach he had used to rally the Silent Majority behind his Vietnam policies. Just as he had used the protest movement against the war as a cultural red flag to mobilize support to continue the fighting, he used the Supreme Court, and its unyielding opposition to segregation, to rally support for slowing the pace of integration. First, he defied the court by having the Justice Department resist its orders. When that strategy failed, he sought to change the court, tailoring it to suit the conservative tastes of his southern supporters. After two of his nominees were rejected, Nixon accused the Senate of "malicious character assassination" and called upon "the millions of Americans living in the South to bear witness to this act of regional discrimination."

By establishing his bona fides with the white South, Nixon consolidated his support there and with the middle class in general. The cost of the turmoil and divisiveness his polarizing cultural strategy had created was a bill that would not come due until later. Meanwhile, his southern supporters helped him gain his overwhelming majority in 1972, a triumph that he was confident would "give the Republican Party the new majority momentum that would give it a new lease on life."

Flushed with that success Nixon began his second term determined to once and for all break the power of the "liberal establishment" and promote the beliefs of his Silent Majority. He had barely begun this struggle when he was suddenly forced to confront another sort of challenge, which turned out to be fatal to his presidency—the scandal of Watergate. The mysterious burglary of Democratic Party headquarters in June 1972, which at first had been dismissed as a trivial "caper," was now taking on increasing and ominous significance as sordid revelations of the behavior of the president's closest advisers began to emerge, first in a trickle, then in a flood.

Nixon fought back, but he was waging a losing battle. Though he could still attack, his defenses were being shredded. "I am not a crook," the president startled the public by declaring at one point in his ordeal. But the preponderance of evidence suggested otherwise. By his conduct he appeared to have repudiated such prime bulwarks of the middle-class cultural values as respect for law and simple truthfulness. Over the years Nixon's leadership appeal to middle-class voters had rested on his assertion that he would use political power to protect their interests and values. Now it appeared he had used that power mainly to advance his own interests and save his own skin, and he was no longer in a position to be of much help to anyone else. He became the first American president to resign his office in disgrace.

"History will make the final judgment on the actions, reactions and excesses of both sides," Nixon said afterward. Three decades removed from the conflicts spawned by Vietnam and Nixon's presidency, that verdict is still evolving. What history would clearly show, though, is that, having been stoked by the Vietnam War and Nixon's presidency, even after both had ended, the fires of the Culture War raged on.

CHAPTER 10

THE RETURN OF
THE RIGHTEOUS

The shocks of Vietnam and Watergate had numbed the political system. The war had so confused and divided the Democrats that its end left them in disarray, lacking purpose and direction. As for Watergate, its aftermath—Nixon's resignation and the GOP debacle in the 1974 congressional elections—had stunned the Republicans, throwing them on the defensive.

But what many politicians saw as a wasteland one saw as an opportunity. His name was Jimmy Carter, the former governor of Georgia. What he lacked in experience or credentials he seemed to make up in ambition and stamina. As the official start of the 1976 Democratic campaign approached, Carter was already running harder than anyone else, campaigning six days a week. And nearly a year before the 1976 primaries got under way he had already visited forty-five states.

But something about the peanut farmer from Plains besides his energy commanded attention. A Southern Baptist, Carter taught Sunday school and made no bones about being a born-again Christian. In fact, he was using his religious faith to energize his candidacy. And Democratic professionals were beginning to pay attention. They realized that Carter's religious background could help him win support among millions of Americans disillusioned with traditional politics and its practitioners in the wake of Watergate and Vietnam. In particular, they suspected that Carter's faith would appeal to a group of conservative

Christians called "evangelicals" who were emerging as a growing force in the political process.

Little was known about the evangelicals outside their churches. But politicians with some sense of the nation's past did not have trouble recalling that the country had a long history of church-based political movements. In fact, the evangelical strain of Protestantism, which rejected any centralized control and regarded the Bible and each individual's conscience as the ultimate authorities on religious matters, had helped to shape relations between church, politics, and society from the earliest days of nationhood.

However much the preaching of some current evangelicals might carry a whiff of theocracy, their predecessors played a major role in implementing the first-amendment guarantees of freedom of worship and church-state separation. Men and women of God had brought energy and purpose to a variety of causes, including emancipation and prohibition. And most recently the civil rights movement had drawn in leaders of the modern church, "progressives" they were called, who were more willing to adjust to cultural changes and take up a battle, like the struggle against racial barriers, that challenged tradition.

But the believers in the Old Time Religion, the evangelicals, including the most hard-edged of their brethren, fundamentalists, had remained on the sidelines since the Scopes "monkey trial" in 1925. This widely publicized confrontation had discredited their great leader, William Jennings Bryan, who had sought to defend the Biblical version of creation, and had thrown their ranks into confusion. They had remained content to tend to their own fires and guard their children against disbelief for half a century, through the Great Depression, the Second World War, and the cultural upheavals of the 1960s. Like their fellow Middle Americans, the evangelicals had been shaken by the uproar and the violence, and they had heard Richard Nixon's rallying cry. Still embittered by their past defeats and frustration, they had not heeded this clarion call, shunning political activity, many of them still unwilling even to vote.

But the forces of change were getting harder to ignore. Turpitude, coarseness, and violence seemed to be escalating at an alarming rate. And the Supreme Court had emerged as a powerful menace to traditional beliefs and values. First, in the 1960s the court had driven the Bible and prayer from the public schools. And then in 1973, in the second term of Richard Nixon, who had set out to change the court so that it would respect tradition, the justices provided evidence of Nixon's failure when they laid down a ruling in *Roe v. Wade*, with even more awful consequences than the banning of prayer. That decision made the killing of the unborn lawful by striking down state prohibitions against abortion.

In addition to the spread of what they regarded as legalized murder, the faithful found themselves threatened at every hand by an encroaching circle of lewdness and depravity, in books and magazines, in motion pictures, and on television, that threatened the corruption of their children. To many evangelicals, it now began to seem that they could no longer afford to wait on the sidelines. The time was coming when they would have to act. And so they awaited their marching orders.

When I asked Jimmy Carter about the political potential of evangelicals in the spring of 1975 in New Hampshire, it was clear that he had given the subject considerable thought. But it was also clear that he was chary of seeming to exploit the political power of religion. The evangelical movement now included nearly 50 million persons, he told me, "people like myself who are deeply committed to establishing government as moralistic and decent." As for himself, Carter said: "Religion is part of my life, part of my conscience. It may or may not be politically significant."

Despite Carter's demurrer, his religion turned out to be the defining agent of his implausible candidacy and the key to his success. It set him apart from the other candidates and infused his drive for the presidency with a moral fervor that was ideally suited for the post-Watergate era, as this visit to New Hampshire demonstrated. At a prayer breakfast in Manchester, Carter was very much at home. "I'm running for president because I am a deeply religious person," he said. "The most important thing in my life is my belief and my commitment in God. We should never deviate from recognizing our own unworthiness, but also our absolute strength when our hand is in the hand of God."

Carter was the first modern candidate for president to use his religion, and the surrounding aura of morality, as a direct reason for voting for him, and this ambience carried over to his stewardship. Though Carter sought to maintain a line of separation between his religious faith and his political career, in reality they were inextricably bound together, as illustrated by his revelation that he was a born-again Christian. While this disclosure puzzled millions of Americans who were strangers to evangelical practices, Carter's words had a powerful and positive impact on true believers who shared with the candidate the experience of being born again—having their lives transformed by making a personal commitment to Jesus Christ as their Savior.

Like other conservative Christians, evangelicals take a stern view of Christian doctrine, put more emphasis on individual morality than on the betterment of society, and regard the Bible as the sole authority on the relationship between God and humanity. What sets evangelicals apart is their conviction that no individual can truly satisfy his Divine maker without going through the born-again experience, as Carter himself had done. By the time Carter was running for president, evangelicals had found a foothold all across the country and in almost every Protestant church. They were particularly strong among Carter's own Southern Baptists, Dixie's most powerful denomination. A Gallup poll showed that half of all Protestants and about one-third of all Americans claimed to have been born again, a total of nearly 50 million adult Americans who maintained they had experienced a turning point in their lives by committing themselves to Christ.

Christian conservatives supporting Carter banded together into a group called Citizens for Carter and four months before Election Day took out a full-page ad in *Christianity Today* under the headline "Does a Dedicated Evangelical Belong in the White House?" a question it answered unequivocally in the affirmative. "In this post-Watergate era, people throughout the country are disillusioned with the moral corruption and incompetent leadership they see in the political arena," the ad declared. And then in lines that echoed one of the main themes of Carter's stump speeches, the ad asserted: "America's problems are a result of a spiritual crisis at its heart. . . . Jimmy Carter stands for a return to open government, competence, honesty and an abiding sense of the importance of morality in our national life."

Still, Carter and the Democrats faced plenty of competition for the souls and votes of evangelicals. Until Carter arrived on the scene, the new evangelical interest in politics had tilted more to the Right. The majority of evangelicals had cast their ballots for Nixon in 1960, 1968, and 1972, and by and large they were believed to have favored Republican candidates in every election since the Civil War.

In 1976 Carter faced a direct challenge for the evangelical vote from his adversary, the incumbent Republican chief executive, Nixon's successor, Gerald Ford. As Election Day drew near, Ford managed to find time to address the Southern Baptist Convention and to give interviews to the National Association of Evangelicals and the National Religious Broadcasters, using these occasions to cast himself as a strong Christian in his own right. Though he was a longtime Episcopalian, a denomination whose practices are far removed from evangelism, Ford let it be known that he himself had had his life transformed by Jesus Christ and that he read the Bible daily. That, together with the fact that his son, Michael, was a student at a leading evangelical seminary in New England, helped him win the endorsement of the Reverend W. A. Criswell, pastor of Dallas's First Baptist Church, the world's largest Southern Baptist congregation.

Trying to gain support of conservative Catholics as well as Protestants, Ford said he would support a constitutional amendment that allowed the states to regulate abortion as they saw fit. This proposal fell short of the absolute ban on abortions that most abortion foes sought, but it helped to atone for First Lady Betty Ford's earlier statement backing the *Roe v. Wade* decision. And it was more than Carter would say against abortion, though early in the campaign for the nomination he had given the impression, misleading as it turned out, that "under certain circumstances" he might back a constitutional prohibition. By the time he had been nominated, the militancy of the feminists and other liberal constituencies among the Democrats in support of abortion ruled out any further such ambiguity on Carter's part. Despite the abortion issue and

Ford's efforts, a Gallup poll a few months before the election gave Carter a 25 percent lead over Ford among evangelicals. But in view of the trend in past elections, the Democratic standard-bearer knew he would have to battle to maintain that advantage, and he did whatever he could to maximize his religious appeal.

He made a start at the convention that nominated him at New York's Madison Square Garden, which took on some of the aspects of a revival meeting, climaxed by the benediction upon the Democratic ticket delivered by Martin Luther King, Sr., father of the slain civil rights leader. "Surely the Lord is in this place," Daddy King declared. "Surely the Lord sent Jimmy Carter to come on out and bring America back where she belongs."

On the campaign trail Carter reached out to Catholics as well as Protestants by stressing the need to bolster the American family. Everywhere he went, Carter declared, "I find people deeply concerned about the loss of stability and the loss of values in our lives. The root of this problem is the steady erosion and weakening of our families." Reeling off a long list of dismal statistics that showed rising rates of divorce, out-of-wedlock births, alcohol and drug abuse, and juvenile crime, he announced that his administration would make strengthening the family "an urgent priority." Indeed, in a decision he would later have reason to regret, Carter promised that soon after he became president he would organize a White House conference that would bring together government leaders, social workers, and ordinary citizens to seek ways to bolster the family.

Not surprisingly, Carter's stress on faith, morality, and traditional cultural values found a responsive chord among religious leaders, particularly evangelicals. Among the most prominent of those who saw Carter's candidacy as opening the gates to the promised land was the Reverend Pat Robertson, perhaps the most politically ambitious of the group of evangelical preachers who had learned to use television to reach congregations that numbered in the millions. "In the next five years we have an unprecedented opportunity for America to fulfill the dream of the early settlers who came right here to Virginia in 1607 that this land would be used to glorify God," he told the huge audience that watched his *700 Club* program, leaving no doubt, within the bounds of Federal Communications Commission regulations, about whom Robertson himself favored for president. Bailey Smith, one of the influential lay leaders of the Southern Baptist Church, was even more fulsome and direct in an address to the church's annual convention. "This country needs a born-again man in the White House," he declared. "And his initials are the same as our Lord's."

As gratifying as all these encomiums were, Carter and his advisers soon began to realize that they were skating on thin ice. All the religious talk by him and his supporters raised doubts among many Americans about the candidate. Had the Democrats nominated some new kind of Southern holy man? Or was he an old-fashioned hypocrite? Most voters did give him positive ratings in opinion surveys, but nearly half of those who thought well of him could not answer most of the specific questions about his qualifications and beliefs. "People were uneasy with him as a person," his pollster, Pat Caddell, warned Carter's other advisers. This was a problem that Carter had difficulty solving. "Because people kept saying that no one knew who Carter was," his press secretary, Jody Powell, observed, "there were repeated and painful attempts by us to explain who this man really was, sometimes to the point of absurdity."

Carter's clumsiest and most harmful effort at self-definition was his notorious interview with *Playboy* magazine. Seeking to alleviate apprehensions about his fundamentalist religious beliefs and prove that he was a regular fellow, Carter volunteered the information that "I've looked on a lot of women with lust. I've committed adultery in my heart many times. Christ says don't consider yourself better than someone else because one guy screws a whole bunch of women while the other guy is loyal to his wife. The guy who's loyal to his wife ought not to be condescending or proud because of the relative degree of sinfulness." These remarks drew intense media coverage. "Sex, Sin, Temptation—Carter's Candid Views," blared the headline in the *Chicago Sun-Times*. The *Washington Star* bannered: "Carter on Sin and Lust: I'm Human . . . I'm Tempted." In his own state of Georgia, the *Columbus Enquirer* ran a pink-tinted "Truth Is Out" headline and later featured a cartoon depicting a Playboy bunny wearing a broad Carteresque grin.

Many in the religious community disapproved of the whole incident—not only of what Carter had said, but of his choice of a forum. "*Playboy* is known for its gutter approach to life," said Dr. Jerry Vines of Mobile, Alabama, a former president of the pastors' conference of the Southern Baptist Convention. "A lot of us are not convinced that Mr. Carter is truly in the evangelical Christian camp." That view was echoed by Jerry Falwell, who had not yet founded the Moral Majority but was already among the most prominent of the new breed of television evangelists. "Like many others I am quite disillusioned," Falwell said. "Four months ago the majority of the people I knew were pro-Carter. Today that has totally reversed."

Falwell's assertion turned out to be hyperbolic. Carter retained enough support from evangelicals, as well as from other Americans of all faiths and beliefs, to eke out a narrow victory over Gerald Ford and become the nation's thirty-ninth president in November 1976. But Falwell's disillusionment was shared by many citizens, even those who chose to vote for Carter as the lesser of evils. It is typical of new presidents to raise expectations that they cannot deliver. But most of these unkept promises have had to do with material things—lower taxes and/or bigger spending on favored programs. Carter had put his presidency and the country at greater risk by placing himself on a pedestal, by making spiritual and moral commitments, by promising to achieve justice with compassion and vowing to make Americans feel better about each other and themselves. He pledged time and again on the stump to give the country "a government as good as its people." Unspoken but implicit in this declaration was the covenant that the people should be as good as the Lord wanted them to be.

The moral foundations of Carter's campaign were underlined by his inaugural address. It was essentially a sermon beginning with a quote from the Old Testament prophet Micah: "And what doth the Lord require of thee but to do justly and to love mercy and to walk humbly with thy God?" Carter talked about affirming the nation's moral strength, bolstering family relationships, and reaffirming the American dream. But the address was notably short, less than 15 minutes, and sparse. Rather than setting forth an agenda for action his speech seemed intended mainly to establish a moral tone for governance. His objectives, Carter said, "are not just my goals. And they will not be my accomplishments but the affirmation of our nation's moral strength and our belief in an undiminished, ever-expanding American dream."

Nor did Carter's moralizing stop with his inaugural speech. A few months after he took office, addressing a group of federal workers on an informal visit to their offices, he felt called upon to urge: "Those of you who are living in sin, I hope you'll get married." Although many Americans welcomed Carter's focus on morality as much needed by a country that had been scarred by scandal and a divisive war, he also created problems for himself. His preachiness conveyed to some citizens the impression of sanctimoniousness, which proved to be politically harmful, particularly after he appeared insensitive to the financial hanky-panky of his budget director, close friend, and confidante Bert Lance, who was accused of ethical indiscretions during his career as a Georgia banker.

But Carter faced an even greater peril. By his rhetoric, and some of his actions, he was raising the nation's consciousness about matters moral and spiritual with consequences that neither Carter nor his party were prepared for or even welcomed. Without intending to, or realizing it, Carter's moralizing had heightened the tensions of the cultural conflict that had seethed since the 1960s, leading to an intense and often bitter debate as to how best to measure the nation's moral strength and fulfill the American dream.

A prime reason for the bitterness was the conflict between Carter's policies on moral and cultural issues as president and the beliefs of many of the evangelicals who had supported him, a discordance which seemed to become more evident as Carter's tenure in the White House lengthened. The first clash in this cultural warfare came over an issue that, when it first emerged, seemed as close to coinciding with the American consensus on social and cultural values as was possible for a political issue. This was the proposed Equal Rights Amendment to the Constitution, or ERA, the pride and joy of the women's movement, a version of which was first proposed in 1923 and which had reemerged with new popular support amid the turmoil of the Sixties. The amendment, which asserted, in part, that "Equality of rights under the law shall not be denied or abridged by the United States or by any state on account of sex," had been approved by the necessary two-thirds majority of both houses of Congress in 1972 and endorsed by twenty-two states within its first year. In 1976 the ERA was backed not only by the Democratic Party platform but also by the GOP, which had had a pro-ERA plank for forty years.

But then the pace of approval slowed markedly and by the time Jimmy Carter moved into the Oval Office, the amendment was stalled, four states short of the required three-fourths. And even supporters had been forced to acknowledge that the goal of ratification was now in doubt. One of the big reasons for this unanticipated difficulty was the rise of the New Right, a term first heard in the Nixon years, in counterpoint to the New Left, as a rubric for an amalgam of religious and political forces drawn together by cultural issues.

For the New Right, casting about for causes behind which to mobilize supporters, the ERA was a godsend. It offered an opportunity to draw a stark contrast between traditional values and the cultural revolution on one of the foundations of society, the importance of distinctions along lines of gender. Moreover, as the New Right soon found, the battle against the ERA helped attract a flood of recruits and energetic leadership, of whom the most formidable was Phyllis Schlafly. A mid-fifties veteran of the earliest cultural conflicts of the past two decades, she had been previously best known as the author of *A Choice, Not an Echo,* the book that had provided the battle cry for Barry Goldwater's presidential campaign. Schlafly's opposition to the ERA reflected, in part, standard conservative doctrine. She regarded the amendment as yet another example of big government intrusion, which she claimed could lead to women being forced to take jobs they did not want and could not handle. But Schlafly also had cultural objections. She viewed the ERA as a threat to that most venerated of American institutions, the family. "Women find their greatest fulfillment at home with the family," she maintained. And the ERA, she believed, would spur women to explore other paths to satisfaction.

Schlafly herself, however, was hardly a homebody. The author of nine books, a monthly political newsletter, and a twice weekly newspaper column, she had a maid to do the cleaning at her home in Alton, Illinois, and a secretary to handle her correspondence. A twice-defeated candidate for Congress, she roamed the country making speeches against the ERA and in support of Right-Wing causes. Nevertheless, she counted herself a full-time wife and mother. Being a housewife, she insisted, doesn't mean a woman must spend 24 hours every day at it. "I certainly do support some type of other interest," she said. "But family demands and concerns have priority. I have canceled speeches whenever my husband thought that I had been away from home too much."

The feminist forces backing the ERA got a taste of how effective an opponent Schlafly could be during Carter's first year in the White House, when she held a conference of her own to counter a throng of some 20,000 women gathered in Houston for the first National Women's Conference. At the National Women's Conference, backed by $5 million in federal funds and chaired by fiery New York Congresswoman Bella Abzug, the feminists had things under control. They adopted a twenty-five-point national plan of action that included not only such noncontentious issues as extending social security benefits to housewives but three more controversial issues: the ERA, abortion, and lesbian rights.

But Schlafly decided to let the feminists stew in their own juice while she led 15,000 ERA opponents to the separate "pro-family" conference in another arena across town from the feminist-dominated conclave. From her point of view, the ERA backers, by having their own way, had done themselves in, particularly by their endorsement of lesbian rights. Schlafly pointed to the impassioned plea by feminist leaders for votes for the lesbian rights resolution, who had argued, "Yes we have to work with lesbians and they have to be part of our movement." Schlafly added: "The American people saw that and they didn't like it."

The Houston conference stoked the resentment of Carter's onetime conservative Christian allies. Recalling that he had "done everything this side of breaking FCC regulations" to help Carter win the White House, Pat Robertson charged betrayal. "I wouldn't let Bella Abzug scrub the floor of any organization I was head of but Carter put her in charge of all the women of America and used tax funds to support that convention in Houston." Another erstwhile Carter admirer, Jerry Falwell, called the Houston conference "anti-family, anti-God and anti-America" and charged that the feminist movement was "full of women who live in disobedience to God's laws."

Within a year of the Houston conference, if the feminist leaders had been willing to be honest with themselves, they would have had reason to question their strategy. No additional states had ratified the ERA; on the contrary, the pressure to get states that had previously endorsed the amendment to backtrack seemed to be building. One locality after another voted down gay rights laws, and the Congress tightened restrictions on federal funding of abortions. "I think it's all gone our way," crowed Schlafly. "Prior to Houston it was difficult to describe the women's liberation movement. Houston made that definition very clear, and showed how anti-family it is," she said.

Events proved Schlafly to be a good prophet. The drive for the ERA went into reverse. During Carter's presidency only one state ratified the amendment; opponents succeeded in getting five others to overturn their previous approvals. As the seven-year deadline for ratification expired in 1979 desperate backers persuaded Congress to extend the deadline another three years. This move was of dubious constitutionality, but more to the point as even ERA supporters privately conceded, correctly as it turned out, that further efforts to gain support would probably be in vain. The tide was running against the ERA, and its backers could not reverse the trend.

Then, as if the forces of the Christian Right did not have enough reasons for rising up against Carter because of his approach to morals and values, he gave them another, by threatening their wallets. This problem arose from a political dilemma confronting Carter. On the one hand he wanted to maintain close ties with evangelicals and with conservative Christians in general. On the other hand he had powerful political obligations to blacks and to civil rights advocates. Carter would not have become the first son of the deep South to get the Democratic presidential nomination if he had not established a reputation as a supporter of civil rights. It was true that he made thinly veiled racist appeals during his campaign for the governorship of Georgia. But once in office he realized that renouncing racism was an absolute necessity for any southerner with national political ambitions. "The time for racial discrimination is over," he declared in his inaugural address. And he followed that statement up by hanging Martin Luther King, Jr.'s, portrait in the state capitol. Moreover, it was his victory over arch segregationist George Wallace in the Florida presidential primary that paved Carter's road to the nomination in 1976.

Under the circumstances, the president was in no position to stand in the way of the Internal Revenue Service when it moved to deny tax-exempt status to private church schools in the South that practiced racial discrimination. Most of these schools had been set up in the 1960s during the turmoil that gripped southern education in the wake of court orders to desegregate public school systems, and they continued to proliferate in the 1970s. Without question, many of the schools were designed mainly to avoid the lifting of racial barriers—and deserved the label attached to them of "segregation academies." But other church schools catered to parents upset about the secularization of public schools—the ban on prayer and Bible reading, the teaching of sex education, and the adoption of texts challenging traditional cultural values.

Whatever the reasons for their existence, nearly all these schools depended heavily for financial support on private gifts, a largesse which was encouraged by the ability of the donors to deduct their donations from their income tax. Withdrawing that deduction would shrink contributions and force most schools to the wall.

In moving against the church schools the IRS was following the path laid down by the federal courts and previous administrations. In 1975, with Gerald Ford in the White House, the IRS had revoked the tax-exempt status of Bob Jones University because it had denied admission to blacks. That decision, appealed by the university, was later upheld by an 8-to-1 majority of the Supreme Court. But in 1978, with the Bob Jones case still in the courts, the questions about tax exemption and discrimination were not yet considered settled. And so when the IRS in the summer of that year issued a set of guidelines for determining whether secondary schools discriminated against students on the basis of race, a huge furor arose in the ranks of the Christian Right, and the target of their outrage was Jimmy Carter.

Under the guidelines, any school that came into existence or suddenly expanded when the public schools in its community were desegregated would be suspect. Such a school would lose its tax-exempt status unless it had a substantial minority enrollment or could show that it was making a good-faith effort to operate on a nondiscriminatory basis. Under the guidance of Paul Weyrich, a canny and well-connected conservative activist seasoned in the ways of Washington, and with the help of such luminaries of the Christian Right as Pat Robertson and Jerry Falwell, conservative Christians mounted a massive protest. "The bureaucrats were so out of touch with real American culture that they assumed racial bias was the only reason somebody would want to start a non-public school," complained Connaught Marshner, an ally of Weyrich. "Not a clue about the real culture decay, or about religious belief."

A campaign of mass mailings and newspaper ads—"Why is the IRS trying to close our private Christian schools?" asked one such advertisement in the *Washington Post*—led to hearings before the IRS itself as well as a congressional subcommittee. In response, the IRS was obliged to modify its guidelines, some of which even civil rights supporters conceded were unnecessarily draconian. Even so, the legal principle that discriminatory schools were not entitled to tax privileges remained intact. But in the long run, the political significance of the furor outweighed the legal issues. The IRS's action had given the Christian Right the most effective incentive it had yet found to mobilize its supporters.

The conservative forces thus were well prepared when Carter presented them with another cause for conflict, the National Conference on Families. On its face, the conference—called in 1980, the final year of Carter's presidency, in fulfillment of a campaign pledge—could not have been more timely. The American family was under enormous strain. Two of every five marriages were ending in divorce; one of every five children lived in a single-parent household; and only one of twenty American families said they could afford to buy a new house.

According to a Gallup poll released just as the first regional session of the conference was about to open, nearly half of all Americans believed family life had deteriorated in the past fifteen years. Asked what was most harmful to family life, most persons surveyed cited alcohol and drug abuse. Also mentioned frequently was a decline in religious and moral values. Indeed, the survey suggested that at least some of the traditional values cherished by conservative Christians were given high priority by most Americans.

Despite the widespread public interest in its subject matter, the conference was marked by squabbling from the very start, when delegates could not agree on the definition of "family." The National Pro-Family Coalition, representing about 150 conservative groups, wanted to limit the forum to "traditional families." To include homosexual and unmarried couples, as some liberals proposed, "lends legitimacy to illegitimate life-styles," contended Connaught Marshner, who emerged at the conference as one of the leaders of the conservative forces.

The breaking point came on the second day of the conference. After preliminary votes on abortion and gay rights seemed to bear out the fears of the conservatives that liberals would dominate the conference, nearly 100 conservatives out of the total of 700 attendees stormed out of the session, which they denounced as "rigged."

The upshot was an embarrassment for Carter at a time when he could least afford one, in the midst of his reelection campaign. Seeking to demonstrate his administration's concern for the cornerstone of American society, he succeeded mainly in providing a showcase for conservative forces deeply opposed to his policies. As Election Day 1980 approached, Carter seemed to have lost control. Humiliated by the Iranian hostage seizure abroad, staggered by runaway inflation at home, most Americans felt when they took stock of their country that it was in sorry shape. As for the president, a good many shared the feelings of one citizen interviewed by pollster Clay Darden who summed up the Carter presidency this way: "The water is six feet deep, and Carter is only five feet nine."

Meanwhile the Christian conservatives and their allies in opposing Carter on cultural grounds had been gaining muscle, prominence, and influence under the banner of the New Right. The New Right mobilized a range of conservative groups, some of which focused on one single issue or another—abortion, homosexual rights, drafting women, pornography, or school prayer—and others that plunged into a wide range of political and cultural concerns. New groups proliferated, increasing from a handful to more than a score, and more traditional groups, such as the American Conservative Union, were becoming energized. Just as important, they were all learning to work together. Richard Viguerie, a direct-mail expert and the nation's leading conservative fund-raiser, defined the new movement as well as anyone: "The Old Right was not that interested in social issues," he said:

> They focused on foreign policy and economics. But when political conservative leaders began to reach out and strike an alliance with social conservatives—the pro-life people, the anti-E.R.A. people, the evangelical and born-again Christians, the people concerned about gay rights, prayer in the schools, sex in the movies or whatever—that's when this whole movement began to come alive.

Basically the New Right represented one of the cyclical developments that defined the Culture War. Much of what energized its leaders and inspired its followers was resentment against the social change and activism wrought by the cultural upheaval of the Sixties. One of the New Right's legislative heroes, North Carolina Senator Jesse Helms, summed it up as "a revulsion at the trends in this country—the permissiveness, the pornography, the drugs, abortion, living together, divorce." He added, "Somewhere you've got to put the flag down and draw the line and say, 'Enough is enough!'"

Only dimly aware of the strength of this threat, Carter desperately tried to revive his old alliances with the evangelical movement. In the closing months of his presidency the beleaguered president invited a dozen or so of the leading lights of the conservative pulpit to a White

House breakfast. Some came, but a number of those he invited, notably Jerry Falwell, were already irrevocably lost to him. In the spring of 1979, Falwell had met with Paul Weyrich and other conservative activists, who urged him to take a leading role in mobilizing Christian conservatives for the political battlefields. Weyrich told Falwell that there existed "what one might call a moral majority," people who could be unified by reminding them that the moral principles they shared overshadowed their seeming differences. Falwell seized on the concept and adopted the name for the organization he created in June 1979. Its main objective was to force the Republican Party into adopting a strong antiabortion plank in its 1980 platform.

That same issue was on the minds of Carter's breakfast guests, particularly because they happened to be meeting on January 22, 1980, the seventh anniversary of the *Roe v. Wade* decision. As they met, thousands of abortion foes were gathering in Washington for their annual protest march. But when Carter was asked about his views, he said nothing to soften his publicly stated support for the court decision. And when pressed about his failure to appoint more evangelicals to posts in his administration, his answer was equally unsatisfactory to the assembled ministers. Afterward, one of them, the Reverend Tim LaHaye, prayed silently to himself: "God we have got to get this man out of the White House and get someone in there who will be aggressive about bringing back traditional moral values." LaHaye remembers that he and his fellow ministers were all glum as they rode in their limousine back to the hotel. But they should have had more faith in the Almighty. For their prayers were about to be answered.

THE CITY ON A HILL

The most conspicuous explanation for Ronald Reagan's success as a political leader was his personality, a blend of warmth and magnetism with calculated nonchalance. His charm was the spoonful of sugar that made his polarizing beliefs go down. "Look, Dick, I don't care what else you do," Michael Deaver, Reagan's principal image maker, told his budget chief, Richard Darman, about making the most of Reagan's persona, "get that face on television. This is a face that when a baby sees it, the baby smiles."

But Reagan's political potency relied on one other pillar, too—his ability to convince people of his commitment to his beliefs, a talent he exhibited on his way to the 1980 Republican presidential nomination when he paid a campaign visit to Plymouth Rock. For almost any other candidate this quick stop would have been just another photo opportunity. Reagan converted the stop at the site of the landing of the Pilgrim Fathers into something more. Returning to the campaign bus, he confronted the traveling press corps and offered this one-sentence epiphany for the voyage of the *Mayflower*. "If they could come all that way in that little boat," he asked, "how dare we be afraid of anything?" With that rhetorical question, farcical from almost anyone else, Reagan demonstrated the intensity that was the secret of his cultural appeal. It was not so much the ideas he espoused as the impression that he actually believed in those ideas that imbued his leadership with an aura of credibility. His apparent sincerity, one of the mainsprings of middle-class cultural values, helped him sweep all before him in his early days in the White House while establishing himself as the hero of the Christian Right.

It was easy for Reagan to seem convincing about his beliefs because most of them were based mainly on his own personal experience rather than on more formal sources. In his later years, when he had outgrown the liberalism of his younger days, Reagan liked to trace his adopted conservative faith back to his formative years in a Midwestern small town. There the institutions of family and church, along with such virtues as hard work and patriotism, were held in high esteem. Dixon, the Illinois town where Reagan grew up, was about 90 miles from Chicago and had a population of only about 10,000.

"It was a good life," he wrote in the autobiographical *Where's the Rest of Me?* "I never have asked for anything more, then or now." In small towns of those days, as Reagan biographer Lou Cannon pointed out, "a presumption of good will" prevailed, undergirding the cultural environment. Townspeople were expected to look after each other, and many of them did. This old-fashioned standard of conduct made it possible, Reagan's admirers suggest, for him to oppose government aid to the less fortunate without feeling that he was being callous. At any rate it offered him a rationale for rebutting the need for government intervention to mend damage to the nation's social fabric.

But Reagan's boyhood in Dixon offered other, harsher lessons, too. Reagan recalled getting into a school yard fight and getting the worse end of it when his father arrived unexpectedly. "He stopped the fight, tongue lashed the crowd—then lifted me a foot in the air with the flat side of his boot. 'Not because you were fighting,' he said, 'but because you weren't winning.'" This, too, was a lesson that conformed to middle-class cultural values: It is okay to empathize with the underdog, but it is better not to be one.

Though his background was secular Reagan infused his rhetoric with a spiritual tone that bolstered his appeal to evangelicals. In 1974, as he was gearing up for his challenge to Gerald Ford for the 1976 Republican nomination, he recalled for a conference of conservative activists on Capitol Hill a passage from the historic sermon delivered by the future governor of the Massachusetts Bay Colony to his Puritan flock on board their flagship, *Arabella:* "We will be as a city upon a hill," Reagan recited from John Winthrop's text. "The eyes of all people are upon us, so that if we deal falsely with our God in this work we have undertaken and so cause Him to withdraw His present help from us, we shall be made a story and a byword throughout the world."

Reagan's repeated use of this quotation from Winthrop in addresses during his campaign for the White House and then as president helped to bind him closer to the evangelical movement. Winthrop's sermon, "A Modell of Christian Charity," along with the Mayflower Compact, the Declaration of Independence, and the Constitution, is among the documents regarded as "sacred" by evangelicals, many of whom view them as supporting their vision of the United States as a latter-day Israel, a land destined to fulfill a mission ordained for it by Divine Providence. In borrowing Winthrop's rhetoric, Reagan typically departed from the facts and from the original text. He referred to Winthrop as a Pilgrim, the term for a different group of Puritans who preceded Winthrop and his group by ten years. The Pilgrims famously landed at Plymouth Rock, where Reagan stopped in his 1980 campaign, about 30 miles south of Boston. Winthrop landed with his group at Salem, and he helped to found the city that later became Boston. And Reagan often interposed the word "shining" so that the model for Americans to follow became that of "a *shining* city on a hill," an embellishment of Winthrop's own metaphor.

Despite these incongruities, Reagan's reliance on this revered passage resonated powerfully with evangelical leaders and reinforced their admiration for the ex–movie star as he challenged Jimmy Carter for the presidency in 1980. By that time the Vietnam protest had long since run out of steam and the accompanying surge of social change had also subsided. As if shaking off a hangover, the nation embarked on a quest for values that would provide spiritual support. The preoccupation with self-gratification that had marked the 1960s and early 1970s had been replaced, according to pollster Daniel Yankelovich, with "a tremendous yearning for escape from the prison of the self—a desire for bonds that aren't remote. There is emphasis on couples and on family. There is emphasis on local community. The nation state is remote; your community is not."

The climate could hardly have been better suited to the message Reagan wanted to preach. In his acceptance speech to the 1980 Republican Convention he appealed to "all those across the land who share a community of values embodied in these words: family, work, neighborhood, peace and freedom." And he called upon the electorate to make a commitment "to teach our children the virtues handed down to us by our families; to have the courage to defend those values and virtues and the willingness to sacrifice for them."

To be sure, Reagan himself hardly seemed to be a paradigm for the values he championed. Instead, with his divorce, his shaky relationships with his children, and his offsprings' aberrational lifestyle, his handlers worried that he might be viewed as another victim of the social turbulence he had long sought to suppress. During the 1980 campaign, "There was a lot of talk about how to handle the Patti (Davis) problem," because of Reagan's daughter's association with the acid rock culture, "and the Ron problem," because of Reagan's son dropping out of college to become a ballet dancer, recalled Richard Williamson, a campaign aide and later a White House staffer. "In the end it was felt that the voters having lived through the sixties and seventies would find RR more humanized because he too had experienced these things. His words offered a vision of an America we wanted to believe in. His experiences showed that his feet had walked the same difficult trail as other American parents."

In the final analysis Christian conservatives and their New Right allies found Reagan's strengths so compelling that they overshadowed his occasional deviations from the path of righteousness they expected him to follow, not only in his personal life, but in his presidency. Most of the disagreements that occurred during Reagan's White House tenure were over matters that were of greater concern to the New Right leaders than to their followers. As disillusioned as they might become at times with Reagan's failure to give more vigorous support on one particular issue or another, they would have had a hard time breaking with Reagan and having to explain that rupture to their rank-and-file members, who were still entranced by Reagan.

The first test of Reagan's hold on the New Right came in August 1980 at the Republican Convention in Detroit when he announced his choice of George Bush as his vice president. Reagan's handlers had turned to Bush only after the collapse of an ill-conceived effort to recruit former president Gerald Ford to be his running mate. Ford's attraction to Reagan's strategists was that his experience in government and his generally moderate record might help mitigate voters' concerns about Reagan's inexperience and extremism. A former congressman, former CIA director, and former UN ambassador, Bush brought some of the same qualities to the ticket. Plus he had been first runner-up to Reagan in the contest for the nomination.

In picking Bush, Reagan and his high command simply disregarded the fact that he was anathema to the New Right on both substantive and cultural grounds. He had been a longtime supporter of abortion rights and the Equal Rights Amendment. More than that, as the scion of one of New England's best-connected families, this son of Yale and member of Skull and Bones epitomized Eastern elitism, which flew in the face of the populism that bolstered the New Right's appeal. As soon as they got wind of Reagan's decision, New Right leaders, including Weyrich, Falwell, Schlafly, and Howard Phillips, founder of the Conservative Caucus, one of the new grassroots conservative groups proliferating around the country, rushed to confront Reagan at the convention in Detroit.

Their objections were in vain. Reagan's strategists deemed Bush as the man most likely to help him win the White House. But the very fact that these newcomers on the Right were granted an audience with Reagan at this critical time demonstrated their growing power within the GOP. Bush himself provided further evidence on that point when as soon as he became Reagan's running mate he abandoned his support for the ERA and reversed his position on abortion.

At any rate, the New Right leaders and followers found enough things to like about Reagan's nomination to forget their disagreements over Bush and to throw their energies into the battle to win the presidency. They vividly demonstrated their enthusiasm a few weeks after the Detroit convention when 15,000 of them packed Dallas's Reunion Arena for a two-day conclave. Those in attendance were hell-bent on preserving America's morals and values by getting conservatives elected to offices high and low, but especially getting Ronald Reagan elected president. "Christians gave Jimmy Carter his razor-thin margin of victory in 1976," said Colonel Donner, the chief political strategist for Christian Voice, a West Coast evangelical group. "We plan to reverse that in 1980."

The speakers held forth on a range of subjects, from theology and scripture to instruction on how to organize without violating tax laws, the practicalities of registering a congregation to vote during the Sunday service, and the importance of keeping a "moral score card" on the voting records of elected representatives. The rafters rang with condemnations of abortion and of the ERA. But mostly those in attendance sat and listened, occasionally dipping into their picnic hampers, which assured that they would not have to miss a single exhortation or denunciation. They were male and female, young and old, preachers and laymen, salesmen and ranchers, with a few moderately well-known Texas millionaires thrown in. But they had several things in common: They were nearly all white, middle class, and clad in their Sunday-go-to-meeting clothes. And most probably had not voted in years. Indeed, according to a survey taken by evangelical ministers in 1976, even with one of their own running for president, 70 percent of born-again Christians had not cast a ballot.

It was the reversal of that behavior that was the main preoccupation of the meeting, as reflected by the conference logotype, much in display on lapel pins and bumper stickers being hawked in the arena lobby—the word "VOTE" with an oversized cross in place of the "T." A procession of speakers marched to the podium to drive that point home. If Christians were distressed because "perverts, radicals, leftists, communists, liberals and humanists" had taken over the country, they had only their own lassitude to blame. "Not voting is a sin against almighty God!" bellowed James Robison, the fire-and-brimstone Ft. Worth evangelist whose weekly TV show was syndicated to 100 stations. But perhaps the biggest inducement for the evangelicals to return to the political battlefields was pointed up by the thunderous ovation accorded the man of the hour, Ronald Reagan himself. Despite Reagan's presence, and the absence of President Carter, the rally organizers, mindful of their need to maintain tax-exempt status, repeatedly insisted their movement was nonpartisan and would make no formal endorsements—although it would "encourage" candidates of Christian principle. Reagan had no difficulty playing along with that legal fiction. "I know you can't endorse me," he said. "But," he added slyly in a line that predictably brought down the house, "I want you to know that I endorse you."

To help preserve the pretensions to nonpartisanship, and to avoid controversy that could hurt him with less moralistic audiences, Reagan's prepared text was scrubbed clean of such hot-button issues as homosexual rights, abortion, and the Equal Rights Amendment. But responding to a question at a press conference, the Republican standard-bearer could not resist suggesting that if public schools teach the theory of evolution, still much abhorred by conservative Christians, then they should also teach the theory of creation. Reagan's words would be the cause of jeers that would dog him for the rest of the campaign, a reminder, if he needed one, that catering to the conservative Christian vote was not without a price.

The big question was whether that price was worth paying. With all the hullabaloo about the power of the Cross at the ballot box, even some New Right leaders were concerned that the incipient movement's strength might be oversold. Some sought to reduce expectations. "Anybody looking for a revolution this year is going to be disappointed," said the New Right's shrewdest mobilizer, Paul Weyrich. "The mechanism for getting out the vote just has not been set up yet. Until they do that, they're just a vague, amorphous group—and vague doesn't win in politics."

Whatever its potential, the political activism of the evangelicals stirred misgivings, even among some of their own leaders, including, remarkably enough in view of his future course, Pat Robertson. "God isn't a right-winger or a left-winger," he argued, only six years before he himself decided to take the plunge into electoral waters. "The evangelists stand in danger of being used and manipulated."

Even harsher criticism came from outside the evangelical family. Richard John Neuhaus, a Lutheran pastor and member of the board of the influential *Worldview* magazine, called the leaders of the evangelical political drive "profoundly immature. . . . They don't really understand the ethical and philosophical traditions of democracy or how to bring about change in a pluralistic society." Particularly disturbed were Jews, who recalled the bigotry attached to the fundamentalist movement in its heyday in the Twenties. By making political judgments based on standards derived from the Bible, they claimed the evangelicals were crossing the constitutional boundary between church and state. "They are violating article six of the Constitution, which says there must not be any religious test for holding office," complained Rabbi Marc Tanenbaum of the American Jewish Committee.

The leaders of the push to the polling booth shrugged off such criticism. "Nobody's ever accused the National Council of Churches of mixing religion and politics," said Falwell. "But when ol' Jerry gets into it, that's violating separation of church and state. The problem isn't violating anything. The problem is that we don't agree with those buzzards—and that we outnumber them."

Falwell seemed to be right about the numbers, according to the election returns, and he and his allies got plenty of credit for their contribution. Given the extent of Reagan's landslide victory over Carter, it was hard for anyone to tell just how much of a difference the Christian conservatives had played in the outcome. But not many stopped to raise that question in the flush of the right-wing triumph. All that mattered was that the leaders of the evangelicals and their New Right allies had promised to help elect Reagan, and that promise had been kept.

Adding to the glory for the Right in the 1980 election were the string of conservative victories in the Senate, where the Republicans had gained a majority for the first time in nearly thirty years. Early in the campaign, Falwell and the New Right political action units had targeted a covey of liberal Democratic senators, and on Election Day they ousted nearly all of them.

Evangelical leaders could hardly control their joy. Ed Dobson, a Falwell aide and board member of the Moral Majority, later recalled listening to reports of the exit poll results on his car radio late on the afternoon of Election Day. Dobson was stunned to hear that not only was Reagan on his way to a huge victory, in what everyone had expected to be a close election, but that the Republicans were taking over the Senate. "But what shocked me most was that much of the credit was going to the Religious Right, the Moral Majority and Jerry Falwell," he wrote. And this from the liberal media! Dobson was persuaded, as he later wrote, that "a new day had dawned on the political landscape. Those of us who were considered anti-intellectual, obscurantist fundamentalists were now a force to be reckoned with. Our agenda would never again be ignored. Had we not been Baptists we would have danced in the streets."

But that mood did not last long. The next twelve years of Republican rule under Reagan and Bush would provide a bitter lesson for the zealots of the New Right. Cultural revolutions, on either side of the fence, are better waged outside the corridors of power. Under this country's awkward political system, with its built-in restraints on government, holding office saps the energy and vitality that infuses the struggle to gain political power, and incumbency becomes synonymous with frustration for advocates of change.

But over the years the fervency of the New Right leaders had become tempered with realism. Despite the glory heaped upon them by the media, polling results showed that the GOP victories owed more to public disgust with Carter's failures than they did to the cultural shibboleths cherished by the New Right and the Christian evangelicals. Carter's economic policies had produced runaway inflation, and his mishandling of the hostage crisis in Tehran, during which U.S. embassy personnel were held prisoner by Iranian extremists for 444 days, had humiliated the country. Given these realities, the New Right leaders realized they had to settle for what they could get from the new president who had been their hero and swallow any disappointment. If that attitude was not likely to make hearts beat faster on the Right, the conservatives were not in a strong enough position to carry out a more inspiring blueprint. That point was driven home to them midway through Reagan's first year in the White House when he named Sandra Day O'Connor to fill a Supreme Court vacancy. Jerry Falwell remembered the moment well. He heard the news from the highest possible source, the president himself. "Jerry, I'm going to put forth a lady on the Court," Falwell later remembered Reagan telling him over the phone. "You don't know anything about her. Nobody does, but I want you to trust my judgment on this one."

"I'll do that, Mr. President," Falwell replied. But other conservatives were not so willing to take O'Connor on faith. That she would be the first woman on the Supreme Court was irrelevant so far as they were concerned. What mattered was her stand on "the right to life," the single issue that more than any other provided the emotional underpinning for the New Right and the evangelical political crusade. They inspected O'Connor's record on abortion as an Arizona state legislator and found it not to their liking, and they let the world know about it. Reagan had no need to make a compromise choice, they argued. With the Republicans in charge of the Senate, the president could get anyone he wanted on the bench.

Within two weeks Reagan was back on the phone to Falwell: "Jerry I've had a chance to talk to her and my people have, and I can tell you that her views will not disappoint you. And I hope you can help me bring the troops in." The reverend dutifully did as Reagan asked. When Cal Thomas, a conservative activist and Falwell ally, went on ABC's "Nightline" to register opposition to her nomination, he soon got a phone call from a Falwell aide at the Moral Majority. Lay off, Thomas was told. Better to accept Reagan's choice than to anger him and lose access to the Oval Office.

The episode left the New Right smoldering. But as the revolutionaries of the Right would soon learn, the benign neglect of Ronald Reagan's White House was not their only serious problem. They also had to contend against the Democrats, who despite the 1980 conservative triumph still had command of the House of Representatives. With the White House, the Senate, and the Supreme Court dominated by conservatives, the Democratic House represented liberalism's last line of defense in the Culture War. And the key bastion within that line was the House Judiciary Committee, which had a long history in the Culture War. It was that committee, under Chairman Emanuel Cellers of New York, which in the 1960s had spearheaded legislation institutionalizing the civil rights revolution and the social reforms of the Great Society—all anathema to the New Right. And it was the same committee, under the leadership of Cellers's successor, Peter Rodino of New Jersey, which had brought a bill of impeachment forcing Nixon, the champion of the Silent Majority, out of the White House.

In those days, with the Left holding the initiative in the Culture War, the Judiciary Committee had been on the offensive, promoting new ideas and new regulations. Now it was in a holding pattern, determined only to preserve liberalism's past achievements. The momentum from the election returns and the vigorous lobbying activities of the New Right organizations had spawned a flood of legislative proposals to turn back the cultural tide of the 1960s. But this was no easy matter. The excesses of big government generated by the Great Society could be curbed to some degree by tightening the federal purse strings. And in this regard, as even right-wingers conceded, the Reagan White House was making headway not only through spending cuts but through massive tax cuts intended to starve the federal monster into submission, paving the way for even more spending cuts.

But the cultural legacy of the 1960s was more difficult to erase than the programs and the taxes. It had come to infuse the bureaucracy, the courts, and ultimately the way Americans lived. The reversal of this inundation of permissiveness, conservative strategists realized, would require more than mere tinkering with the budget. Nothing less than constitutional change would do the job. So in the first months of Reagan's first term the legislative hoppers on Capitol Hill overflowed with proposals for amending the Constitution. Some measures would ban abortion, either absolutely or with exceptions for incest and to protect the life of the mother. Others would overturn the court rulings prohibiting Bible reading and prayer in school. Still others would nullify court-ordered school busing as a tool for desegregation. And other proposals, though not technically amendments to the Constitution, would have just as fundamental an impact because they were aimed at restricting the jurisdiction of the federal courts.

All these proposals faced a common obstacle—the House Judiciary Committee. And there the majority Democrats—Chairman Rodino and his chief lieutenants—seemed to have the same motto as the World War I French troops who defended Verdun against the Kaiser's legions: "They shall not pass." And so these House Democratic leaders served as a strong counterweight to the ultraconservative Judiciary Committee of the Senate. The faithful conservatives who ruled that committee, led by Chairman Strom Thurmond of South Carolina, swiftly endorsed the constitutional amendments put forward by the advocates of the New Right and sent them on to their counterpart panel in the House. And there, if

Rodino and his colleagues had anything to say about it, and they almost always did, these measures would all die a lingering death.

By the end of Reagan's first term, Capitol Hill had turned into a graveyard for the legislative dreams of the New Right. Its leaders' only success had come on the issue of abortion, where they managed to put through a bill restricting federal funding of abortions almost to the vanishing point, even banning federal workers from using government-funded health insurance plans for abortions. As unwelcome as this bill was to supporters of abortion rights, it was seen as only a limited victory by the conservatives. They had not been able to achieve their most cherished goal of curtailing a woman's right to an abortion, as decreed by the Supreme Court. A constitutional amendment to permit legislatures to ban abortions failed in the Senate in 1983.

On other issues, the New Right had even less to show for their support of Reagan and their lobbying efforts. An amendment to permit prayer in public schools languished and eventually perished, despite periodic rhetorical boosts from Reagan. The Senate did pass anti-busing legislation in 1981 designed to slow the pace of court-ordered school desegregation, but it was immediately bottled up by Rodino's Judiciary Committee. Tuition tax credits failed to win passage even in the Senate, losing by more than twenty votes.

For the most part, the White House, heeding the advice of the centrist Republican leadership in the Senate, deferred any push on major social issues lest the highly emotional debate they were certain to generate distract from efforts to gain approval of Reagan's top priorities, which were economic. But by the time the decks were clear of economic proposals, the blush was off the rose of the Reagan revolution.

A bitter recession in 1982, pushing unemployment to the highest rates since the Great Depression, robbed the president of much of his influence and prestige. And serious GOP losses in its House membership in that year's midterm elections weakened the Republican hand on Capitol Hill. Reagan continued to reiterate his support for the whole gamut of social issues, but as New Right leaders complained, this lip service was about all he provided.

Any hopes the New Right might have nurtured that Reagan's second term might bring rewards denied in his first term were obliterated by the 1984 campaign. The country was in a complacent mood as a result of the beneficent state of the economy. Sure, it was far from perfect. Unemployment was still over 7 percent. The rich were getting richer faster than ever, while the poor and the middle class lagged behind. The federal budget deficit was mounting. But carps about such conditions from the president's critics faced one overwhelming reality: For most middle-class Americans the conditions of their lives seemed vastly better than they had been in 1980. And there was a sound basis for their satisfaction. The misery index—the combination of inflation and unemployment that had reached over 20 percent under Jimmy Carter—had been cut in half under Reagan.

Reagan's gifted image marketers did all they could to exploit the prevailing prosperity. Their most memorable television ad, called "It's Morning Again in America," set the tone for the campaign. It presented a series of vignettes—a white farmhouse at dawn, a happy wedding party, an elderly man raising an American flag while glowing, youthful faces looked on. As the flag filled the screen and misty music played, a narrator intoned: "It's morning again in America. Today, more men and women will go to work than ever before in our nation's history." And the narrator went on to talk about the wonders of low inflation and low interest rates, concluding with this assertion: "Our country is stronger and prouder than ever. . . . Why would we ever want to return to where we were less than four short years ago?" The message of that television spot, to those who wanted to lead a conservative cultural revolution, boiled down to this: If you did not get much out of the first four years, you can expect even less in the next four.

If Reagan's campaign set the stage for inertia in his second term, circumstances also assured the persistence of the status quo. The first two years of the second term, like the first half of the first term, were dominated by economic concerns—this time of Reagan's own creation, a result of the sweeping tax cuts and Pentagon spending hikes he had pushed through Congress at the start of his tenure. In the 1986 midterm vote, the economy, particularly the farm economy, slowed enough to cost the GOP a net of nine Senate seats and control of that body.

Even worse news broke after the congressional elections—the Iran Contra scandal. In pursuing a cause the New Right heartily endorsed, combating communism in the Americas, Reagan had allowed his overzealous aides to operate with such reckless abandon that it almost cost him his presidency. Fighting to regain his grip, Reagan offered conservatives probably the greatest gift he had made to the New Right as president, the nomination of Judge Robert Bork to the Supreme Court. But the rejoicing on the Right over Bork would soon turn to grief.

Prior to nominating Bork, Reagan, as if trying to make up to conservatives for the choice of O'Connor, had used one vacancy, the resignation of Chief Justice Warren Burger, to make two moves to shift the court to starboard. In 1986 he promoted William Rehnquist, by far the most conservative of the sitting justices, to replace Burger as chief justice, and Appeals Court Judge Antonin M. Scalia, who was just as conservative and at least as brilliant as Rehnquist—and far more aggressive—to take the latter's position as associate justice. Yet even with the two new conservative appointments, the court remained in a precarious balance between Right and Left.

It was clear to both liberals and conservatives that the next appointment would see a renewal in the long struggle for the court. Setting the stage for that battle was the success scored by the Democrats in the November 1986 elections when they regained control of the U.S. Senate by a 55 to 45 margin. Apart from the psychological boost, the election results gave Democrats an advantage they had lacked for six years in battles over appointments—control of the Senate and its procedures.

The new balance of power in the Senate was soon tested when Supreme Court Justice Lewis Powell announced his retirement in June 1987. He had functioned as the ideological middleman on a sharply divided court. By filling the Powell vacancy with a true conservative, Reagan would be able to shift the course of American jurisprudence in a conservative direction for many years to come, giving the New Right an enormous boost. The obvious choice for Reagan and his advisers was

Judge Robert Bork of the U.S. Circuit Court of Appeals, a man possessed of both unquestioned conservative beliefs and formidable intellectual powers acknowledged even by his enemies.

Democrats believed that Reagan made that decision, and risked a nasty confirmation battle, to satisfy the New Right. Administration officials claimed they disregarded warnings that Bork would meet stiff opposition because Bork had twice won Senate confirmation before, first as solicitor general and then as Circuit Court of Appeals judge. But the stakes were much higher now, nothing less than control of the Supreme Court, and the liberals, with a Senate majority, put up a much tougher fight than they ever had before.

At issue was every flash point in the Culture War from abortion to race, from pornography to crime. In mounting their successful assault on Bork the liberal activists drew on the lessons they had learned the hard way—from their past defeats by conservatives in using the media to shape opinion on cultural conflicts. "We learned during the Reagan years that the conservatives knew how to frame the debate," Ralph Neas, director of the Leadership Conference on Civil Rights, told me. "They had sophisticated techniques to define issues. For four or five years we were relegated to the second to last paragraph of stories. But by 1985 and 1986 we started to frame the debate and catch up with them." Indeed in 1987, the Bork battle provided evidence that in this regard the liberal groups had not only caught up but shot ahead of their right-wing enemies.

To mobilize support against Bork the liberals sifted through polling data and focus group interviews, targeted ads at the constituencies of fence-sitting senators, flooded the print media with op-ed pieces, and enlisted a seemingly unending stream of point persons to argue their case on radio and television talk shows. And when it came to appealing to the public's emotions, few efforts by the conservatives could match the raw impact of the opening statement by Massachusetts Senator Edward M. Kennedy in attacking Bork. "Robert Bork's America," Kennedy charged, "is a land in which women would be forced into back alley abortions, blacks would sit at segregated lunch counters, rogue police would break down citizens' doors." What the liberals succeeded in doing was what the conservatives had accomplished before: They swamped the media. "Everybody reported the speech," wrote Ethan Bronner of the *Boston Globe,* pointing out that Kennedy's hyperbolic rhetoric amounted to a distortion of what could be reasonably inferred from Bork's record. "The more sophisticated news organizations made clear that it was unusually sharp, pointing to the partisan nature of the looming battle. But even columnists who later criticized the Kennedy attack as irresponsible did so only in sweeping terms without specifically analyzing the basis of the charges."

Bork did little to help his own cause, tending to obscure his defense in legalisms. Kennedy, his chief accuser, by contrast showed a better understanding of the cultural values at stake, using populist appeals to advance his case. "With all your ability I just wish you had devoted even a little of your talent to advancing equal rights rather than criticizing so many of the decisions protecting rights and liberties," he told Bork when the nominee came before the Senate Judiciary Committee. "Lawyers can always make technical points but justice ought to be fair." Bork, as *Washington Post* media critic Tom Shales wrote, "looked and talked like a man who would throw the book at you—maybe like a man who would throw the book at the whole country." When the hearings on the nomination began before the Judiciary Committee, polls showed that the public was about evenly divided for and against Bork's confirmation. After he testified, the nays were ahead by eight to ten points. Bork's nomination went down by a 52 to 48 Senate vote. Reagan ultimately filled Powell's vacancy by appointing another federal appeals judge, Anthony Kennedy, also a conservative, but by most measurements more moderate than Bork. Kennedy easily won confirmation. Over the years, the difference between Justice Kennedy's votes and the votes that probably would have been cast by a Justice Bork gave liberals ample grounds for claiming their efforts had paid off.

Seven years after their great victory in the 1980 election, the New Right and the Christian conservatives had suffered a stinging defeat. Most striking about the rejection of Bork was the resurgence of the forces on the cultural Left and their ability to seize the initiative, dominate debate, and win middle-class Americans to their cause. That skill was unsettling for the conservatives, but they were at least as much aggrieved by their betrayal at the hands of the leaders they had helped gain power. So with a new election looming in 1988, they were determined to even the score, not only with their foes but with those who had presented themselves as their friends.

CHAPTER
12

"THE CHRISTIANS
ARE COMING"

It was a pleasant spring evening and most of Vice President Bush's aides had gone home to relax with their families. But one staffer was still on duty. He was Doug Wead, who served as Bush's liaison to the Christian community, a position unique in national politics, and on this particular evening, May 27, 1986, he faced a critical test of his judgment and political insight.

The son of an Assemblies of God minister, Wead had founded and operated an international famine relief organization, work that brought him into contact with political leaders in countries around the world and with both Democratic and Republican leaders at home, among them Bush. He had helped to draft a speech Bush had delivered to the National Religious Broadcasters, and his efforts had gained him a job in Bush's nascent presidential campaign.

Before most other contenders to succeed Ronald Reagan in the White House in the 1988 election, Bush and his top political advisers had caught on to the idea that conservative Christians were becoming increasingly active in GOP politics. They wanted Wead's advice on how best to deal with this new force. But as is the way of such things, seeking Wead's counsel did not necessarily mean that Bush's more senior strategists would listen to him.

For some weeks now Wead had been sounding the alarm about developments in the state of Michigan, where under a peculiar new process, the competition for the 1988 Republican nomination was starting more than two years in advance of the party's national convention. The reason for this premature beginning was the desire of Michigan's Republicans to gain attention and influence for their state and their party. This was an aspiration they shared with nearly all the other state Republican parties. The difference was that Michigan's ambitious party chairman, a Harvard law–trained conservative named Spencer Abraham,* was willing to go to greater lengths than anyone else to accomplish that purpose. Abraham had designed, and gotten his state party to adopt, a multitiered scheme for delegate selection that would climax at a state convention in January 1988, the election year, but would begin on May 27, 1986, more than two years before the general election. The first step would be the filing of petitions by Republicans who wanted to be delegates.

Bush, as vice president to an incumbent still popular among Republicans, was the heavy favorite to win the party's 1988 nomination. He had initially greeted the news of Michigan's early start with equanimity. After all, he had won the state's primary in 1980 when he was running for president. The victory had given his ultimately unsuccessful campaign for the nomination a badly needed shot in the arm and helped to make Bush the logical choice as Reagan's running mate. And the state's voters were considered for the most part to be the sort of solid, moderate types who would be natural Bush constituents.

All of this made Bush's advisers inclined to discount Wead's warnings that there might be trouble in Michigan. Wead early on had come to believe that the Christian conservatives had become such an important part of the GOP that one of their leaders was likely to run for president in 1988. And through his soundings among evangelical leaders and followers around the country he soon realized who that candidate was likely to be—Marion G. (Pat) Robertson, the silvery haired preacher with the beaming countenance and the vast television following.

---

*Later U.S. senator from Michigan and then secretary of energy in the George W. Bush administration.

The fifty-five-year-old Robertson was a natural for the role. Politics was in his blood and breeding. His father, the late Willis Robertson, had been a fixture in the Democratic Party and in the U.S. Senate for years. Moreover, better than anyone else, Robertson, as the progenitor of a multi-million-viewer, multimillion-dollar religious broadcasting empire, seemed to possess the resources and talents to tap the energies of the millions of evangelicals who had been organizing and registering voters at a furious pace in one of the most striking political phenomena of the 1980s. "We are moving on a flood tide of revival in America," is the way Robertson himself put it earlier that year, addressing the National Religious Broadcasters convention, where the audience was sprinkled with members of "Christians for Robertson" wearing "Pat Robertson '88" buttons.

In simplistic terms, a Robertson presidential campaign would help determine whether the revival wave he had heralded swept onward or whether, in keeping with historical cycles, it already had crested and was about to recede. Few Republicans, not even Wead, gave Robertson a serious chance of winning the nomination. But most conceded that he could have a significant impact on the campaign and on the Republican Party by focusing attention on such emotionally explosive cultural issues as abortion, homosexual rights, and school prayer. Through parts of his speeches, Robertson sounded like any other conservative Republican— for example, calling for support of "freedom fighters" against communism around the world and proclaiming the need to cut federal spending. What set him apart was the fierce intensity with which he addressed cultural concerns.

In his talk to the National Religious Broadcasters, Robertson inveighed against divorce, drugs, crime, and pornography. And in a bitter double-edged attack on modern education and abortion, he charged that, for today's children, "school has become the most dangerous place to be, probably, outside the mother's womb—which is the most dangerous of all." These issues engendered fierce commitment among evangelicals, and Robertson and his adherents believed that his candidacy could further energize the evangelicals as well as other similarly minded Christians, including conservative Catholics.

Indeed, from what Wead could tell, Robertson was already doing that in Michigan, where he had set up a grassroots organization called the Freedom Council to enlist the faithful in his cause. A couple of weeks before the May 27 filing deadline for would-be convention delegates, Robertson himself had given his followers a pep talk—speaking to 3,000 people in Detroit's Cobo Hall and at least that many more around the state via satellite television. "You have an extraordinary opportunity here in Michigan to influence the whole nation," he declared. And one of his lieutenants followed up, providing explicit directions on what had to be done to become a precinct delegate.

As the filing deadline approached, Wead warned Bush that he expected the number of Robertson followers filing for precinct delegate to reach close to 5,000, which would top the number for any other candidate, Bush included. The vice president shook his head in disbelief. His campaign manager, Lee Atwater, widely regarded as the keenest of GOP strategists, had estimated the number would be no greater than 500. Wead saw no point in arguing. He decided to let events speak for themselves.

They spoke loudly. Lee Atwater ended Wead's long wait on the evening of May 27 with a phone call. Atwater had just heard from Bush's operatives in Lansing that Robertson's supporters had turned in thousands of precinct delegate filings just before the deadline. Atwater was frantic. "You gotta get back here," he told Wead. "We gotta talk."

There was plenty to talk about. Wead's guess of 5,000 petitions for Robertson had been close to the mark. As for the supporters of Bush, and of former congressman Jack Kemp, another presidential contender, the confusing nature of the process made it hard to arrive at their exact totals. But everyone agreed that Robertson had upstaged the competition, turning out far more filers than expected and more than any of his rivals. "Pat Robertson hit a home run today," said the clerk of Wayne County, Michigan's most populous county, who estimated that of the roughly 1,600 petitions filed in his jurisdiction half were brought in by Robertson's Freedom Council. "They dumped and dumped" petitions all day, he said. Robertson, never hindered by excessive humility, summoned up his favorite metaphors to describe the results of the recruiting drive: It was a "tidal wave," he said, adding that the showing of his supporters "reinforces the fact that a lot of people would like me to run for president."

In a letter to his supporters he put it more bluntly. "THE CHRISTIANS HAVE WON!" Robertson wrote. "What a thrust for freedom!" Robertson's letter continued. "What a breakthrough for the Kingdom! . . . As believers become involved in this process, they will be able to turn this nation back to its traditional moral values."

The *Washington Post's* justly esteemed chief political columnist, David Broder, noted that Robertson's big score in Michigan came hard on the heels of upset primary victories by Republican candidates with strong evangelical support in a pair of Indiana House districts. He also mentioned the 43 percent showing of a fundamentalist Baptist minister challenging veteran Oregon Senator Bob Packwood. "The pattern was enough to send a murmur, if not a shock wave, through this city," Broder wrote from the nation's capital. "Suddenly everyone was proclaiming, or warning, 'The Christians are coming!'"

What it all boiled down to was that more than a decade after the Vietnam War's ending and the fading of the counterculture, the Culture War was erupting on a new front. This development could be traced directly to realities of the competition for the Republican presidential nomination in 1988, the leader of which, if all went well, would serve as Ronald Reagan's successor.

If the forces of the cultural counterrevolution had been disappointed with the fruits of the Reagan presidency, they had reason to fear greater frustration in the political future. For even as Reagan struggled through the last two years of his lame duck term, the line of Republican succession as envisaged by the GOP hierarchy was already clearly drawn, and it led directly to the bête noire of the Right—Vice President George Bush. The trouble was that conservatives were united in their disdain for Bush, but on little else.

For the first time in a generation the conservative forces that had first rallied behind Barry Goldwater and then followed Ronald Reagan through thick and thin had no clear champion to lead them. It was in this wide open environment, where presidential candidates selected themselves, that

Pat Robertson stepped forward. It was true that only a few years before, during the 1980 campaign when evangelists had rushed to rally behind Reagan's banner, Robertson remained on the sidelines, cautioning his brethren that they might be manipulated. But that was then. This was now—the twilight of the Reagan presidency, and Robertson had learned something from the passing years. He had been right when he said that evangelicals could be manipulated. That was what had happened under Reagan. But it was also clear to Robertson that the same thing would happen again. The Republicans had learned to tap into the political energy of the Christian Right, and they were bound to keep coming back to the same source. And the evangelicals would respond as enthusiastically as they had before. If the evangelicals were going to be manipulated, it seemed to Robertson, it might as well be done by one of their own.

In 1980 the evangelicals had hitched a ride on Reagan's bandwagon even as they worked hard to propel it to victory. For their efforts they reaped plenty of glory but little in the way of tangible benefits. In 1988, with Reagan not in the running, and no traditional politician with a comparably strong appeal to evangelicals, the circumstances were right for preacher Robertson. His chances of winning the nomination were slim. But if he managed well he could emerge from the process with enough delegates and enough prestige so that if victory once again crowned Republican efforts, the evangelicals would have a greater role in portioning out the spoils.

As sound as this strategy was, its success depended on how well Robertson executed it. In some ways he was well suited to the job—he was bright, attractive, articulate, and energetic. But what he lacked was the discipline to control his own ambition and ego, and this flaw would cost him dearly.

Robertson came by his outsized sense of self-importance honestly. From his childhood in Lexington, Virginia, where he was born in 1930, he was the cynosure of his parents' conflicting hopes and dreams. His senator father, Willis, who had come to Washington with Franklin Roosevelt in 1932 and left in 1966 when Lyndon Johnson was in the White House, served seven terms in the House and another twenty years in the Senate.

He wanted his son to follow the political career path he himself had blazed. His mother insisted that her son follow another paradigm, established by Jesus of Nazareth.

For her part, Gladys Robinson, a born-again Christian who prayed and read the Bible without let-up, thought her husband's chosen field had little to recommend it. It was all right for Willis, but for her son Pat she wanted a higher calling, a ministry in the church. Young Pat at first seemed to disregard that advice. He graduated from Washington & Lee University magna cum laude in 1950, just as the Korean War broke out. After a two-year stint as a Marine Corps second lieutenant—a period that would later become the cause of bitter controversy and litigation— Robertson earned a degree from Yale in 1955. He was well on his way to following in his father's footsteps. Together with his new wife, Dede, he moved to New York City and joined a group of old law school buddies as a partner in an electronic components company. His interest in politics and his ties to the Democratic Party were both still strong enough that when the 1956 campaign got under way Robertson became chairman of the Stevenson for President Committee in Staten Island, where he and Dede had settled.

Robertson was earning enough money to begin "to enjoy some of the social life, the Stork Club, Le Pavillion and trying to cut a little bit of a figure in the Big Apple," as he later recalled. Yet something was amiss. For one thing, Robertson had signed up for the New York Bar exam, and excellent student though he was, he had discovered that when he started the grueling work of preparation neither his heart nor his mind were in it. He failed the test, stunning all who knew him. When his dejected father asked what had gone wrong, Robertson could offer no explanation, even to himself. "I had tried pleasure, philosophy, a profession, nothing satisfied," he later wrote. "Life was empty."

His mother, of course, had a solution. All these years she had refused to abandon hope that her son would follow the path of faith. She had never relented on bombarding him with Gospel literature through the mail. Since all else had failed, Robertson tentatively decided he might as well take her advice. He agreed to enter the ministry. But his pursuit of his new vocation was rather aimless until his mother arranged for him to meet with a Baptist missionary whose faith and manner were so compelling that, by Robertson's later account, the experience transformed him into a prayerful man of God.

The next day, seated at his desk at the electronics firm, the full realization of the change came to him. Leaning back in his chair, Robertson suddenly burst out laughing. "I had been saved. I had passed from death into life. I was suddenly aware that I was living in an entirely new world. It was an indescribable sensation of joy and peace."

Before long, thanks to what Robertson claimed was heavenly intervention, a buyer came along for his $2,000 interest in the electronics firm. He left the business world and enrolled in New York Theological Seminary. Soon after his graduation, as Robertson recounted the story, the Lord stepped in again. And so did his mother, who passed on to her son word of a defunct UHF television station in Portsmouth, Virginia, that was on the block for the proverbial song. Robertson, who later claimed that at the time he did not even own a television set and had only $70 in his pocket, nevertheless managed to raise the funds to buy the station. And in 1960 the Federal Communications Commission issued to Robertson's brand new corporation, the Christian Broadcasting Network, the first license for a television station that would devote more than half of its air time to religious broadcasting.

WYAH-TV, the station's call letters, formed an abbreviation for "Yahweh," the ancient Hebraic name for God. Robertson went on the air in 1961. In 1963, needing $7,000 a month to keep operating, Robertson thought of a telethon. He would offer membership in a viewers' club for 700 subscribers willing to give $10 a month. Robertson got more than enough pledges for the $7,000. He soon began airing *The 700 Club,* a sort of religious variety show headquartered in the resort town of Virginia Beach, Virginia, that became one of the mainstays of CBN broadcasting. By 1985, according to an A. C. Nielsen study commissioned by CBN, *The 700 Club,* carried on cable and also on about 200 UHF and VHF stations around the country, reached more viewers than any other religious broadcast—with 16.3 million households tuning in at least briefly once a month, though the average weekly audience for the program was much smaller—about 1.4 million households.

Over the years Robertson kept adding stations as outlets, some through outright ownership, some through syndication, and expanding his reach through satellite technology. In the early 1970s he emerged as one of the most prominent entrepreneurs in the rapidly growing Christian broadcasting field. Along the way he founded CBN University, which eventually became Regent University, on a 187-acre site in Virginia Beach. By the time Robertson was preparing for his run for the presidency, his various endeavors in communications and education operating under the CBN corporate umbrella were producing revenues he estimated at more than $200 million a year. Though his soul may well have burned with spiritual fervor, Robertson retained the easygoing demeanor of the bon vivant he had been in his secular days. In contrast with other television preachers who seemed to be spewing fire and brimstone at unrepentant sinners, he projected a more amiable image. His presentation was conversational and his visage invariably brightened by the smile that had become his hallmark.

Nevertheless, Robertson, both on and off the air, had given his adversaries plenty of ammunition, even before he decided to run for president, and much of it was on tape. He often called for the help of the Almighty on television to heal the victims of specific afflictions and—among other things—to chase away hurricanes, notably Hurricane Gloria, which in September 1985 was on a destruction path headed right toward Virginia Beach and CBN headquarters. As it turned out the hurricane veered from its course and headed harmlessly out to sea. "So it was, of course, a miracle," he said. "There's no other explanation."

On another sensitive issue, the status of women, Robertson also appeared to be heading for trouble. "The husband," he had said, "is the high priest of the family." And in *Shout It from the Housetops,* his own chronicle of the start of his religious career, Robertson quoted his wife, Dede, as telling him: "I know you think a wife is supposed to submit herself to her husband, and I think that, too."

Such departures from the post-Sixties mainstream culture did not slow down Robertson's presidential bandwagon when it began to roll in

1986. Few people outside the relatively small circle of his ardent supporters were paying any attention to Robertson, whose prospects were not highly rated by established politicians. Helped by this temporary grant of immunity, Robertson pushed ahead in Michigan.

Following his early success in the delegate filings in May, Robertson made another strong showing in the August primary balloting. At that time voters elected delegates from among those who had filed their petitions in May to attend a county convention, yet another step in Spencer Abraham's Rube Goldberg–like design for choosing the state's delegation to the GOP national convention. Robertson came in second, just behind Bush and well ahead of Jack Kemp. That result paved the way for another milestone in his campaign—his conditional declaration of his candidacy.

Taking over Washington's Constitution Hall in September 1986 for an address beamed by closed-circuit TV to more than 200 gatherings around the country, Robertson announced that if, by September 1987, a year hence, his supporters could get signed pledges from 3 million registered voters to back him, he would become a candidate for the White House. In making his decision to edge closer to mounting a campaign, the critical question Robertson stressed was: "What is God's will for me in this? Let me assure you I know God's will for me."

As Robertson moved ahead in the presidential arena, he concentrated on building support from his brethren within the evangelical and fundamentalist Christian community. Many of these leaders had at the start viewed Robertson's prospective candidacy with a distinct lack of enthusiasm. Some, jealous of his prestige and influence, were reluctant to see Robertson become the whale in the sea of Christian conservatism while they followed him like minnows. Beyond that, by supporting Robertson they would be giving up the chance to bargain for leverage and influence in the nonevangelical campaigns of Bush, Kemp, and Robert Dole.

But Robertson kept getting endorsements from the likes of Jimmy Drapper and Charles Stanley, both former heads of the Southern Baptist Convention, the largest Protestant denomination. And each endorsement increased pressure on other conservative Christian leaders to climb aboard the Robertson express. Some, like Jerry Falwell, had been persuaded by Bush's man Doug Wead to endorse the vice president before Robertson had become a serious presidential prospect. But with Robertson picking up steam, Falwell announced that he intended to back away from active political involvement. Then, when Robertson announced his possible candidacy, television evangelist Jimmy Swaggart abandoned his former opposition to the Robertson campaign, declaring, "For the first time in human history, the possibility exists that the hand that is laid on the Holy Bible will be joined to a shoulder, a head and a heart that are saved by the Lord Jesus Christ."

Swaggart's involvement gave the Robertson candidacy an extra dimension in the Culture War. Unlike some of his brethren, Swaggart had never been reluctant to criticize other religions, particularly the Catholic Church, which he had described as a "false cult" promoting the "doctrines of devils." While that sort of rhetoric might go over well with some fundamentalists it also provided potential ammunition for Democrats seeking to undermine the ties Republicans had been building to working- and middle-class Catholics, long a reliable Democratic constituency.

Democratic National Chairman Paul G. Kirk, Jr., was among the first to zero in. In a fund-raising letter, he described Robertson as "an ultra-fundamentalist leader of the Religious Right" and warned Democrats not to dismiss Robertson's chances in 1988 "because, when President Pat Robertson finishes his Scripture reading and begins his televised State of the Union address, it will be too late."

Republicans, who saw Robertson as ruining a good thing—namely, their hegemony over the morality realm in national politics—joined in the assault. Education Secretary William J. Bennett sharply seized upon Robertson's off-the-cuff suggestion that Christians "maybe feel more strongly than others do" about "love of God, love of country and support for the traditional family." Bennett, who harbored presidential ambitions of his own, declared: "This sort of invidious sectarianism must be renounced in the strongest terms. The vibrant families and warm patriotism of millions upon millions of non-Christians and nonreligious Americans give it the lie."

The fiercest broadside came from the opposite cultural pole, the liberal People for the American Way, established by television producer Norman Lear to counter the religious Right. Lear's group held a "Robertson

Film Festival" with clips from *The 700 Club*. They showed Robertson claiming to have changed a hurricane's course, arguing that "non-Christian people and atheists" are using the Constitution "to destroy the foundations of our society," and assigning to the husband the role of "high priest" of the family unit. Then cartoonist Gary Trudeau piled on, with a "Doonesbury" panel depicting Robertson, being interviewed by a skeptical journalist, calling on Jesus to "drive the hiccups from this reporter."

All this was too much, even for some defenders of the mainstream culture. "I think some of what we are seeing and hearing comes uncomfortably close to ridiculing others' religious beliefs—something that should not be part of American politics," complained columnist Michael Barone.

> Every faith is vulnerable to ridicule. Faith healing, speaking in tongues, proclaiming the father as head of the family and belief in the efficacy of prayer are equally central to the lives of millions of Americans. You will not find many of them in Ivy League colleges, Capitol Hill offices or Georgetown restaurants. In some quarters of this culturally variegated nation they are as rare as Moslems or Hindus. But the Americans who hold these beliefs are entitled to the decent respect of their fellow citizens.

However such counsel for restraint went largely unheeded by most of the media, political operatives in both parties, and that relatively small portion of the public that was paying heed. The impulse to ridicule evangelical leaders became particularly hard to resist in the wake of the eruption in the righteous world of evangelicism of a scandal so grotesque that it stretched credulity. In the center of the uproar was forty-six-year-old Jim Bakker, the cherubic Pentecostal proprietor of the PTL (which stood for "People That Love" and/or "Praise the Lord") Network in Charlotte, North Carolina, a television program ranking second only to Robertson's own CBN in Christian cable. Its featured offering, the counterpart, so to speak, to *The 700 Club*, was the daily *Jim and Tammy Show*, a variety-and-talk program with Bakker and his wife as hosts on a lavish make-believe hacienda with orchestra, singers, and live audience. Bakker's revenues totaled more than

$100 million a year, much of which he had invested in his Heritage USA theme park, opened in 1978 near Fort Mill, South Carolina, which had become the third-largest such attraction in the country with nearly 5 million visitors a year.

Suddenly, in the spring of 1987 this godly empire was rocked off its foundations by the revelation that six years previously Bakker had enjoyed a roll in the hay with a former church secretary named Jessica Hahn, whose silence on the affair had then been bought for $250,000. It hardly mattered that, as Bakker protested in a weepy farewell to the viewers of his PTL Club, he had long since repented and been forgiven.

What made the episode even messier was the charge by Bakker and his friends that fellow evangelists had only brought his indiscretion to light to pave the way for a "hostile takeover" of PTL's $129 million in annual revenues. The conspirator-in-chief was none other than Jimmy Swaggart. For his part, Swaggart defended his tattling as his Christian obligation to hate sin and love the sinner; in Bakker's case, Swaggart argued, he had helped to cut a cancer from "the body of Christ." That same sense of obligation also prompted him to deplore the conduct of evangelist Oral Roberts, who had said that unless his followers came up with $8 million for medical missionaries, God might "call me home." On television, Swaggart described Roberts as "a dear brother perched up in a tower, telling people that if they don't send him money, God's going to kill him. Then we got this soap opera," Swaggart said, referring to Jim Bakker. "I'm ashamed, I'm embarrassed. The Gospel of Jesus Christ has never sunk to such a level as it has today."

Most of Swaggart's evangelical colleagues agreed with him on that score. Some joined his condemnation of Bakker; others faulted Swaggart himself, including, not surprisingly, Oral Roberts, who accused Swaggart of "sowing discord among the brethren" and told his own followers to "go to your checkbooks" on Bakker's behalf. Jerry Falwell, striving at Bakker's request to put the tattered PTL empire back together, tried to stay neutral.

As for Robertson, who was in the process of withdrawing from his involvement in CBN in preparation for his presidential candidacy, he declared at first that he welcomed the house cleaning. But new revelations emerged, principally about the exorbitant salaries paid to both the Bakkers, along with allegations of homosexual activity by Bakker, which he denied. Bakker was stripped of his ministerial credentials. Robertson felt himself obliged to assert: "I'm just not involved in this at all."

In literal terms, that was perfectly true. But in the eyes of many Americans the PTL scandal tainted all television evangelists, sparking indignant calls for fuller financial disclosure by the electronic ministry and increasing uneasiness about Robertson's candidacy. Polls showed support for his presidential campaign slumping and his negatives rising, and reporters bombarded him with questions about the whole mess.

Having no choice, Robertson pressed on with his campaign, trying to limit questions on the scandal to one or two per press conference so he could still get his message out. Fortunately for Robertson, the PTL furor broke during a lull in the campaign, at least so far as official competition was concerned. With the Michigan struggle more or less settled, he was able to spend his time preparing for the formal announcement of his candidacy in the fall. Meanwhile, the Iowa precinct caucuses, which traditionally start the official battle for convention delegates, were quickly approaching.

The caucuses would not take place until February 1988. But there was plenty of work to be done in the state beforehand. From the beginning Robertson and his advisers realized that Iowa offered them special advantages. For one thing the state's population included a substantial number of conservative Christians, likely recruits for Robertson's campaign. Second, because the Iowa delegate competition was based on caucuses, or meetings of political activists, rather than a primary, the turnout was always relatively small and the payoff for organizational effort was bound to be relatively great. Those circumstances worked in Robertson's favor because his supporters, whatever they lacked in numbers, made up for it by the intensity of their loyalty to the candidate.

To the Hawkeye State Robertson dispatched his top organizer, Marlene Elwell, a key figure in his success in Michigan. Elwell soon decided Robertson's chances in Iowa would depend on a straw poll conducted by the state party in September 1987. Only a few thousand people would vote—the franchise was limited to those who showed up for the state party convention in Ames, a town about 25 miles north of Des Moines, and paid a $25 poll tax. Elwell knew she would have plenty of competition from Kemp, Bush, and Dole. But she had an edge—the names Robertson had been gathering for his signature drive to usher in the formal announcement of his candidacy. Elwell turned up names of these already established supporters from all of Iowa's ninety-five counties and phoned them all, urging them to show up for the straw poll and to bring their friends and the friends of their friends—as many as they could.

When the 3,843 total straw votes were counted—more than twice the turnout of the most recent contested poll in 1980, when Bush had attracted national attention with a surprising win—Elwell and Robertson savored their triumph. Robertson had stunned his opponents with 34 percent of the votes, to 25 percent for Dole, 23 percent for Bush, and 14 percent for Kemp. Never one to understate his own success or an adversary's misfortune, Robertson declared: "The Vice President has been wounded very badly."

But when his turn came to address the assembled convention delegates Robertson sounded a harmonious note, driving his point home with the practiced cadences of a sermon giver. "Whether we're rich, whether we're poor—whether we're management, whether we're labor—whether we're black, whether we're white—whether we're educated, whether we're uneducated—We—Are—All—Americans!"

This was a fine ecumenical credo, but it really did not advance his ambitions. Those unifying sentiments could have been expressed just as well by any of Robertson's rivals. They did not express his own political identity, which was what attracted the fervent support that won straw polls for him—the sense of moral righteousness and sanctified mission that infused his candidacy. Moreover, many in the broader Republican constituency for whose support he seemed to yearn had already been turned off by the very moralistic and religious qualities that appealed to his core followers.

The difficulties Robertson faced became more apparent after he formally launched his candidacy in October 1987. Polls showed that the harder Robertson campaigned and the more he succeeded with his own evangelical constituency, the more he disturbed the rest of the electorate.

Six out of ten Republicans surveyed had an unfavorable impression of him, while only two out of ten viewed him favorably. By contrast, for Bob Dole, despite his deserved reputation for abrasiveness, the positive and negative figures were roughly reversed.

Some of this aversion to Robertson reflected ignorance and suspicion of evangelical religious beliefs and practices, fostered by the press coverage of Robertson's candidacy and exacerbated by the disclosures of the antics of the Bakkers and Swaggart. Few reporters—outside of the relative handful who covered church affairs—knew much about evangelism or religion in general, and their coverage reflected this deficiency, wrote Garrett Epps, a liberal columnist for the *North Carolina Independent*.

> Robertson believes that God speaks to him, that God answers prayers, that God can heal the sick and that God works miracles in the affairs of nations. As a charismatic, he expresses these beliefs in flamboyant and sometimes disturbingly literal fashion, but the beliefs themselves are part of mainstream Christianity. In my own Episcopal parish, which serves a sophisticated academic congregation, they are taken for granted.

Shrugging off his critics, and boosted by his success in the Iowa straw poll, Robertson stepped up his efforts to win support in the state's precinct caucus showdown in February 1988. His efforts began to make the opposition nervous. Following the straw poll results, Sanny Thompson, the Bush campaign's chairman in Marshall County just north of Des Moines, made it her business to convince other Bush supporters that Robertson was a serious threat, thereby exhorting them to greater labors for the vice president.

But she had an uphill task. "A lot of people here aren't aware of what Robertson can do," she acknowledged to a reporter. The *Des Moines Register* Iowa Poll found Robertson supported by only fewer than 8 percent or so of would-be caucus voters statewide. The vice president's Iowa campaign manager, attorney George Wittgraf, reported that Robertson likewise barely showed up in Bush's samplings. But still, Wittgraf worried. He realized that Robertson was gaining support outside the boundaries where Republican caucus goers were usually found.

Many Robertson backers were new to presidential politics. They were not on precinct voter lists, contributor lists, or volunteer lists; nor were their phone numbers on the party Rolodex lists. They were not on the same channels of political gossip; they attended different social functions. And so they defied the normal political measures. Sanny Thompson, who had lived in Marshall County for more than thirty years, attended a Robertson event which drew 200 Marshall County Republicans. "I knew hardly a soul," she said later. "And they sat there enraptured, mesmerized by him." "Enraptured" and "mesmerized" were words not commonly used to describe the reaction of Bush or Dole supporters to their candidates.

Among those inspired was Roberta Edgar, a ripely pregnant Marshalltown housewife who drove an hour to Des Moines to hear Robertson speak one November night, ignoring the twinges in her swollen abdomen. The following evening, Edgar gave birth on schedule to daughter Rachelle Rae. Two days after that, Edgar was out with the crowds cohosting a Marshalltown event for Robertson. "My husband and I believe he's the man who is going to turn the country around," Edgar explained.

All of the passion and energy expended by Edgar and other Robertson followers paid off in spades on caucus night. By that time, Bob Dole's victory in the competition was a foregone conclusion. Aided by his own Midwest roots and the lethargy of the Bush campaign, Dole came in first with 35 percent of the vote. But no one was prepared for the candidate who came in second—Pat Robertson. His showing was made even more dramatic by the fact that he finished well ahead of Bush, the longtime favorite of the Republican establishment.

No one could accuse Robertson of understating the significance of the results. "My campaign for the presidency has been given an enormous boost," he told reporters while supporters cheered. "It's going to be like I've got a rocket strapped to my back and I'm going to be taking off. I was looking for an opportunity to broaden my base and that's exactly what happened," Robertson said.

But of course this was exactly what had not happened. In Iowa, as in Michigan in 1986 and in Hawaii, where he had captured 80 percent of the delegates the previous week, Robertson had only succeeded in energizing his base among Christian conservatives. By no means had he reached beyond those parameters, and the aftermath of his Iowa success was going to make it that much harder for him to accomplish this goal.

By defying expectations Robertson had brought down on himself the full glare of the mass media, particularly the television cameras. And while he seemed to think this attention was exactly what his candidacy needed, it was soon clear he was not prepared for his moment in the sun. The trouble started on caucus night when NBC anchor Tom Brokaw interviewed Robertson live and on camera. When Robertson was a television evangelist, Brokaw recalled, he often said he had followed "God's advice." As a candidate, Brokaw asked, was he still getting counsel from the same source?

Robertson's hallmark grin never left his face. But he was obviously furious. That question, Robertson told Brokaw, was a sign of "religious bigotry." Anyhow, Robertson said, he had been a "Christian broadcaster" and not a "TV evangelist," a distinction without a difference to most Americans, though it was a point Robertson kept trying to make throughout the campaign. And this incident was only the beginning of his troubles with the media. Robertson kept running afoul of reporters who insisted on bringing up things he had said in the past—things that made him seem like just what he denied being—a television evangelist. Sometimes Robertson dealt with these unwelcome reminders of past controversial statements by denying he had ever made them. This was the case when he was asked about his comments in January 1985 that only Jews and Christians who had submitted themselves to Jesus—his definition of a born-again Christian—should be entitled to jobs in government. Robertson told reporters that he never said such a thing until he was confronted with a videotape of the comment.

Despite being harried by journalists Robertson exuded confidence. Speaking in a fundamentalist church in Bedford, New Hampshire, two days before the state's primary and six days after his strong showing in Iowa, Robertson told the congregation, "This is where God wanted me to be, here in New Hampshire, before a major primary." He then said, "I assure you that I am going to be the next president of the United States."

Forgetting that while the enthusiasm of New Hampshire's Christian conservatives matched Iowa standards, their numbers did not, Robertson declared that he would finish "at least a solid third" among Republican candidates in the state, adding, "The only question is how much beyond third we can go." As it turned out, Robertson came in fifth in a five-man field.

Shrugging off that debacle, Robertson pointed to the South Carolina primary little more than two weeks later, on March 5. He predicted that the Palmetto State's large population of born-agains, including charismatics and Pentecostals, would put him over the top. And first indications were that something of the sort might indeed take place as the faithful flocked to Robertson's rallies around the state.

The Republican primary in South Carolina was especially important because it occurred three days before the so-called Super Tuesday primary on March 8. That date would see no fewer than seventeen delegate contests—fourteen of them in southern and border states. And Robertson's strategists anticipated that a victory in South Carolina would give them a huge burst of momentum for the Super Tuesday competition elsewhere in Dixie, the region of the country where Robertson's potential strength was believed to be greatest.

In South Carolina Robertson's field workers displayed the same intensity that had paid off in Iowa and Michigan. But his advantages extended beyond the inspirational to the material realm, to the mother's milk of politics, money. He was spending far more than any of his rivals in the states to be contested on Super Tuesday. By January 31, a few weeks before the vote, Robertson's campaign had shelled out more than $3 million on these critical contests, $1 million more than his closest Republican rival, Bob Dole. Overall, Robertson had raised more money than any other Republican except Bush—a total of about $22 million, compared to Bush's $26 million. But Robertson was outspending Bush by an even wider margin—$22 million to Bush's $16 million. That left Bush in a far better financial position, particularly since Robertson had borrowed $6 million to help grease the wheels of his bandwagon.

But just as Robertson's prospects appeared promising for the southern primaries, his candidacy was staggered by blows from his worst enemy, himself. Less than two weeks before the South Carolina primary, Jimmy Swaggart, the man who had pointed the finger at Jim Bakker, was forced himself to resign from his ministry when word got out that he had been photographed escorting a prostitute into a New Orleans hotel room. At first Robertson sought to minimize the impact from the Swaggart scandal on his own campaign. Why should he bear the blame for someone else's sin, he asked?

It was a reasonable point, and Robertson might indeed have escaped serious damage if he had only let matters rest there. But this sort of discretion was not in his nature. Instead he tried to pin the blame for the disclosure on Vice President Bush. To believe that the timing of the disclosures about Swaggart had not been by design "would stretch the credulity of almost anybody," Robertson told reporters. Admitting he had no hard information about who might have done such a deed, Robertson nevertheless unleashed a broad and bitter attack on Bush's campaign. "Knowing the quality of the people surrounding George Bush," Robertson said, "there is nothing that I would not believe that they would do sleazy."

Was he accusing Bush of putting out the story about Swaggart? "I'm not saying any such thing," Robertson said coyly. "You're the reporters. Go out and find out for yourselves." Anyhow, he said, his campaign had been a victim of numerous other "dirty tricks," including the cutting of telephone lines and the cancellation of hotel reservations. While he implied that the Bush campaign was behind the incidents, he provided no evidence. "People don't leave tracks," he said.

"It's crazy," said Bush when asked about Robertson's accusation. "It's an absurd charge." In the long run the attack on Bush, offered without any evidence to support it, hurt Robertson far more than it did Bush, giving ammunition to those who regarded the reverend as more than a bit loony.

The truth was that for all the natural advantages the South seemed to offer Robertson, and for all the resources and organizational effort he poured into the campaign, the religious broadcaster, as he preferred to be called, had hard going there as elsewhere in broadening his reach. He clearly realized this difficulty himself, and his frustration led to his foolish fulminations about Bush and Swaggart. These outbursts diminished whatever chance he had of reaching the goal that would have allowed his candidacy to continue. As it turned out, the Lord himself could not have made the handwriting on the wall any clearer.

In South Carolina, where he had predicted victory, Robertson finished third, behind Dole, getting less than 20 percent of the vote, while Bush came in first with nearly half the vote. Robertson blamed his loss on "distortions" of his public comments and insisted that a third-place finish and failure to capture any delegates was not a loss. "I've always had modest delegate goals in the South," he said. "What happened today is right in our game plan."

But the results contravened the major tenets of his campaign. He had counted on thousands of evangelicals registered as Democrats crossing party lines to vote for him in the Republican primary. In reality, fewer than 10 percent of the Republican primary voters were Democrats, and Bush and Dole each got more of their votes than Robertson did. With half the citizens of the state considering themselves born-again Christians, Robertson planned on drawing enough of their votes to win. As it turned out, his portion of the Christian vote was no larger than Bush's.

Defeat in South Carolina set the stage for debacle on Super Tuesday. Bush won nearly everywhere, in effect locking up the nomination. In the seventeen statewide contests across the country that day Robertson came in first only in the Washington state caucus. In his native Virginia, he ran behind not only Bush but even Dole. Trying to put the best face on things, Robertson claimed that his string of third-place finishes was "not too bad for an amateur" and insisted he could carry his fight to the GOP convention in New Orleans. But in effect, his candidacy was over. And he provided the most fitting epitaph himself. "I spoke too much and I should have kept my mouth shut," he said.

For all of his personal shortcomings, and consequent comeuppance, Robertson's candidacy had far-reaching impact on the Culture War. His flamboyance and abrasiveness helped to mobilize the mainstream culture against the evangelicals. As a result of his candidacy, charges of bigotry and narrow-mindedness against the GOP became a staple in the Democratic arsenal. The use of this weapon fell off after Robertson's defeat, but it would be revived in future years with consequences that cut both ways. The Democratic efforts to create a bogeyman of the Christian Right probably helped the party with its liberal base, making these constituents more likely to vote and more willing to organize. But the attacks also had as least as much reverse impact by galvanizing Christian conservatives. Accustomed to seeing themselves as beleaguered and embattled, they reacted vigorously to the thrusts from the Democrats.

Of more immediate significance was the energy and enthusiasm Robertson brought to efforts to politicize the Christian Right. Even after his Super Tuesday defeat had obliterated his chances of success, Robertson kept his candidacy alive to encourage his followers to battle for places on state delegations to the nomination convention and for positions in state parties. At the convention several score Robertson delegates carried on the fight for the goals of his candidacy and made their voices heard. In fact, Robertson and his backers could feel quite comfortable with the 1988 Republican Platform, particularly its intractable opposition to abortion. Meanwhile, zealous, well-organized Robertson supporters took control of the party machinery in a handful of western states and made significant inroads in several other states, notably Georgia, Virginia, Texas, Louisiana, Minnesota, and the Carolinas.

Their satisfaction with this progress was dimmed in the aftermath of the election by Bush's presidency, which served in the main to confirm the misgivings of conservative Christians about the new chief executive. Like Reagan himself, Reagan's hand-picked vice president and successor did very little in a practical sense to advance such cultural goals as restoring prayer in the schools and banning abortion. And his rhetoric, for whatever that was worth, was nowhere near as stirring as Reagan's had been. Conservatives were gratified by Bush's nomination of Clarence Thomas for the Supreme Court but they never forgave him his earlier selection of David Souter, who turned into one of the foremost liberals on the bench. Bush's choice of Souter, as right-wingers saw it, forfeited the chance to establish a solid conservative majority on the high court.

The Gulf War represented another lost opportunity to conservatives. In the wake of the success of Desert Storm, Bush's approval rating soared in the polls to stratospheric heights. Jack Kemp, one of the conservative movement's heroes in the post-Reagan era, whom Bush had appointed as his secretary of Housing and Urban Development, argued that the time was right for Bush to launch a broad new approach to cultural politics. Bush should take advantage of his high standing in the polls to broaden the Republicans' appeal, Kemp urged the president. Kemp proposed waging "an audacious, aggressive kind of dramatic war on poverty," and pushing such ideas as privatization of public housing and enterprise zones. "Bush has a chance of going beyond where Ronald Reagan went," especially with minority voters, Kemp said.

What was lacking for this strategy to be carried forward was presidential leadership. Bush had no commitment to the bold ideas for advancing conservative cultural goals that Kemp advocated, nor did he have the will to challenge the Democratic majorities on Capitol Hill. He regarded his post–Gulf War popularity as a treasure to be hoarded, not as a resource to be deployed, and as a result he watched it evaporate in the dismal statistics of the 1992 recession.

Nevertheless, for all their disappointment with Bush, conservative leaders made a pragmatic bargain to support him in his 1992 campaign against Bill Clinton in hopes of gaining concessions on cultural issues in Bush's second term, which of course never materialized. As for Robertson, though in the wake of the 1988 campaign he and his aides had talked cockily about making another try for the presidency in 1992, he himself concluded, as he later put it, that he had "more important things to do." One of these things turned out to be establishing the Christian Coalition, which under the leadership of a young political operative named Ralph Reed provided a new and broader outlet for the energies of conservative Christians. Although the Christian Coalition was a grassroots organization, ostensibly nonpartisan, its impact and goals were much the same as the Robertson candidacy. Like Robertson himself, it sought to shift the cultural agenda of American politics to focus on the moral concerns of conservative Christians. And like the Robertson candidacy, it would serve to energize both its allies and its foes.

The years after the 1992 election were filled with peaks and valleys for Christian conservatives. They would find it easier to accept Bush's defeat than the presence of Bill Clinton in the White House. Once again, they would feel themselves betrayed by a president. Though few of their leaders had supported him, many of the rank and file had taken Clinton's gestures toward cultural conservatism to heart. Though they believed the allegations of his sins, they also believed in redemption for sinners. Their outrage would be that much greater when Clinton's public policies and personal conduct transformed him in their eyes into something resembling the Antichrist. They achieved a measure of revenge with the Republican conquest of Congress in the 1994 election.

But as noted earlier, Ralph Reed had forebodings about that victory from the start, and with good reason. Indeed, with hindsight it is apparent that disappointment for cultural conservatives was etched into the design for Republican victory. The GOP field marshal, Newt Gingrich, for all his bold cultural rhetoric, had avoided taking stands on cultural issues in the much ballyhooed Contract with America, preferring to focus on economic issues and procedural reforms, which he regarded as safer ground. And though the impact of the contract on the election results was greatly exaggerated, it was the blueprint that Gingrich chose to use as the instrument of counterrevolution in the ill-fated Republican-controlled 104th Congress.

Reed and his cultural conservative allies were forced to introduce their own "Contract with the American Family," a sort of facsimile of the GOP's campaign manifesto. The difference was that Reed's contract emphasized the social and cultural issues that had been excluded from the original because Gingrich deemed them too polarizing and risky. But Reed never had a real chance to test his own contract. By the end of the 104th Congress's first year, the new Republican majority was in full retreat. They had been embarrassed not over some instance of countercultural excess but by allowing Clinton and the Democrats to portray them as extremists determined to ravage health care, education, and the environment and to shut down the federal government to get their way.

Cultural conservatives had to learn to swallow their disappointment with the 104th Congress and the conservative revolution that flopped, along with another presidential defeat in 1996. This loss was made more bitter because it was inflicted upon them by Bill Clinton. But Clinton's second term was barely a year old before the president once again demonstrated his vulnerability to his own appetites and with the Monica Lewinsky affair furnished what appeared to be devastating ammunition to his adversaries on the Right.

It can be said that for most of the last decade of the twentieth century the Culture War was dominated by the conflict between Clinton and the cultural conservatives. This struggle in large part accounted for the two defining events of that period, the Republican seizure of Congress in 1994 and Clinton's impeachment in 1998. Moreover, the tensions and concerns stirred by the impeachment battle did not end with Clinton's acquittal in 1999 or even with his presidency. Instead they spilled over into the new century to dominate the contest to choose his successor.

PART FOUR
NEW
MILLENNIUM

CHAPTER 13

THE PRINCE
OF COMPASSION

The Senate's acquittal of President Clinton on impeachment charges on February 12, 1999, was commonly hailed as a triumph for him and his party. And many in the media predicted that the Republicans would suffer dire consequences for having sailed against the wind of public sentiment on this issue. Indeed, the *Washington Post* sounded the alarm even before the vote. "The impeachment of President Clinton has inflamed long-standing ideological divisions within the Republican Party, weakened the party's image among independent and swing voters and now threatens to inflict long-term political damage," warned two of the *Post*'s top political writers, Thomas B. Edsall and Dan Balz.

But the Senate's actions had broader significance than those early judgments suggested. The fact that more than four-fifths of the Senate membership went on record as condemning the president's behavior in the Lewinsky affair was an early warning of the dramatic impact of morality and cultural values on the political debate in the 2000 presidential campaign. Far from concluding the Culture War, as many expected, the struggle over impeachment assured the extension of that conflict into the first presidential campaign of the new century, and then into the administration that followed. The campaign elevated matters of religious faith on the agendas of both parties, raising such concerns to a prominence not seen since Al Smith's first Catholic presidential candidacy in 1928.

The failure of the public and the press at first to grasp the import of the Senate action on Clinton had to do with their dependence on and confusion over polls. Most polling data during the impeachment controversy suggested that the public opposed Clinton's impeachment and approved of his performance in office. This led many politicians and journalists to conclude that the public was little disturbed by the Lewinsky scandal, a judgment that reflected a failure to grasp the limitations of the polling process. Because of the superficial design of their questions, most polls tend to be more reliable about simple, explicit questions, such as voting choices, than about more complex issues such as marital fidelity, adultery, lying under oath, and the meaning of high crimes and misdemeanors.

Even so, a close look at the available data revealed a more nuanced, enigmatic, and fluid impression of public opinion than was commonly advertised. A majority of Americans, according to a Fox News poll taken in the midst of Clinton's Senate trial, believed the president perjured himself before the grand jury in August 1998. According to another poll, taken a few weeks earlier by John Zogby International, 55 percent also viewed perjury as an impeachable offense. Similarly, a survey conducted by the *Washington Post* in collaboration with Harvard University and the Henry J. Kaiser Family Foundation in the summer of the Lewinsky scandal found that more than seven in ten said adultery was unacceptable and "should not be tolerated." Yet fewer than half of those who said adultery "should not be tolerated" said Clinton's affair with Lewinsky was an important matter. This and other data profiled an electorate that was desperately seeking a reason not to remove Clinton from office.

Another finding in the survey underlined sharp divisions among Americans on the relevance of personal behavior to political performance—perhaps the central question raised by the Clinton scandal. About half of those interviewed—49 percent—said it was performance alone that counts in a president, agreeing that "as long as he does a good job running the country, whatever he does in his personal life is not important." But just as many disagreed: They said the president has a "greater responsibility" to set "an example with his personal life," a view that was in accord with Clinton's rhetoric during the 1992 campaign, when he sought to depict himself as a paragon of middle-class cultural values.

One man who well understood the significance of these findings was the then governor of Texas, George W. Bush, who was already preparing to run for the presidency. For Bush, heightened concern with morals and values held twofold significance, presenting both an opportunity and a risk. On one hand Bush knew that finding a formula for dealing with cultural issues was a necessity for him if he was to gain the nomination of his party. For the GOP, cultural issues were both a bane and a blessing. It was cultural issues that were needed to mobilize the Christian Right, whose energies Republicans needed to tap if they were to become a majority party. On the other hand, as Bush well knew, it was the same zeal of Christian conservatives which Republican leaders counted on to fuel their bandwagon that also alarmed millions of other Americans who were not as committed as the religious Right to the application of Christian values to politics.

For the resolution to this dilemma Bush turned to an ex-Communist, ex-atheist, born-again Christian named Marvin Olasky. Olasky had become a savior of sorts among Republicans, who saw in his theories of what he called "compassionate conservatism" a way to shed their image as the party without a heart and still maintain their opposition to what they derided as government "do good" programs. As it happened, Olasky was conveniently located right in Austin, where he taught journalism at the University of Texas. But he already had a national reputation, in large measure because of Newt Gingrich. The leader of the conservative revolution of 1994 never hesitated to tell the world how much he had been influenced by Olasky's seminal work, *The Tragedy of American Compassion*. In that volume, published in 1992, Olasky made a great point out of his contention that charities and voluntary associations, many of them church-based, were more effective than government in helping the poor and instilling a sense of personal responsibility.

Gingrich's conservative revolution soon collapsed as a result of overreach, a debacle that eventually consigned its prophet, Gingrich, to political oblivion. Olasky's ideas did much better. His faith-based welfare approach found its way into a piece of legislation that, though signed by President Clinton, who hailed it as one of the proudest achievements of his presidency, amounted to the most enduring monument achieved by the abortive conservative revolution.

This landmark statute was the welfare reform act of 1996, a measure which as Clinton's liberal critics complained essentially shifted government's role from providing for the poor to reforming them. Almost overlooked among all the new law's drastic provisions slashing benefits right and left was an amendment—which had the sotto voce support of the White House and was sponsored by a conservative stalwart, Missouri Senator John Ashcroft—that let churches and religious groups bid on government contracts to provide job training and other services.

But the governor of Texas did not choose to await action by the federal government to put Olasky's doctrines to political use. While Congress was still debating the welfare reform bill Bush recruited Olasky to lead a task force assigned to find ways to implement faith-based programs in Texas. For Bush, Olasky's formula was just what the doctor ordered to placate the conservative Christians in the Republican Party who viewed his candidacy with suspicion and also to confound the critics who charged the GOP had no interest in aiding the downtrodden.

Actually, so far as Bush was concerned, the significance of compassionate conservatism extended beyond the public policy realm to the personal. The concept seemed well suited to helping refurbish not only his party's reputation for cold-hearted callousness toward the poor but also Bush's own reputation as a sower of wild oats during a carefree youth that had lasted in his case well into early middle age. It was by no means a secret that young Bush had been something of a hellion. "George had a good time and there were a lot of gin and tonics and a lot of fun and a lot of wise guy remarks," his cousin and friend since childhood, John Ellis, told me. Not only did Bush, by his own admission, drink more than was good for him, but by some accounts, which he would never flatly deny, he had also snorted a bit of coke on the side.

But the years had altered his mores and lifestyle. On his fortieth birthday, Bush, reputedly with some prompting from his wife, Laura, and impelled by what he later described as a rededication to religion, decided that alcohol was "interfering with my energy level" and quit drinking cold. And as governor, fusing the zeal of a reformed sinner with the theories of Olasky, he also had turned himself into something of a moralist.

I learned about all this firsthand, months before Bush officially announced his candidacy for the presidency, when as a national political
correspondent for the *Los Angeles Times,* I spent a day with him as he
campaigned in his home state for reelection to the governor's office
he had won four years before. We traveled in great comfort in his sleek
chartered jet. The plane, as Bush pointed out, "is what you get when you
have $14 million in your war chest."

The rolling countryside stretching from Austin to San Antonio across
which the governor ranged on this hot, dusty day is rich in Lone Star state
history. Hays County, Bush's first stop, was named for Jack Hays, a celebrated Texas Ranger captain who directed a bloody rout of the Co-
manches a century and a half ago. San Marcos, the county seat, is home
to Southwest Texas State University, alma mater of the first Texan president, Lyndon Baines Johnson. Next we visited Floresville, about 100
miles south, the site of the 200-acre ranch that once belonged to John B.
Connally, another self-made Texas titan and Republican presidential aspi-
rant, a domain to which Connally clung even after he went bankrupt.

But in his stump speeches, Bush was less interested in the past than in
foretelling new history of his own. George W. Bush is no more electrify-
ing than was his father, the first President Bush. Yet the son's straightfor-
ward, folksy manner creates an impression of conviction and authenticity
that his father rarely achieved. Though he was nominally only running
for reelection as governor, Bush promised the admiring south Texas
crowds that his candidacy would be the precursor of nothing less than a
profound shift in American culture to what he heralded as "the responsibility era." "I'm worried about a culture that says, 'If it feels good, do it, if
you've got a problem just go ahead and blame somebody else,'" Bush told
the folks in the San Marcos County courthouse, testing out phrases he
would reiterate all across the land two years later as he ran for president.
"I see a more compassionate time which says that each and every one of
us are responsible for the decisions we make in life."

Becoming a teetotaler did not turn Bush into an advocate for prohibition. But during our travels that day he did put considerable stress on
urging young people not to drop out of school, not to use drugs and

alcohol, and in particular, not to have children out of wedlock. He spoke highly of a Baptist program called "True Love Waits" that advocates sexual abstinence before marriage.

"Do you think a presidential candidate needs to practice what he preaches?" I asked him after the speech making, when we were chatting aboard his campaign jet.

Bush glared at me, a glance that betrayed his irritation with the question. "I have never committed adultery, if that's what you're asking," he snapped.

But on other matters he was good-natured and responsive to questions. Not long before Bush set out on this campaign swing, Trent Lott, the Republican leader of the U.S. Senate, had called homosexuality a sin and compared it to alcoholism and even kleptomania. The Senate's assistant majority leader, Don Nickles of Oklahoma, agreed that Lott was "biblically correct." And over on the House side, Republican Majority Leader Dick Armey of Texas averred, "The Bible is very clear on this." Lott's outburst had been occasioned by a recent Culture War skirmish over Clinton's nomination of James Hormel, a gay San Francisco philanthropist and heavy Democratic contributor, as ambassador to Luxembourg.

"I stand by my statement that the role of governor is to be a uniter, not a divider, and to treat people with dignity and respect," Bush told me. "The truth of the matter is that when it comes to sin we're all sinners and the degree of sin ought to be left to the Almighty."

I mentioned to Bush that some people had suggested that Lott's remarks were a way of getting the GOP's conservative Christian base energized for the 1998 elections. "I think there is a better way of handling the issue," Bush said. "I don't think you can lead by dividing. I think you lead by uniting. We're all sinners. I think it's important to recognize that."

Bush acknowledged that his own experiences as a young man influenced what he said to young people now as governor and how he said it. "I made a lot of mistakes when I was young, and I learned from my mistakes," Bush said. "I've asked people to adhere to a higher standard than I did. I'm not trying to be holier than thou. I'm trying to be realistic."

In his standard stump speech I heard Bush allude to the cultural upheavals of the Sixties. I asked him how he felt about what the Sixties had wrought and how he proposed to change that. "There were some good things and some bad things," Bush said. "The good things were renewed interest in civil rights, renewed interest in trying to reconcile the races, renewed interest in people expressing themselves. On the other side of the ledger were 'the not so good things' of the Sixties." "One product of that decade," he said, returning to a theme he had established in his stump talks, was the "if it feels good, do it" culture. "There has been a disregard for persons accepting the consequences of the decisions they make in life. . . . My point is that since I've seen one change in the culture, I'm optimistic that it can change again."

Mindful of Olasky's dicta, Bush stressed that government, for all its power, is not the sole reason cultures change. Change, he said, depends mainly on each individual, a point he had advanced in our San Marcos visit and expanded on in our second stop at Floresville. "My priority will always be the education of children," he told the crowd in Floresville. "But we have to teach our children more than just reading and writing and adding and subtracting. As a society we must teach our children that there are wrong decisions to make in life and right decisions to make in life." The audience, a mixture of Anglos and Latinos, gnarled ranchers and weather-beaten farm hands, brown-skinned *mujeres* with their *niños* in arm, was alert and attentive, sometimes nodding in agreement as their governor went on.

"There are three prescriptions for a difficult life in Texas," Bush said. "Abusing drugs, abusing alcohol, and having a child out of wedlock." He repeated what he had said earlier: "Our culture today essentially says if it feels good, do it, and if you have a problem, blame somebody else."

On our way back to Austin I asked Bush about the role of churches in compassionate conservatism. "I don't want to use my position to proselytize for a particular religion," he said: "But the role of government is to encourage people of faith to be actively involved in their communities. The best welfare program is a Sunday school adopting a welfare family, or a synagogue or church helping with recidivism issues with prisoners. All this takes advantage of the law that says states can encourage faith-based organizations to become an integral part of delivery of compassionate welfare."

When Bush and I talked in Texas in the early summer of 1998, he was still a relatively unknown figure on the national political scene. Though his name was famous, his identity remained a mystery. There were far more questions about what he believed than there were answers. Over the next year and a half the world was to learn a good deal more about George W. Bush—up to a point. There still remained questions about his beliefs, questions that might never be answered. But what would become unalterably clear during that time was that Bush was well suited to be the new leader of the counterrevolution, wearing the mantle of Ronald Reagan in a way his father could never manage.

Yet he owed a great debt to his father, whose legacy propelled him to the White House, just as his father, the first President Bush, owed a lot to *his* father, Prescott Bush, the senator from Connecticut and partner in Brown Brothers, Harriman. The Bush family legacy had little to do with ideology. It was composed of influence, wealth, and celebrity, with a dollop of personal charm thrown in. The eldest son's achievement was to exploit the assets of the inheritance while countering the parts that it benefited him to oppose.

The fame, the network of friends and acquaintances, the wealth, which created access to more wealth, as much as he could ever need, all of this enabled George W. Bush, or "Dubya," as he was often called, to soar to the first ranks of national politics before anyone knew anything about him except that he was his father's son. On the other side of the ledger was the elder Bush's preppie, elitist manner, his remoteness from ordinary people and the real world that cost him dearly during the recession that wrecked his presidency.

George W. Bush did not need to do anything to remind people that he was his father's son. But sometimes he felt it convenient to point out differences between them. When he talked about the cultural influences that shaped him, Bush emphasized growing up in Texas, not in New England like his father. The difference between himself and his father, he would say, was that "he went to Greenwich Country Day School and I went to San Jacinto Junior High in Midland, Texas." This was an artful reference. The school in Greenwich, in Connecticut's fashionable

Fairfield County, epitomized the preppy aspect of the Bush family. San Jacinto, in contrast, was of course the site of the battle against the Mexican generalissimo Santa Anna that avenged the Alamo and made Texas free: the land of rough-and-ready, red-blooded Americans, free of sham, who worked hard, played hard, cared hard for their children, and stood as a bulwark against the counterculture.

The trouble with that allusion was that young George W. Bush attended San Jacinto Junior High for exactly one year. And though he spent eight more years at other Texas schools the total was no greater than his nine years back East at Phillips Academy, Andover, and Yale, where he got his bachelor's degree, and Harvard, where he earned a master's degree in business administration.

How Bush responded to the challenges at Andover and Yale, the same schools his father attended, offers an early clue to his character. He managed to make good use of both sides of his father's legacy growing up in an age beginning to scorn the old traditions that his father honored. Bush could not match his father's record as a scholar or an athlete. What he would use to make a place for himself were his exceptional social skills—the gifts of a politician. "My ability to make friends," Bush calls it; "It's just who I am. I can make friends well." Of course what Bush did not always mention was that being his father's son was a big part of who he was and helped no end in making friends and meeting life's other challenges.

With the confidence that comes with being well born, Bush was not afraid to make himself conspicuous, to challenge the establishment that he knew would never dare to reject the son of George H.W. Bush and the grandson of Prescott Bush. Andover had a dress code, of course, at which Bush thumbed his nose by wearing a tie with a T-shirt. Lacking the talent to become a star athlete, he became head cheerleader, breaking new ground by wielding a giant megaphone like a stand-up comic, making barbed comments about players and spectators, and organizing skits in which the cheerleaders dressed up once as a motorcycle gang and another time in drag.

Still, his grades were down at the middle levels, prompting a counselor, who noticed that Bush was applying only to Yale and the University of Texas, to urge the young man to think of fallback schools. But Bush was less naive than his counselor. He never forgot for a moment that at Yale his father had been Skull and Bones and his grandfather, Prescott Bush, was a trustee of the university. He knew he had little need of a fallback school.

Sure enough, Old Eli welcomed him with open arms. College in many ways was just a continuation of Andover, with hard liquor added. Bush got to know a lot of people, made friends with most of them, and led a social circle notable for its carefree view of academic life. He joined his father's old fraternity, Delta Kappa Epsilon, known for the biggest and best parties, and became its president. He also followed the family path into Skull and Bones.

It did not seem to matter greatly to him that by his senior year in 1967–1968, the protest against the war was building at Yale, as on campuses around the country. Bush did not join the protest movements; he claimed not to share those views. Anyhow, for him to raise his voice against the Vietnam War, or any war Americans were fighting, might have seemed like a slap in the face of his family, particularly his father, whose plane had been shot down over the Pacific in World War II and who had returned home with three Air Medals and the Distinguished Flying Cross.

Nor did young Bush sit around and wait to be drafted and shipped to Vietnam. Instead he joined the Texas Air National Guard. Bush claimed afterward that his motive was not to avoid combat in Indochina but rather to follow in the footsteps of his fighter pilot dad. Circumstances led critics to charge that the influence of his father, then a Houston congressman, helped him get preferential treatment from the Guard. Certainly Bush's career in the Guard moved ahead swiftly, and without his having to submit to some of the inconvenient requirements imposed on others. Indeed, according to documents unearthed by the *Boston Globe,* he had apparently stopped flying early in 1972, thus, in effect, dropping out of the Guard two years before his service commitment ended.

War or peace, life for the Bush family went on as before. George Herbert Walker Bush, having lost a U.S. Senate bid in 1970, moved to New York as President Nixon's ambassador to the United Nations. A turn as Republican National Committee chairman while the Watergate scandal unfolded followed. As the father switched positions, so the son bounced from one job to another, but without the design that drove the elder Bush, whose course to the top was already charted.

His son was like flotsam drifting in the sea. "I didn't know what I wanted to do, and I wasn't going to do anything I didn't want to do," he said. One thing was certain: The coat-and-tie routine "wasn't for me." One night in 1973 Bush had taken his younger brother out drinking during a visit to Washington; returning home, he managed to steer into some trash cans belonging to a neighbor who happened to be Supreme Court Justice Potter Stewart. When his father summoned George W., the son, a couple of sheets to the wind, challenged his father. "Let's settle this *mano a mano,*" he demanded.

Instead his parents sent their rebellious offspring off to bed that night and then shipped him back to Texas to work with a mentoring program that tried to help underprivileged youngsters in Houston. One summer of that and Bush entered Harvard Business School, where not only his father's name, but also the name of his grandfather, Prescott, who died in 1972, carried weight. He emerged two years later with Harvard's coveted MBA. The young man decided to make his start in the business world where his father began, in the oil fields of Texas, which were then still booming because of the 1973 Arab oil embargo. Back in his old hometown of Midland, Bush began investing in oil leases and exploration. He continued to live the life of the carefree bachelor until 1977 when he met and married Laura Welch, a librarian, who by all accounts exerted a stabilizing influence on her husband, not least by giving birth to twin daughters, Jenna and Barbara.

Right after his marriage, in 1978 Bush plunged into the first political race of his life for an open congressional seat in the 19th district, which encompasses a good part of the flat, dusty plains and tree-filled skyline of west Texas. He won the GOP nomination easily, knocking off the favorite with the help of old friends and neighbors from Midland. But in the general election he was overmatched against veteran State Senator Kent Hance.

A nominal Democrat, at least as conservative as Bush and much cannier in the ways of Texas politics, Hance was shrewd enough to turn the legacy of Bush's father against him. Before Bush could work out a way to explain himself on the hustings, Hance created a lethal cultural identity for him that fit all too well—the privileged son of a privileged father.

As he campaigned Hance used to like to tell of walking along a country road when a fancy car rolled up. "It was a Mercedes," Hance would say, and the crowd would begin to laugh, sensing what was coming next. "The guy rolled down the window and wanted to know how to get to a certain ranch." Hance related giving directions, telling the driver to turn right after a cattle guard, a metal grate common in those parts to keep livestock from straying. Then Hance delivered the punch line. "The driver of the Mercedes asked 'what color uniform will that cattle guard be wearing?'" The audience roared with laughter, and just to be sure that the voters knew he was talking about his Connecticut-born opponent, Hance would add that he had noticed something else about the Mercedes George W. Bush was driving: "It had Connecticut license plates."

By branding Bush as an Eastern elitist Hance was able to isolate him from the middle class just as handily as if he had been able to stigmatize him as a Sixties radical. Both the elite and the radicals were outside the Texas cultural mainstream. "Kent Hance gave me a good lesson in country boy politics," Bush said later. "He was a master of it, funny and belittling. I vowed never to get out-countried again." It was a Culture War lesson he would carry with him up the political ladder.

Returning to the oil business after his defeat, Bush found that the boom was over, ruling out his chances of gaining the success his father had in those same oil fields twenty years before. Indeed Midland, which had been a flourishing symbol of the oil industry's prosperity, had been devastated by the downturn. The First National Bank, the second largest bank in the country, crashed, and office buildings and homes were deserted.

It was during this stressful period that Bush, for the first time in his life, became seriously interested in religion. His childhood exposure, attending the First Presbyterian Church of Midland with his family, had not had much impact on his mind or soul. But now he was drawn into a more meaningful experience by fellow businessmen who, stunned by the downturn in their fortunes, began holding regular Bible reading sessions.

"We were most of us baby boomers, men with young families," Don Jones, one member of the group, told the *Washington Post*. "And we suddenly found ourselves in free fall. So we began to search for an explanation. Maybe we had been too involved with money. Maybe we needed to look inwardly and find new meaning in life."

Even in this environment Bush remained a smart aleck. When the leader of the class asked, "What is a prophet?" Bush replied: "It's where revenue exceeds expenses. No one's seen that around here since Elijah." Though he never stopped wisecracking, and was reluctant to discuss his inner feelings, his classmates believed that he was looking at life differently. Bush had long been reluctant to discuss his reawakening with journalists. But in the closing weeks of his presidential campaign, he referred to the experience briefly in an interview with Beliefnet, an Internet magazine devoted to religion and spirituality, when asked how his faith affected his notion of compassionate conservatism. "A lot," Bush said: "A genuine philosophy reflects the experience of a person. And in my case I was raised a Christian, recommitted myself to Christ, got into the Bible. My life changed in many ways. An outward manifestation is I quit drinking. I was a more dedicated, focused person. Not to say I wasn't dedicated beforehand, but it was a life changing moment."

Bush soon made other changes in his life. He sold off his oil business and went to Washington to take up a post as an adviser to his father's 1988 successful presidential campaign. One of his chores, which turned out to pay long-range rewards, was working under the supervision of Doug Wead as a liaison between his father and emissaries from the Christian Right, activists who would ultimately become Bush's own allies in future political wars. "He came in and said, 'We're gonna take this thing over,'" recalled Wead. "And it was such a relief. Because I could see right away with this guy I wasn't going to have to write a 20-page memo explaining what 'born again' means." Bush met with evangelical leaders around the country and impressed Wead by his ability to answer their theologically coded questions. "He could see them coming from a mile away," recalled Wead. "'I know what it means to be right with God,' he would say."

After the elder Bush won the White House in 1988, the legacy paid off again for George W. Returning to Texas, and cloaked with the prestige of his father the president, Bush assembled a group of investors who bought the Texas Rangers. His selection as managing partner seemed inevitable and he immediately launched a successful campaign to get public backing for building a new stadium, funded by a local bond issue, in Arlington, the home of the baseball team. Not all Bush's decisions as a baseball executive worked out well. He has had a hard time trying to laugh off his decision to trade the slugger Sammy Sosa to the Chicago Cubs where Sosa made baseball history by hitting more than 60 home runs for two successive seasons.

But if the Sosa deal was a mistake, Bush did not pay for it financially. When the team was sold in 1994 his original $600,000 investment repaid $15 million. More important, the experience acquired at the helm of the Rangers helped Bush to deal with the downside of the legacy, the slur that Hance had tarred him with during the campaign. As Bush told *Time* magazine, the biggest liability to his running for office in Texas was that people would think he was simply trading on his father's name. "Now I can say, 'I've done something—here it is.'"

In 1993, after his father lost the presidency to Bill Clinton, Bush announced his candidacy for the governorship of Texas. His opponent, the Democrat incumbent Ann Richards, was known for her aggressive style and sharp tongue. She had entertained the 1988 Democratic Convention by claiming that Bush's father had been "born with a silver foot in his mouth," and she referred to his son derisively as "shrub" and "junior." It was the same tactic that Kent Hance had used against Bush, putting him on the wrong side of the cultural conflict between the elitists and the middle class.

But Bush did not rise to the bait. Instead, he made a point of treating his opponent respectfully. He referred to her only as "Governor Richards," behavior that was consistent with middle-class standards as to how a gentleman should treat a lady, even if the lady was trying to cut the gentleman's political throat.

More than that, mindful of the criticisms leveled at his father for seeming out of touch with everyday life, and made wiser by the lesson in cultural politics that he had learned from Hance, the younger Bush made a point of being casual and approachable. And he tried to demonstrate how politics affected ordinary people. He concentrated on four issues: welfare reform—limiting benefits to two years and requiring job training; juvenile crime—requiring adult prison for violent offenders as young as fourteen; legal reform—limiting damages from lawsuits; and education reform—upgrading local school systems. His agenda could be considered his own Texas version of the Contract with America that Republican congressional candidates ran on nationwide, except that Bush's program was shorter, more relevant to the lives of the voters he was trying to reach, and far better advertised in Texas than the contract was nationally. In November 1994, a banner year for Republicans, the same electoral tide that carried Newt Gingrich and his zealous cohorts to power on Capitol Hill helped Bush defeat Richards and win a four-year term as governor.

Once in office he gained approval for most of his campaign platform. To fight crime, he also signed a law that permitted Texans to get a permit to carry concealed weapons. The crime crackdown and welfare reform established his bona fides as a conservative. His claim to compassion was based mostly on his educational reforms. Bush called for an end to "social promotion," the term for moving children on to the next grade regardless of their academic success or failure. "You either believe that people can learn or not," he declared. "And I refuse in my state to condemn anybody to failure." He also sought to reach out to Hispanic Americans. Unlike other Republicans, he opposed cutting off aid to legal immigrants. And he kept an open mind on the idea of schools offering some courses in both English and Spanish, an approach rejected by many others in his party, saying, "My deal on bilingual education is that if it works, if it teaches children, we ought to support the program."

As his first term drew to an end, Bush was so popular that Democrats had a hard time finding a candidate to oppose him. They finally drafted the state land commissioner, Gary Mauro, who started out light years behind Bush and never caught up. Bush would sweep to victory in November 1998 with nearly 70 percent of the overall vote and almost half the Hispanic vote, the first Texas governor to win two consecutive four-year terms. The stage was set for his presidential candidacy.

Nearly a full year passed between the day I followed Bush on the campaign trail in South Texas and the day he launched his bid for the White House in the summer of 1999. But nothing had happened in those intervening months to alter his compassionate conservative theme. Standing in an open-air exhibition hall, with the rolling green farmland of Eastern Iowa as a backdrop, the governor promised as president to give a greater role to faith-based organizations—churches, synagogues, mosques, and charities—to help address the nation's social problems. "I will lift the regulations that hamper them," he vowed. "I will involve them in after-school programs, maternity group homes, drug treatment programs and prison fellowship programs. Supporting these men and women—the soldiers in the army of compassion—is the next bold step of welfare reform."

And in New Hampshire he reiterated the other part of the cultural mantra. "My first goal is to usher in the responsibility era, an era that stands in stark contrast to the last few decades where our culture has said that if it feels good, do it; and if you've got a problem, just go ahead and blame somebody else. Each American must understand that we are responsible for the decisions that each of us makes in life."

A few weeks later, in what his aides described as his first major policy speech, Bush spelled out the explicit undergirding for his themes of compassion and responsibility. The setting was well planned for his purposes—an Indianapolis church with an enthusiastic, interracial audience. Its members cheered Bush's talk of funneling billions through religious charities to help the needy, along with creating tax incentives and grants to give neighborhood groups a central role in tackling problems from day care to drug addiction.

But at least as significant as the proposals was the rhetoric he used to dispel the image some voters hold of the Republican Party as cold and mean-spirited. "In this campaign, I bring a message to my own party," he declared. "We must apply our conservative and free-market ideas to the job of helping real human beings, because any ideology, no matter how right in theory, is sterile without that goal." It was not enough, Bush said, for politicians to merely advocate tax cuts without proposing solutions for social problems. Nor was it enough just to promote values. Rejecting one of the pillars of conservative belief, Bush said that government had a clear role to play in dealing with society's problems, and that role was to promote community solutions. Bush pointedly separated himself from President Reagan's famous declaration that "government is the problem," as well as the rallying cry of congressional GOP conservatives that Washington "bureaucrats" should simply "leave us alone." "The American government is not the enemy of the American people," Bush insisted. "At times it is wasteful and grasping. But we must correct it, not disdain it."

In all, the speech made clear that Bush, very much like Bill Clinton in 1992, was hoping to change his party's image with a message that blended its traditional goals with ideas usually associated with the other side of the political spectrum. That approach had worked for Bush back in Texas, where his talk of compassion had gone over well with Democrats who were quick to hail Bush as a moderate. But it needs to be remembered that the Democratic Party in Texas had never recovered from the years when Texas, like most of the rest of the South, was a one-party state. In those days Democrats smothered genuine disagreement and conservatives made themselves at home within the party. With a few exceptions, such as Ann Richards, whom Bush had ousted from the governorship, that attitude still prevailed in the Democratic Party of Texas. Many of the party's leaders were glad to regard Republican governors like Bush as allies and collaborators if they offered the slightest encouragement by way of conciliatory gestures.

But the best clue as to what Bush believed and where he was really heading came from paying attention to what conservatives were telling other conservatives. "More conservative than his father, George W. has a proven record of conservative accomplishment that the media have largely ignored," Ralph Reed, former executive director of the Christian Coalition, wrote in the *National Review* of July 1998 as Bush was campaigning for reelection. "A Bush victory in November 2000 would be a conservative triumph, not a moderate one."

It was Reed, a close adviser to Bush, who explained to me around that time how Bush planned to fuse the themes of compassionate conservatism and the responsibility era into a powerful generational appeal. It was an appeal that played off the reaction to Bill Clinton, which had been dramatized by Clinton's condemnation by four-fifths of the Senate at the climax of his impeachment. If Clinton was the Antichrist, as many conservatives had come to believe, then Bush was to be presented as the anti-Clinton.

"He is a baby boomer who basically believes his father's generation saved the nation from fascism and communism and his own generation kind of mucked it up," Reed said. "That through a philosophy of 'if it feels good, do it,' we sort of lost our moorings as a culture." Just as Clinton believed that his own life story, his rise from a broken home and meager circumstances to power and prominence, epitomized the American Dream, Bush believed that his personal saga was an individualized template for the whole boomer generation experience.

Bush had had some wild days and was a little rebellious and eventually came to adulthood and married and had a family. And he came to realize, as Reed explained it, that he was an adult and could make a contribution to efforts to restore traditional values to their pre-Sixties standing. "That theme overlays very nicely with religious conservatives," Reed said. "But it is distinct and different because it flows as much or more from generational aspirations than religious and spiritual beliefs. Not that he isn't a man of faith because he is," Reed added. "But there are generational aspirations which are connected with all this, there is a sense that Clinton was the first member of the generation to be president. Many members of his generation are embarrassed." And now George W. Bush could help them feel better about themselves, their country, and their culture.

And so this is how George W. Bush was offering himself to the electorate, and this was the real meaning of compassionate conservatism as he saw it: He was more than just a moderate Republican, he was the redeemer of his generation. And to underline that point and highlight the contrast between himself and the first member of that generation to gain the presidency, everywhere he went Bush repeated what he had said on his very first campaign foray into New Hampshire: "I think it's important for any of us who assume high office to understand that when we put our hand on the Bible, that we're swearing not only to uphold the laws of the land, but that we are swearing to uphold the dignity of the office to which we've been elected." And then, while the cameras clicked away, he would add: "It is a pledge I made to the voters of Texas and a pledge that I have upheld, so help me God."

Still, Bush's strategy presented complications. In a way it was like walking a tightrope: He had to shed the extremist image that had hurt Republicans in the past while paying his dues to the Christian conservatives, who formed a significant part of the GOP's base and of the party's primary electorate. This balancing act was particularly difficult in Iowa, where Christian conservatives were a potent force, but success was all the more important there because the state's precinct caucuses marked the official beginning of the delegate selection competition for 2000. What eased the pressure on Bush was that he faced three rivals—magazine magnate Steve Forbes, talk show host Alan Keyes, and conservative activist Gary Bauer—who were eager to demonstrate their loyalty to the Christian Right. As the campaign heated up in Iowa, Gary Bauer conducted a memorial service at a Des Moines cemetery for "the one and one-half million babies that don't get a name." Forbes, after seeming indifferent to the social and moral issues in his 1996 campaign, had transformed himself into an avatar of Christian principles and stumped with antiabortion stalwart Phyllis Schlafly, singing the praises of an antiabortion Supreme Court.

But no one could top Alan Keyes. He had made the antiabortion cause the cornerstone of his campaign in 1996, and he escalated the same emotional appeal in 2000 in a way that stirred more emotion among the faithful than had anyone since Pat Robertson. Visiting a fifth-grade class one day, he asked the youngsters, "If I were to lose my mind right now and pick one of you up and bash your head against the floor and kill you, would that be right?" When the students said no, Keyes said abortion was no different.

Outwardly all this brouhaha might seem like it would have created a problem for Bush by making the competition greater for pro-life votes. But if one takes a more practical view, as the Bush strategists did, it makes sense that the number of ardently antiabortion contenders worked to Bush's advantage. By dividing the pro-life voters among them, they kept this group from rallying behind any one candidate who might pose a threat to Bush. In vain did his rivals taunt Bush at every turn by branding him, as Forbes described it, a "pro-life pacifist."

Indeed, no one seemed more indignant about Bush's unwillingness to go all out against abortion than Forbes, for reasons that were not hard to understand. In 1996, Forbes had said that he would support a constitutional prohibition against abortion—but that it made no sense to push for one until the country was willing to accept it. That view was too wishy-washy to suit pro-life forces. So in his 2000 candidacy Forbes made a point of aggressively supporting the bid to put an immediate end to partial-birth abortions and strengthened his commitment to introducing a constitutional amendment banning all abortions. In doing all this to win over the social conservatives, Forbes risked damaging his appeal to economic conservatives who held more moderate views on abortion. Having run this risk and endangering his candidacy, it naturally angered Forbes to see Bush trying to get away with a less than wholehearted commitment to the antiabortion cause. "I have taken the pledge in selecting a pro-life running mate," he complained as he stumped through Iowa, pointing out that Bush had backed away from any such commitment. "I've pledged to appoint only pro-life judges. He has not done so. I think this underscores that it's not enough just to say one is pro-life."

But the fact was, to Forbes's great frustration, Bush seemed to be operating on that principle and getting away with it. In the main Bush chose to burnish his credentials on issues of importance to social conservatives in other ways. He praised religious charities ministering to the down-and-out and talked about parenthood as his most important job. Now and then he would drop in a reassuring word for the more extreme factions of the cultural conservative crowd. Asked about *Roe v. Wade,* he said simply, "It overstepped the constitutional bounds, as far as I'm concerned."

For the most part his talk on abortion was dominated by generalities. "We ought to have the goal that every single child—born or unborn—should be protected in law and welcomed into life," he told Iowans. "We ought to have a culture that respects life in America—not only the life of the unborn and the life of the soon-to-be-born—but the life of the elderly and the life of the people living in tough situations. Life is valuable."

Rather than get into the hard-edged specifics that cultural conservatives doted on, but that also turned off moderates, Bush chose to appeal to the Christian Right with statements of his religious faith in a way that sometimes seemed jarring, at least to nonevangelicals. Thus when he and other candidates were asked during a campaign debate to name their favorite philosopher-thinker, Bush replied: "Christ, because he changed my heart."

The TV anchor who had asked the question wasn't satisfied. "I think the viewers would like to know more on how he's changed your heart," he prodded. But Bush resumed his customary taciturnity about his religion. "Well, if they don't know, it's going to be hard to explain," he replied. "When you turn your heart and your life over to Christ, when you accept Christ as the savior, it changes your heart. It changes your life. And that's what happened to me."

Gary Bauer, who followed Bush in the order of questioning, also offered Christ as his favorite philosopher, but Bauer, probably the most thoughtful and articulate of all the Republican seekers after the presidency that year, expanded on the notion by quoting Scripture. "I was hungry, and you fed me. I was thirsty and you gave me drink. I was a stranger and you welcomed me," Bauer said. "Christ, with those words, told all of us about our obligations to each other." But for all his own eloquence, Bauer realized that Bush had stolen a march on him. "He thought he was trumped," Bauer's senior policy adviser, Jeff Bell, said. "And others felt the same way."

Indeed, Alan Keyes, who must have felt that by his references to the Son of God Bush was trampling on Keyes's own turf, struck out at Bush, accusing him of misunderstanding Jesus. "I found it kind of shocking, and I think a lot of people did because G. W. Bush thinks that Jesus Christ was a philosopher, and this is not possible," said Keyes. "Philosophers are people who seek the truth. Jesus is the truth, and there is a vast difference."

But for all the carping, Bush had accomplished his purpose, which was to advertise his devotion to religion. And despite the criticism, Bush's discussion of Jesus had helped to advance his broad strategy. For a candidate like Bush, trying to maintain a centrist stance, his frequent avowals of faith, a Bush adviser explained to the *New York Times,* were "almost like a surrogate for the more hard-edged moral agenda of the party." In other words, the *Times* was given to understand that Bush was in effect telling the Christian conservatives, "I can't say everything you want me to say, or propose everything you want me to propose, but I want you to know that in my heart or in my soul, I'm where you are personally. And what I can accomplish, I will accomplish, and you can trust that."

Whatever the flaws in this approach, it had, as it turned out, one great virtue—it worked. It allowed Bush to win Iowa ahead of Forbes, who divided up the Christian conservative vote with Keyes and Bauer. And when Forbes and Bauer dropped out of the race after New Hampshire, the Christian conservatives joined ranks behind Bush and helped him recover from his drubbing in New Hampshire at the hands of John McCain.

In the end Bush would coast to the nomination as the candidate of the Christian Right. Even if he was not their first choice, he was the last one because he was all that stood between the nomination and John McCain. McCain's emergence as the enemy of the Christian Right stemmed in part from tactics and circumstance but also from a collision of beliefs and style.

Not that McCain did not have much to commend him to the Christian Right. The son and grandson of admirals, a bona fide war hero from his long imprisonment by the North Vietnamese, his Senate record showed him to be staunchly antiabortion and anti–gun control. The liberal Americans for Democratic Action had given his overall voting record in 1999 a minuscule 5 percent ranking.

But from the beginning of his candidacy, McCain, like Bill Bradley on the Democratic side, seemed reluctant to join in with the effusive professions of faith exhibited by his rivals and apparently preferred by the leaders of the Christian Right. His faith, McCain declared, was "something that's between me and my family." And in his best-selling memoir, *Faith of My Fathers,* he avoided using his five and a half years' imprisonment during the Vietnam War as an occasion for a sectarian sermon. Instead, he emphasized the broader beliefs that had inspired his forebears.

On more practical grounds, the Christian Coalition and other conservative groups viewed McCain's campaign finance reform proposal as a threat to their political influence in the GOP. The problem was that it would limit what they could spend on advertising to promote their favorite causes. The Christian Coalition would lose much of its clout under McCain's reform proposal, and Pat Robertson, who had founded the organization, felt that McCain's support of such a bill made him unfit to be president. "It would absolutely gut organizations like the Christian Coalition," he said. "He will not talk to our lawyers. He will not listen to reason."

McCain soared to prominence in New Hampshire following a strategy of his own that owed little to the Christian Right or any of its causes. A long shot, with little support among party leaders, and having no real base in the GOP, McCain sought to create favorable coverage in the media by stressing his commitment to campaign reform and by making himself infinitely accessible and supremely candid. To emphasize this openness, McCain cruised the highways of the Granite State in his van, which he dubbed "The Straight Talk Express." He romanced the members of the press mainly by answering their questions bluntly and without great regard for the sensitivities of others, particularly Christian conservatives.

It was one such session that led to McCain's first brush with the Christian Right. The imbroglio began when a reporter on board McCain's Straight Talk Express asked him whether, if his fifteen-year-old daughter, Meghan, faced an unwanted pregnancy, he would refuse to allow her to get an abortion. On the day before this question was asked McCain had said he would support changing the GOP platform, which favored an absolute ban on abortions, to allow for exceptions in cases of rape, incest, or to protect the health of the mother. That position happened to be one that he held in common with George W. Bush. In answering the reporter's question about his daughter, McCain was careful and deliberate. He said he would talk to his wife, Cindy, and his daughter and that both he and his wife would make clear to Meghan that her baby would be brought up "in a warm and loving family." But, he added: "The final decision would be made by Meghan with our advice and counsel."

But no sooner had the Straight Talk Express pulled to its next stop than alarm bells began to go off in the McCain high command. The senator quickly had the word passed to the press contingent that he had modified his position. "What I believed I was saying and intended to say is that this is a family decision," McCain said. "The family decision would be made by the family, not by Meghan alone. And other than that I believe that it is a private family matter." And that, or so McCain fervently hoped, was the end of that.

Of course it was not. That very night, at one of the seemingly countless debates that filled the presidential primary schedule, Alan Keyes, seeking to capitalize on his own record as a fervent abortion foe, charged that even making such a decision a family matter "displayed a profound lack of understanding" on McCain's part of the primacy of a fetus's life. McCain at first tried to brush off Keyes by referring to his own consistent record of antiabortion votes in Congress. But like a dog with a bone, Keyes would not give up until finally McCain cut him off: "I will not draw my children into this discussion," he said.

Keyes was unrelenting. He did not think he could support John McCain if he were the GOP nominee because of what McCain had said about his daughter's abortion. "It is the classic pro-choice position," Keyes said. "If that in fact reflects John McCain's heart, he's not pro-life. He's pro-choice."

In moderate New Hampshire, the flap over abortion did little to damage McCain's candidacy. He shook up the political world by trouncing Bush by 19 points. But when the GOP presidential competition moved on to its next stop, South Carolina, which Bush had counted on as a firewall to protect his candidacy, the Christian Right got its revenge on McCain for his defiance of their interests on campaign finance.

In a sense the battle against McCain served to rejuvenate the Christian Right and the New Right generally, which had fallen into a slump after the impeachment battle had ended in their apparent defeat. The Christian Coalition, the cutting edge of social conservatism in political battles, was beset by a substantial debt and weakened by the departure of Ralph Reed from its helm.

More broadly, social conservatives seemed to suffering from a crisis of confidence signaled by a letter written by one of their most militant leaders, Paul Weyrich, to his supporters in February 1999. In the letter, Weyrich questioned the basic premises of the New Right. "Let me be perfectly frank about it," Weyrich wrote. "If there really were a moral majority out there, Bill Clinton would have been driven out of office months ago." He continued:

> I believe we probably have lost the Culture War. That doesn't mean the war is not going to continue, and that it isn't going to be fought on other fronts. But in terms of society in general we have lost. That is why, even when we win in politics, our victories fail to translate into the kind of policies we believe are important.

What Weyrich suggested, in view of this sobering development, was dropping out of the Culture War. "We need to take another tack, find a different strategy," he wrote.

But Weyrich was not surrendering, only rethinking. And that reappraisal did not last for long. Once the call of battle sounded for the 2000 campaign, it was hard for Weyrich and other veterans of past skirmishes to ignore the trumpet. Weyrich himself gave his enthusiastic backing to Steve Forbes. "He issued press releases, did media interviews and was a surrogate for us at two of the debates," Greg Mueller, Forbes's press secretary, later told me. And others in the movement also took one side or another. It was true that no one candidate had inspired them as Reagan once had. But by the time the South Carolina primary loomed, with Bauer and Forbes out of the race and the choice between Bush and McCain, most religious conservatives had no difficulty deciding which side to take.

Bush set the tone for the struggle in the Palmetto State with a speech at that twenty-first-century stronghold of old-fashioned fundamentalism, Bob Jones University, notorious for its support of segregation and for sheltering bigotry. "I am the Right. I am the conservative candidate," he declared when he arrived behind the black iron gates circling the 200-acre campus. In one 32-second segment of his speech, Bush said the word "conservative" six times.

Even before Bush arrived the National Right to Life organization had begun running radio ads pointing to McCain's support in the Senate for fetal tissue research as evidence of his apostasy on abortion. The group also sent out a mass mailing that said McCain "voted repeatedly to use tax dollars for experiments that use body parts from aborted babies." Another mailer, featuring a photograph of a baby, said: "This little guy wants you to vote for George Bush."

McCain and his supporters fought back as best they could, sounding their own spiritual organ notes. "God has placed John McCain here for a reason, in the right spot at the right time," Representative Lindsey Graham of South Carolina, McCain's chairman in the state, declared. "We have in our midst a man who can heal the wounds of the nation. Really, he shouldn't be alive," Graham said, recounting the grievous injuries McCain had suffered when his plane was shot down over Hanoi and his North Vietnamese captors tortured him. "John McCain was supposed to die, but he didn't." And then, turning to the somewhat embarrassed senator, Graham said, "You're here because God wants you to be here. And God has given us in South Carolina the opportunity to raise you to the needs of the nation."

But the words of praise from McCain's supporters were drowned out by the din of Bush's radio ads and the thunderous condemnation from no one less than the Reverend Pat Robertson. "If McCain wins the nomination, it will destroy the Republican Party," he declared. "The Christian Coalition would not put out 75 million voter guides, would not urge its membership to vote for anybody in the general election. I'm not going to go raise great sums of money to get somebody elected when I don't feel good about him. And I think others are the same way."

South Carolina turned into a debacle for McCain, with Christian conservatives voting against him by two to one. But even before those returns rolled in, McCain's campaign had launched a massive telephone campaign in the next critical primary battleground, Michigan. His workers were pointing out to Catholic voters there that in visiting Bob Jones University, Bush had "stayed silent" about "anti-Catholic bigotry" while "seeking the support of Southern fundamentalists." Despite the criticism from McCain and others, Bush at first refused to admit to any error about his visit to Bob Jones, not while the critical South Carolina battle raged. But soon after those votes were cast, with the campaign shifting to locales in northern states with big Catholic populations, Bush made public a letter of apology to John Cardinal O'Connor of New York. In it, he expressed his "profound respect for the Catholic Church" and, for the first time, apologized for his appearance at Bob Jones University in South Carolina. "On reflection, I should have been more clear in disassociating myself from anti-Catholic statements and racial prejudice," Bush wrote.

But if Bush thought that his apology would bring a truce in the Culture War, he was mistaken. On the same day that his letter to the cardinal was released, McCain took the offensive. He lashed out not only at Bush but at his two most prominent allies among Christian conservatives—Pat Robertson and Jerry Falwell. Bush he dismissed as a "Pat Robertson Republican who will lose to Al Gore." And then he let Robertson and Falwell have it in no uncertain terms. "Neither party should be defined by pandering to the outer reaches of American politics and the agents of intolerance," McCain said, "whether they be Louis Farrakhan or Al Sharpton on the left or Pat Robertson and Jerry Falwell on the right." McCain added: "We are the party of Ronald Reagan, not Pat Robertson. We are the party of Theodore Roosevelt, not special interest. We are the party of Abraham Lincoln, not Bob Jones."

To underscore his defiance McCain chose to deliver his speech in Virginia Beach, site of the nerve center of Robertson's broadcasting empire—and on the eve of the Virginia primary. His apostasy brought swift condemnation from his adversary. "It sounds like Sen. McCain has taken to name calling, needless name calling," Bush said. "Ronald Reagan didn't point fingers. He never played to people's religious fears like Senator McCain has shamelessly done." And a Bush adviser was even harsher. "This is more than just a throw of the dice," he told the *Los Angeles Times*. "This is a little bit of a burning down of the Republican Party on the way out."

McCain advisers said the speech marked a new stage for his insurgent candidacy—one that could cast a huge shadow over the remaining weeks of the campaign. "It's the defining speech of the campaign. It's a defining moment for the party," said John Weaver, McCain's campaign director. Indeed it was nothing less than an attempt to redefine the party, in McCain's terms. With that speech McCain essentially wrote off the remaining southern primaries. His hope was that by taking such a strong stand against Robertson—an enormously polarizing figure—he could attract voters elsewhere who were socially moderate or who simply preferred that the GOP focus on economic issues. "Bush has already carved out turf as the Confederate candidate," one McCain strategist explained. "He's the candidate of the Deep South, and in staking out that turf he's effectively ceding the rest of the country. This speech puts up a fence around him."

But as it turned out it was McCain who had fenced himself off. In their desperation, McCain and his aides had seized upon the hope that the anticipated wrath of the Christian conservatives would be visited upon them only in the South, a region where they knew their chances were doomed. They were right about one part of their analysis: McCain was overwhelmingly defeated in Virginia, the day after his Virginia Beach speech, and in the southern primaries that followed a week later on Super Tuesday. But as the returns on Super Tuesday also demonstrated, religious conservatives exerted a powerful influence in GOP primaries throughout the country, not just the Deep South. More than a quarter of GOP presidential primary voters in 1996 classified themselves as members of the religious Right in such states as Illinois, Ohio, Florida, Colorado, Oregon, Washington, and California. In the thirteen delegate contests of March 7 McCain won four New England states but Bush won everything else, including New York and California.

The exit poll in New York said all that needed to be said about McCain's desperate bid. In the Empire State, far from Bob Jones University, cultural politics still wielded a terrible swift sword. Asked to name the most important issue, Republican voters put moral values first. And among the moralists, Bush, the errant post-adolescent, beat war hero McCain by a three-to-two vote. Two days later McCain suspended his candidacy. George W. Bush had the nomination in his grasp.

What McCain's losing battle demonstrated was that the religious Right had become part of the Republican establishment. That had not been true in 1988, when Robertson ran for president and the party establishment held solid for Vice President George Bush. Since 1988, however, the religious Right had joined forces with the GOP hierarchy. In 1992 and 1996, religious Right leaders had resisted the appeals of Patrick J. Buchanan and succeeded in holding their voters in line for, respectively, President Bush and Bob Dole. In 2000 the religious Right made common cause with the GOP establishment against a different kind of threat: McCain. When McCain attacked the leaders of the Christian Right and called Robertson and Falwell "agents of intolerance" comparable to Louis Farrakhan and Al Sharpton on the Left, he cast himself not as someone trying to save the conservative cause from corrupt and self-interested leaders but rather as someone trying to discredit the conservative cause.

In losing, McCain did Bush and his party a great service, certainly without intending to. He forced Bush and the religious Right into each other's arms. Some thought that alliance would weaken Bush's chances in the general election by stigmatizing him as the candidate of the Christian Right. Instead it liberated him from the burden of having to placate the Christian Right. He was free to run from the center—as the prince of compassion—and then to govern from the Right. He still had one more adversary to face, Democratic standard-bearer Al Gore. But it would turn out that just as McCain's strategy ultimately benefited Bush, so did Gore's battle plan play out to Bush's advantage.

14

THE FAITH THAT FAILED

What made the immersion of George W. Bush's candidacy in religion even more striking was the fact that his Democratic counterpart, Al Gore, in launching his own drive for the White House, also seemed to have chosen the Lord above as his running mate. Both politicians were impelled by similar motivations, though the pressures on Gore were greater because of his link to President Clinton.

Like Bush, Gore had to face questions about his past conduct likely to cause misgivings among voters concerned with traditional cultural values. Not that Gore had ever used alcohol to excess, as Bush admittedly had done, or snorted cocaine, as Bush was suspected to have done. But he had played fast and loose with the federal campaign finance laws. Heavily involved in the fund-raising excesses of Clinton's 1996 reelection campaign, he had to defend himself for attending a political gathering at a Buddhist temple in Los Angeles where money was raised, then for making dozens of fund-raising phone calls from his White House office—barely skirting a federal law that banned activity of that sort.

Gore said he did not know the meeting in the temple was a fundraiser. As for the phone calls, Gore contended in a disastrous press conference that there was "no controlling legal authority" prohibiting the phone calls, repeating that legalistic phrase so often that he made himself a laughingstock. The vice president got a huge break when the Justice Department decided the charges against him did not merit investigation by an independent counsel, a probe that well might have wrecked his presidential ambitions. Afterward, Gore avoided defending or explaining his conduct, relying on his advocacy of campaign finance reform to help erase the stain on his integrity.

Gore had other problems, too, stemming from his tendency to improve on the truth to his own advantage. It was a typical failing for politicians but it took on extra cultural resonance because of the misgivings about President Clinton's integrity, leading to disproportionate attention from the media. Thus when Gore announced that he "took the initiative in inventing the Internet," he opened himself to derision from reporters who pointed out that when the Internet was launched in 1969, Gore was just graduating from Harvard.

It mattered not that, as even Newt Gingrich acknowledged, Gore had genuinely played a role in popularizing the Internet while he was in Congress. Such facts were drowned out by stories reminding the public that earlier Gore had claimed that he and his wife, Tipper, had been the models for the ill-starred couple in the celebrated tear-jerker novel *Love Story;* he was, in part, according to author Erich Segal, though Tipper was not. But it was not only his own past that posed a cultural problem for Gore; it was also the besmirched record of the president whom he had loyally served for more than six years and enthusiastically supported during his hour of supreme travail, the Lewinsky affair. Clinton, Gore had said on the day of his impeachment, would "go down in history as one of our greatest presidents."

As the weeks passed following the end of the impeachment trial, Gore had increasing reason to regret that utterance and similar remarks. To be sure, with the economy roaring along in high gear, Clinton's job performance still got high grades. The trouble was, public disapproval of the president's behavior—of his cultural profile—instead of evaporating, seemed to intensify.

Even the military success achieved in the Kosovo war did nothing to help. Usually defeating a foreign bogeyman is a surefire prescription for boosting a leader's standing. When Saddam Hussein crumbled after Operation Desert Storm in 1991 George Bush's ratings soared into the stratosphere. And certainly Slobodan Milosevic fit the role of villainous tyrant as well as Saddam. But when in June 1999, after weeks of bombardment by NATO forces, the Serbian strongman finally agreed to withdraw his troops from Kosovo, polls showed that most Americans did not share in Clinton's exultation. Instead, the surveys indicated that Americans were no more convinced by Clinton's promises of peace in the Balkans in 1999 than they were by his denials of adultery in 1998. Moreover, public rating of his moral stature dipped to a record low. A *Wall Street Journal* survey at the time put Clinton at a disreputable 15 percent on a "good standards" scale, compared to 45 percent for his wife, Hillary Rodham Clinton; and 57 percent for Republican frontrunner George W. Bush.

Indeed, disapproval of the president on cultural grounds was so pervasive that pundits and pollsters had coined a new phrase to describe it: "Clinton fatigue." An early demonstration of this phenomenon was a Pew Research Center poll taken early in February 1999, hard on the heels of Clinton's impeachment acquittal by the Senate. Although a majority of Americans wanted the next president to offer policies and programs similar to Clinton's, the survey showed, by a four-to-one margin most wanted a president with different personal qualities.

More significant for the future, the weariness with Clinton seemed to be undermining Al Gore's prospects for the White House. Noting that his surveys found Gore trailing Bush by double figures, Pew poll director Andrew Kohut blamed "personal image problems and fallout from the Clinton Administration scandals." Also worrisome for Gore was the finding that three out of four Americans said they were "tired of all the problems associated with the Clinton administration," a reaction that seemed likely to influence their attitude toward Gore's candidacy in 2000.

Realizing that Clinton fatigue was a potentially fatal affliction, Gore set about separating himself from the sleazy side of the Clinton presidency as soon as he declared his candidacy. Indeed, he began this task the night before his June 16 announcement speech, when in chatting with reporters he bemoaned "that awful year we went through"—the year of Clinton's impeachment. "What was most upsetting about it," Gore told reporters, was "the wasted time. I'm even more anxious to move forward swiftly to make up for that waste of time," he went on. "We shouldn't have had to go through it." Next day, in a formal address in Carthage,

Tennessee, Gore pledged to "bring a new wave of fundamental change to this nation," change that would include, he made clear, a fresh moral start in the Oval Office. "If you entrust me with the presidency, I will marshal its authority, its resources, and its moral leadership to fight for America's family," Gore pledged, taking care to make that declaration with his own family, including his eighty-seven-year-old mother and his pregnant twenty-five-year-old daughter, creating a tableau behind him.

Detaching himself from Clinton was only one part of the vice president's efforts at cultural redemption. Even before he officially became a candidate he had begun moving to link religion to the politics of his candidacy, leading him to strike some of the same spiritual notes that his Republican rival George Bush was sounding. Gore made sure that no one missed his new emphasis on churchly values. He unveiled his strategy in an address in which he decried "the allergy to faith that is such a curious factor in much of modern society" and called for Washington to work more closely with religiously oriented charities in delivering social services to the needy. With a Salvation Army center in Atlanta as a setting, Gore proposed installing the solutions being pioneered by faith-based organizations at the center of the national social welfare strategy, just the sort of thing Bush had already explored in Texas and would soon propose as federal policy.

"National leaders have been trapped in a dead-end debate" on church-state questions, Gore said, faced with a false choice between "hollow secularism or right-wing religion." "If you elect me your president," he pledged, "the voices of faith-based organizations will be integral to the policies set forth in my administration."

The sources of Gore's own religious beliefs were eclectic, to say the least; as he himself put it: "I had a real smorgasbord of religious experiences." He considered himself a Southern Baptist, the church of his father, Senator Albert Gore, Sr. But when he and his family were back home in Carthage, Tennessee, they would alternate between his mother's Church of Christ and his father's Baptist church. During the school year, Gore would attend Sunday services at the Presbyterian Church around the corner from the Fairfax Hotel, where the Gores lived in Washington.

And at St. Albans prep school the daily chapel services he attended followed Episcopalian ritual. Though neither of Gore's parents were greatly taken with religious matters, Gore developed an interest on his own, even as a young man. His Harvard roommate remembered him reading the Bible and talking of the need for prayer to cultivate the soul.

After graduating from Harvard and serving in Vietnam, Gore went to Vanderbilt Divinity School where he spent three semesters, focusing on ethics. He also took a course called Theology and the Natural Sciences and eventually came to see environmentalism as a religious obligation to protect creation. That turned out to be one of the main themes of *Earth in the Balance,* his 1992 book about the environment, in which he argued that the spiritual link between man and nature is threatened by the economic pressures of Western civilization.

It was while he was attending Vanderbilt, when he was still in his twenties, that Gore became a born-again Christian, a fact he chose to reveal after he announced his candidacy. "It's very personal," he told a television interviewer, "and I don't want to be advertising all of the particulars and details but, yes, when I was a young man, I had an experience that would come under that heading, which was a very intense awareness of the presence and the meaning of Jesus and the message of God through Jesus." Inevitably, Gore's emphasis on religion and his attempts to separate himself from Clinton met with criticism and skepticism, all the more so since both tactics represented departures for him as a politician. Whatever his innermost feelings about God, he had not chosen to externalize these beliefs in the past, even when he had first run for president in 1988. Moreover, liberals, who had grown accustomed to Republicans invoking the Almighty, found it particularly jarring to hear spiritual themes from a leader of the Democrats, who were usually chary about injecting God into politics. "It almost cheapens faith and spirituality and beliefs," said Abraham Foxman, national director of the Anti-Defamation League of B'nai B'rith, of Gore's invoking of religious beliefs in political forums. "When you appear in church, it's fine—but not on the political stump."

And the vice president's pledge to use the "moral leadership" of his office "to fight for America's family" brought jeers from Republicans. "Al

Gore was totally silent" while the controversy about the White House sex scandal was at its height, contended the most recent Republican vice president, Dan Quayle, an early contender for the Republican presidential nomination. And Elizabeth Dole, also a candidate for the GOP nomination, asked pointedly: "Where was Al Gore when his partner, Bill Clinton, robbed the Oval Office of its moral authority?"

That was a question that mattered less to Democratic loyalists, who dominated their party's nominating process and generally viewed the impeachment effort as a partisan scheme, than it would matter to the general electorate. Indeed, the continuing criticism of Clinton by Republicans helped his vice president gain support from many Democrats who viewed Gore, not unreasonably, as a proxy target for Clinton's enemies.

In these circumstances, Gore had little difficulty defeating what turned out to be a feeble challenge from New Jersey Senator Bill Bradley. At first glance Bradley appeared to be just what the doctor might have prescribed for the Democrats to beat back the attacks of cultural traditionalists. Here was a man whose character was impeccable, whose integrity had never been questioned even by his rivals, a former Rhodes scholar and star pro basketball player who exuded idealism. Bradley was also known to have strong religious beliefs. But like McCain, and unlike Gore and Bush, he concluded that he would not advertise his faith as part of his presidential candidacy.

Bradley's restraint, however, did him little good on the stump. "My abilities match the national moment," Bradley was fond of telling voters in Iowa and New Hampshire. That claim was scarcely enough to inspire resistance to the juggernaut campaign of the incumbent vice president, and Bradley's candidacy, like McCain's, was buried under an avalanche of Super Tuesday votes.

But once Bradley was out of the way, Gore's real troubles began, a development that demonstrated the dramatic negative cultural fallout from the Clinton presidency. Gore found himself in serious difficulty, trailing Bush in the polls. This predicament seemed almost incredible given the salubrious national condition—the same circumstances that had helped Clinton weather the impeachment storm should by all past indications have favored Gore's election in his place.

To say that the economy was in good condition would be a gigantic understatement. While stock averages had been dropping during the year, this slippage merely represented a retreat from record levels which had brought paper wealth to millions. Every other single economic indicator of note—unemployment, inflation, productivity, gross domestic product, household income—was in a more favorable state than at any time in recent memory. Moreover, gauges of social conditions told a similar and not unrelated story. Among teens, the school dropout rate, the pregnancy rate, the suicide rate, and the use of alcohol was in decline; in the general population, the divorce rate was headed downward and violent crimes were at or near their lowest levels in twenty-five years.

Almost invariably, when times are good, and they could hardly have been better than they were in the spring and summer of the election year, political history shows that Americans do not turn an incumbent administration out of office. Only twelve years earlier, in the election that serves as the closest analog to the 2000 campaign, George Herbert Walker Bush had won the presidency not mainly on the basis of his own merits but because he happened to be Ronald Reagan's vice president during an era when the sun smiled on the American economy. Reagan, like other presidents during years of prosperity, was given much of the credit. In the baker's dozen of presidential elections fought out in the post–World War II era, only once has there been an exception to this good-times-helps-incumbents rule. And that was in 1968, when despite a booming economy and low unemployment, Hubert Humphrey, Lyndon Johnson's vice president, was toppled by Republican Richard Nixon. But there were big reasons for the break with tradition. The Vietnam War and the anguish it brought with it was the most evident cause. The tide of violence and crime that engulfed America's cities was another. And for that matter, the economic picture was not entirely problem-free because of increasing concern about the threat of inflation.

At any rate, it was clear that conditions in the year 2000 were a far cry from those that had prevailed in 1968. And yet, from the way the public was treating Al Gore in the polls, the nation might have been caught in the coils of some terrible tragedy. For instead of running far ahead, coasting toward a seemingly inevitable victory, Al Gore, vice president of an

administration that by all past precedents should have been the beneficiary of the good times it presided over, pitted against the presumptive Republican nominee, a man possessed of nondescript talents and limited experience, whose intellect seemed strained by the challenge of explaining
his own policy proposals, in the spring of the election year was actually
trailing George W. Bush.

Journalists were obviously puzzled by the poll standings, and some of
the explanations offered were notably vague. "While many Americans
find Vice President Al Gore's stands on issues more appealing," the *New
York Times* reported, "*he is not as well liked* or considered as commanding
a leader as Gov. George Bush" (emphasis added). But a story by the veteran *Washington Post* political writer Tom Edsall cut through this haze to
focus on the heart of Gore's problem, the cultural backlash. "White male
voters are rejecting Vice President Gore in numbers reminiscent of the
failed Democratic presidential campaigns of the 1980s, posing a serious
threat to his hopes of gaining the White House," Edsall wrote.

Not only was Gore losing, but he was losing the same way Democrats
had lost in the Eighties, that wasteland of a decade when their party lost
three presidential elections with candidates the likes of Carter, Mondale,
and Dukakis. White men had spearheaded the Republican surge in the
1980s, largely driven by cultural considerations. They were revolting
against the Democratic Party's seeming obeisance to pressure from various
interest groups, particularly blacks and feminists, but also organized gays,
whose cultural objectives white males viewed as at war with their own.
These white men were the most conspicuous cohort of the broader group
of white middle-class voters whom Clinton and his New Democrat allies,
including Gore, had spent the better part of a decade winning back.

But this endeavor was a never-ending struggle that ebbed and flowed
as issues came and went. For example, the April 1999 massacre at
Columbine High School in Littleton, Colorado, which claimed twenty-
five lives, had energized Democratic interest in gun control as an issue
with appeal to middle-class Americans. On Mother's Day, 2000, hundreds of thousands of mothers and family members massed in Washington and seventy other cities for what its sponsors called the Million Mom
March, making it the largest public demonstration for gun control in

U.S. history. "Politicians, take heed. We are watching you. The hands that rock the cradles rule the world," Dawn Anna, mother of Lauren Townsend, a student killed at Columbine High School, told the crowd.

But if the marching mothers viewed gun control as an antiviolence measure, many white males saw it as a threat to their way of life. As Tom Edsall put it in his *Post* story, for many white men guns were "as much a part of growing up as baseball and senior proms, a way to train children in mastering danger, and for adults a crucial means of protecting family and home." Tommy Hawk, who worked at a Ford assembly plant for thirty-one years and now owned a shooting range, told Edsall that his children "were raised with guns. To the best of my knowledge they never used one for anything outside of hunting. I raised two girls and a boy, and all of them have kids. I think that you teach a kid to use it, let him be on the range, let him feel the recoil, let him actually see what it'll do. Then you take the questions out of his mind as to what is going to happen."

But other polling data suggested Gore's problems were broader than any one particular issue, such as gun control or abortion, and related instead to the glaring contradiction between Clinton's personal conduct and the middle-class value system he had championed as a bulwark of New Democratic belief. During the pre-Lewinsky years of his presidency, Clinton had cut sharply into the traditional Republican advantage among married voters, almost wiping it out. But in the spring of 2000, a *Los Angeles Times* poll showed that gap had been reestablished. Married voters, who tended to be more conservative on cultural issues than single men or women, preferred Bush over Gore by a commanding 21-percentage-point margin. More disturbing for Gore and the Democrats, Bush was leading decisively not only with married men but also married women. Indeed his strength among married women was offsetting Gore's strong appeal to single women and allowing the Texan to run step-for-step with the vice president among women overall. This trend eliminated the solid Democratic gender gap advantage that had helped propel the party's ticket to the White House in the previous two elections.

How could this be happening to Al Gore, by all accounts a happily married and faithful husband, a devoted father and doting grandfather, and a conscientious advocate for families? The answer, operatives in both parties agreed, was mainly widespread anxiety among married women (especially mothers) about the nation's culture and morals—an anxiety exacerbated by disappointment with the example Clinton had set. "It's values and Clinton," one senior Gore adviser told the *Los Angeles Times* in explaining his candidate's poor showing. The past four years under Clinton have been "a black spot on our country," Valerie Gerheiser, of Crofton, Maryland, a stay-at-home parent of two teenagers, told the *Boston Globe* as she chaperoned several dozen middle-schoolers on a pre–Memorial Day field trip to George Washington's Mount Vernon home, "I'm sure there are some things George Bush and I disagree on. But no way will I vote for Al Gore, who stood there in Clinton's shadow, not if you paid me. It's time for a change."

As the campaign ground on, the polls gave no reason for Gore to believe that he had at last found a way to exploit the splendid national condition. Instead of his prospects improving, as August approached, bringing with it the Republican Convention, things seemed to get worse.

The Republicans naturally sought to milk their cultural advantage to the fullest. In his acceptance speech at the Republican Convention, Bush, along with adumbrating the canons of his compassionate conservatism credo, once again promised to usher in "a responsibility era"—adding with unmistakable emphasis—"and to lead this nation to a responsibility era, a president himself must be responsible." He mentioned "the vision" of America's founders: "Their highest hope as Robert Frost described it," Bush said, was to "occupy the land with character. And that, 13 generations later, is still our goal: to occupy the land with character."

Veteran *New York Times* correspondent R. W. Apple, in commenting on the speech, noted, "Few if any of the thousands who filled the First Union Center here and few of those watching on television can have missed the allusion to Mr. Clinton's sexual involvement with an intern, which led to his impeachment."

Gore now was persuaded that his candidacy was in danger of being vaporized by the middle class's cultural backlash against Clinton. Facing a crisis, he sought a drastic solution. He found it in the junior senator from Connecticut, Joe Lieberman, and by choosing this little-known lawmaker as his running mate, redefined the course of his own candidacy.

Until the summer of 1998 there was not a great deal to distinguish Lieberman from other Washington politicians. His rise up the ladder had been neither particularly rapid nor dramatic. Born in Stamford, Connecticut, to Henry Lieberman, a liquor-store owner and realtor, and his wife, Marcia, he had been educated in the public schools of his hometown before going on to Yale University, where he earned a bachelor's degree in 1964 and a law degree in 1967. He got his first taste of politics as a Washington intern on Capitol Hill and then won a state senate seat in 1970. After ten years in the Connecticut legislature Lieberman tried for Congress and lost, but then two years later he won election as state attorney general. The reputation he earned as a defender of consumers and a guardian of the environment helped boost him into a U.S. Senate seat in 1988.

As a senator, Lieberman was known to the public, if he was known at all, for his moderate politics, conservative enough so that he often found himself allied with Republicans. In pursuit of his beliefs he had become chairman of the Democratic Leadership Council, the same centrist group Clinton had used as a platform for his run to the presidency.

Washington insiders who followed the Senate closely knew Lieberman to be the only orthodox Jew to serve in the Senate and a man who took his faith seriously. Strictly observing the Sabbath, in more than three decades of public life, Lieberman had shunned campaigning and purely political activities from sundown on Fridays to sundown on Saturdays but considered it his duty to attend legislative sessions, to vote, and to sit in on important public meetings. In 1988, he refused to attend the Democratic Convention that nominated him for the Senate because it met on a Saturday. But when the Senate itself met on Saturdays, Lieberman made it his business to get there, walking the five miles to and from his home in Georgetown to the Capitol, where he cast 75 votes during Sabbath sessions.

Unlike most other Jews in Congress, who have limited themselves to secular concerns, Lieberman had made his piety a major force in his public career. Joining with the GOP's William Bennett, he had lashed out at the entertainment industry for excessive depictions of violence and sexuality. Movies, television, and popular music, Lieberman warned, had "enormous power to shape our culture, to affect our lives, particularly our children's lives." In their struggle to arrest the coarsening of the American culture, Lieberman and Bennett embarrassed Time Warner into selling its Interscope label for gangsta rap records. Then they bestowed the "silver sewer" award on the record company's new owner, the Seagram Co., for failing to clean up the lyrics. They also dissuaded a number of advertisers from backing daytime TV shows they labeled as trash and helped to convince video game producers to establish a voluntary rating system.

All this was merely a prelude to the most significant act of Lieberman's political life—the speech he delivered in the Senate in August 1998 to denounce Clinton. The president had been a twenty-four-year-old volunteer in Lieberman's first campaign for the Connecticut State Senate, a favor Lieberman had returned in 1992 when he became the first senator outside the South to endorse Clinton for president. While few outside the Senate knew or cared about these details of Lieberman's resume, his ideological kinship with the president endowed his address in the Senate with great political significance.

This assault on Clinton came not from the ideological Left of the democracy, the onetime stronghold of party discontent and dissent, the forces that a generation earlier had brought down an incumbent Democratic chief executive, Lyndon Johnson, at the height of his power. Instead it was a leader of the Democratic Right who spoke out, a cultural conservative who not only had joined with Bennett in condemning obscenity but also was the sort of Democrat who could speak favorably of partly privatizing Social Security on the one hand while voicing misgivings about affirmative action on the other. And as such he represented the forces in the party who were most threatened by the contradiction between Clinton's behavior and the middle-class values he had advocated while leading the Democratic reconquest of the White House in 1992.

After delivering his address on the Senate floor, Lieberman made plain the depth of his feeling. He was angry, Lieberman explained, at Clinton's own weak apology offered when finally after months of denying the truth, he admitted to his affair with Lewinsky. "I was angry," he said, "because I felt the misconduct was so at variance with the values that he had championed, that we and a lot of others had worked together on in the New Democratic movement."

Lieberman's complaint had all the appearance of a *cri de coeur* but it also reflected an important element of calculation. As Rutgers political scientist Ross K. Baker, himself an old Senate hand, pointed out, far more was at stake in the Lewinsky scandal than the fate of a single president. "The scandal also had ominous implications for Clinton's party, particularly his New Democratic cultural comrades, like Lieberman and Gore," Baker wrote. "For the contagion from a diseased presidency quickly infects the ideas and philosophies that it has embraced." It was clear that no one understood that point better than Lieberman, an insight that particularly commended him to Gore.

Presidential candidates typically spend hours and sometimes days struggling over what they perceive as decisions critical to their ambitions, but in most cases once they decide they find the consequences hard to compute, or sometimes even to discern at all. The political world appears to go on as if nothing had been decided at all. But that was not the case with Al Gore's choice of Joe Lieberman. It reverberated with tremendous impact, getting more attention than any event of the presidential campaign since the emergence of John McCain as some new kind of national hero.

On Friday, August 4, a *USA Today*-Gallup poll had shown Gore trailing Bush by 19 points. On the following Monday, the day the choice of Lieberman was revealed to the world, pollsters found Bush's lead essentially erased—he now had a mere two-point advantage. And the media, which for months had devoted their energies to picking and carping at Gore's every move, now exploded with praise and commendation unlike anything Gore had received in all his years in national politics. Gore, the media concluded, deserved extra points for boldness—a trait not often associated with him in the past. He had seen what had to be done—sever his symbolic link to the Clinton scandals—and had gone ahead and done it, even at the risk of picking a Jew whose selection might bring down the curse of anti-Semitism upon his candidacy.

"Lieberman is a daring choice for Gore, in part because it is unclear how voters will react to having a Jew on the ticket," wrote Naftali Bendavid of the *Chicago Tribune*, voice of the nation's Heartland. And then, to underline the point, Bendavid wrote: "The boldest aspect of Gore's decision is that he has for the first time selected a non-Christian to sit one step from the presidency in an overwhelmingly Christian nation." Gore's aides were quick to compare the occasion to John F. Kennedy's battle to become the first Roman Catholic president. And in case anyone had missed the point, Bendavid quoted Lieberman himself as paying tribute to Gore's boldness: "Let us be very clear about this: It isn't me, Joe Lieberman, who deserves the credit and congratulations for taking a bold step," Lieberman modestly declared. "It is Al Gore who broke this barrier."

Amidst the accolades, left unanswered was the question raised by the *Chicago Tribune:* How would voters react to having a Jew on the ticket? Remarkably enough, one of the few politicians to even raise this issue in public was the national chairman of Lieberman's own party, Ed Rendell, who is also Jewish. Even before the choice was announced—when Lieberman was just one of several senators considered to be on Gore's short list—Rendell told reporters, "I don't think anyone can calculate the effect of having a Jew on the ticket. If Joe Lieberman were Episcopalian, it would be a slam dunk." That comment drew an immediate and infuriated response from some Jews, among them Nathan Diament, political director of the Union of Orthodox Jewish Congregations of America, who charged that Rendell by his comments was giving legitimacy to "whatever anti-Semitic views are out there."

Actually, that charge was probably unfair to Rendell, who had a tendency, unusual in a politician, for making gratuitous remarks that happened to be true. Rendell was right. No one could compute the impact of Lieberman's Jewishness on the ticket. But more important, what no one could predict was that as the campaign went on the issue of anti-Semitism would be obscured by other aspects of Lieberman's candidacy and their impact on Democratic prospects for better and for worse.

For the time being such calculations were set aside as the Democrats were swept away with something close to euphoria over Lieberman and the huge benefit their presidential candidate drew from his selection. Some of Gore's gains were undoubtedly due to the Democratic nominating convention, which traditionally gives presidential candidates a shot in the arm, especially since Gore had used it as an opportunity to once again declare his independence of Clinton. So sensitized was the public, not to mention the media, to Gore's determination to break away from the president that when he bestowed on his wife, Tipper, a particularly long and ardent kiss as he came to the podium, it was immediately seized upon as a gesture of cultural contrast with Clinton. Asked later by a television interviewer if he was trying to "send a message," Gore replied: "Actually, I was trying to send a message to Tipper."

Whatever Gore meant to convey by his embrace, there was no mistaking the intent of his words: "I stand here tonight as my own man," he told the cheering delegates, "and I want you to know who I truly am." In substantive terms, the speech represented something of a gamble that had been forced upon him by the painful cultural legacy of the Clinton presidency. Instead of resting on the laurels of the booming economy, which many believed was his greatest advantage in the election, Gore made clear he intended to extend the good times to those who had not thrived in the so-called new economy. "Let's make sure our prosperity enriches not just the few but all working families," he declared. To drive that point home, Gore infused his speech with a class-conscious rhetoric that portrayed him as the defender of "working families" against "powerful interests" such as "the big polluters," "the big drug companies," and "bean-counters at HMOs."

Gore's turn toward this populist appeal was all the more significant because of the decade-long argument among Democratic strategists over how to build a winning presidential coalition. Many of the centrist "New Democrats" around Clinton had favored concentrating on the upper middle class, with government playing the role of benign referee. But the more traditional Democrats wanted to aim at down-scale voters and promote a more vigorous role for government in curbing the excesses of free enterprise. Gore had adopted the latter approach.

The aggressive tone and content of Gore's acceptance speech established a pattern he followed through the general election campaign. They were very different from the moderate themes that had dominated Gore's utterances in the past, however, not only as vice president but also in his own campaign for president in 1988 and in his drive for the nomination itself. In weeks to come, and after his defeat, Gore would be resoundingly criticized by many in his party who claimed he should have stood firmly on the Clinton record. He would have been wise to tell the American people, or so the argument went, as another incumbent vice president, George Bush, had told them in 1988, how much better off they were than they had been eight years before, assuring them that the good times would roll on. But it would have been a tricky course for Gore to follow. By doing so he would have tied himself to his boss, the president, even more securely, thus undercutting his efforts to set himself apart from the immorality that concerned American voters.

The heart of Gore's dilemma was to find a way to benefit from the Clinton-era prosperity and still keep his distance from the Clinton presidency. But that was next to impossible to do. And he himself had made it particularly difficult by his choice of Lieberman, best known for his condemnation of Clinton on the Senate floor. So Gore ran as an agent of populist change, and just as important, as champion of traditional cultural values, rather than a defender of the Clinton status quo, because Clinton had left him no other choice. And ultimately this dilemma cost him the presidency.

Just as Clinton created one dilemma for Gore, Lieberman created another. By playing his role as a champion of middle-class cultural values and morality to the hilt, he would run the risk of offending the Democratic base. And so, once Lieberman became Gore's running mate, he lost no time in backing away from substantive positions he had held in the past that irritated hard-core Democrats, such as his resistance to affirmative action and his trumpeting of school vouchers. "I think this is an important idea," Lieberman had told me of his cosponsorship of legislation to authorize pilot school choice programs around the country. "I'm on a long march here."

As it turned out, Lieberman's long march came to a screeching halt with his vice presidential nomination. He backed as far away from supporting vouchers as he could, saying he viewed them as "a temporary lifeline" for poor children. His focus, he said, would be on improving the public school system. And the only mention of vouchers in the acceptance speeches at the Democratic Convention came not from Lieberman but from Gore, who denounced them in no uncertain terms.

There was another controversial position that Lieberman held from which he would not back away. It involved the role of faith in public life, which he viewed as of great importance, as he had made clear in his collection of essays called *In Praise of Public Life,* published only a few months before his nomination. Remarking on the surge of religious talk on the stump in the presidential campaign, Lieberman disagreed with the "cynics" who dismissed such talk as merely politically expedient. He saw deeper roots, "a sincere reflection of the need the American people have to rebuild around themselves what has come to feel like a crumbling moral framework in the life of our nation."

The Lewinsky scandal, the Littleton shootings, the entertainment industry's promotion of violence and vulgarity, Lieberman contended, all contributed to the growing anxiety that "the traditional sources of values in our society, such as faith, family and school—are in a life and death struggle with the darker forces of immorality, inhumanity and greed." Faced with such crises in the past, Lieberman wrote, without saying which crises he meant, "Americans had turned to God and to America's civil religion for strength and purpose." So it was only to be expected, and quite appropriate, that in the current crisis, "we are again turning to faith and experiencing what may be a spiritual awakening that can lead to social and political renewal."

No one who read those words should have been surprised that Lieberman would seize upon the bully pulpit of his vice presidential candidacy to do what he could to promote this new awakening. Indeed, no sooner had he hit the campaign trail after his nomination than his stump speeches, laced with effusions of religion, caused anxiety among leaders of the B'nai B'rith Anti-Defamation League, the recognized authority in the Jewish community not only on anti-Semitism but on questions of religion and society. They attributed those remarks, at first, as one said, to the "rush and the excitement" of his selection. But then, arriving in Detroit to address the congregation of Fellowship Chapel, one of the Motor

City's largest African-American churches, only a fortnight after his nomination, Lieberman, in the view of the ADL's elders, went over the top.

Declaring that belief in God is the basis of morality and of the nation, Lieberman, in unequivocal language, called for a greater role for religion in American public life. "As a people we need to reaffirm our faith and renew the dedication of our nation and ourselves to God and God's purpose," he said. Lieberman found ample precedent for his argument. "John Adams, second president of the United States, wrote that our Constitution was made only for a moral and religious people," he noted. "George Washington warned us never to indulge the supposition 'that morality can be maintained without religion.'"

Even amidst the widespread spiritualism of the 2000 campaign, Lieberman's remarks commanded attention. As the *New York Times* pointed out, "His words, if spoken by a conservative Christian, would probably be received with alarm by many factions in Mr. Lieberman's own party—including many Jews—who are wary of the political activism of the religious right." Indeed, Lieberman used phrases very like those often uttered by conservative Christians in his Detroit speech. He spoke of reaching out "to those who may neither believe nor observe and reassure them that we share with them the core values of America, that our faith is not inconsistent with their freedom, and that our mission is not one of intolerance but one of love." But he made no bones about arguing not merely that the presence of religion in politics should be tolerated but that it should be deemed a prime requisite for meaningful political debate.

His own nomination, he claimed, in addition to shattering the previous barriers against putting a Jew on the national ticket, would also eliminate obstacles to the infusion of faith in politics. "I hope it will enable people . . . to feel more free to talk about their faith and about their religion. And I hope that it will reinforce the belief that I feel as strongly as anything else, that there must be a place for faith in America's public life."

That was about all the Anti-Defamation League wanted to hear about that. If no one should have been surprised at Lieberman's revivalism then Lieberman himself should not have been surprised at the bitter criticism it provoked. On Monday, the day after Lieberman's address in Detroit, the ADL's top officials released a letter to Lieberman in which they argued that his regular infusions of biblical language and allusions to a heavenly creator were "inappropriate and even unsettling." "To even suggest that one cannot be a moral person without being a religious person is an affront to many highly ethical citizens," stated the letter, written to Lieberman by Abraham H. Foxman, the group's national director, and Howard P. Berkowitz, its national chairman. "The United States is made up of many different types of people from different backgrounds and different faiths, including individuals who do not believe in any God, and none of our citizens, including atheistic Americans, should be made to feel outside of the electoral or political process."

Joining in the ADL protest, although for somewhat different reasons, were evangelical Christians, smarting at the praise many had heaped upon Lieberman for expressions of faith which when uttered by believers in the New Testament stirred sharp criticism. "For people to applaud Sen. Lieberman for taking his Judaism seriously but then to diss Gov. Bush for saying in reply to a question that Jesus Christ was the philosopher who influenced him the most is a double standard," said Richard D. Land, president of the Ethics and Religious Liberty Commission of the Southern Baptist Convention. Land contrasted the hosannahs for Lieberman with the reaction to Pat Robertson's 1988 candidacy. "The very existence of Pat Robertson as a candidate somehow threatened separation of church and state," Land said. "That's a double standard."

In the wake of the criticism, Lieberman denied that his comments were part of a campaign strategy to blunt the "moral issue" Republicans were using to their advantage. "I said what I have been saying for 20 years," the senator claimed. "There was nothing in these statements that was either encouraged or cleared by what we refer to as Nashville," the site of Gore's campaign headquarters. But of course what went unsaid is that when Gore chose him as running mate he had every reason to expect he would perform just as he did. Indeed, in the wake of the criticism, Lieberman said, "some people" in Gore's campaign "were uneasy" about his comments, "but when Al and I got together on the West Coast, he was very supportive."

Lieberman's insistence on blending politics and morality caused him further discomfit in September when he became embroiled in the continuing controversy over one of his favorite grievances, the entertainment industry's alleged responsibility for violence. The issue came to a head in large part because of the Clinton administration's effort to make political capital out of the Columbine school shootings. It was only to be expected that after the tragedy Clinton would take out after the gun makers and the National Rifle Association, longtime foes of the president and his party. But in a move that stunned and angered his friends and hefty campaign contributors in Hollywood, who had stood by him during his impeachment ordeal, Clinton took aim at them, too, ordering a Federal Trade Commission probe of the entertainment industry's marketing of violent movies, music, and video games to children. The FTC report, issued in September, condemned such products and marketing techniques, whereupon Gore and Lieberman immediately rushed to the attack, denouncing the movie makers and vowing to give them six months to shape up or face new laws punishing deceptive marketing.

This threat was much stronger than the response from George Bush, who said, mildly enough, that his priority would be voluntary negotiations with the industry. Other Republicans were quick to point out that Democrats had raised more than $13.6 million from the entertainment industry in the current election cycle. That was $5 million more than the amount raised by Republicans. And these amounts were swollen with three massive fund-raisers headlined by entertainment figures within a week of the release of the FTC report. The largest of these events had been arranged by Harvey Weinstein, whose Miramax studio had distributed a number of films criticized for their violence and sexual content, most notably *Pulp Fiction,* which established a new benchmark for graphic mayhem.

And it was not just Republicans who saw hypocrisy in the Democratic stand. In a stinging editorial, the *New York Times,* which ultimately would endorse the Gore-Lieberman ticket, pointed out that the Democratic Party had "a tradition of protecting free expression." Gore and Lieberman, the *Times* said, "had crossed a line no Democratic presidential candidate should ever cross." The editorial accused Gore of "sophistry" in promising to fashion punitive legislation aimed at "deceptive advertising" that would be "consistent with the First Amendment."

The public criticism of the Gore-Lieberman position, along with private grumbling from film executives, seemed to have an impact. At a $4.2-million Beverly Hills fund-raiser the week after release of the FTC report, Lieberman told the assembled moguls that he did not want to censor Hollywood but instead intended merely to "nudge" movies and television in a more acceptable direction. That softening brought a swift rap on the knuckles from chief Republican moralist William J. Bennett, who accused his onetime partner in denouncing entertainment violence of "trimming his views." "I did not realize that when Joe Lieberman and I were denouncing the filth, sewage and mindless bloodletting of the popular entertainment industry, calling it what it is—degrading and dehumanizing—we were just being 'nudges,'" Bennett said in his written statement. "Sen. Lieberman and I were doing more than 'nudging' the entertainment industry; we were trying to shame them," he added.

Bennett also said he was aghast at Gore and Lieberman's apparent acceptance of a joke told at the Monday fund-raiser by Larry David, who was executive producer of "Seinfeld." David, according to reporters present, said, "And like Bush, I too found Christ in my 40s. He came into my room one night. And I said, 'What, no call? You just pop in?'" Gore and Lieberman should have left in protest, Bennett said.

For his part, Lieberman agreed that David's joke was "in bad taste" and conceded that he "winced" when he heard it. But he responded with a jab of his own at Bennett. "He is my friend and he will be my friend," Lieberman told reporters. But he could not resist noting that Gore had moved ahead of Bush in the polls. He remarked: "I wonder whether this is a sign of a campaign that is faltering or kind of anxiously trying to figure out how to regain the momentum."

Lieberman was gloating too soon. It was true that his own selection as vice presidential candidate, along with the apparent success of Gore's acceptance speech, had seemed to reverse the trend of public opinion in Gore's favor. Suddenly, instead of trailing Bush and Cheney, Gore and

Lieberman had moved into the lead. Confidence surged among Democratic leaders. Now they told each other Gore would claim the victory that had been predicted for him all along. Yet Gore, even with Lieberman's help, could not close the deal. After all, the benefits Lieberman could bring to the ticket were limited. He had to deal with the contradictions between his own support for middle-class values and the realities of Democratic politics, a point underlined by Bennett's criticism.

Anyhow, Lieberman was only the number two man. It was Gore who was running for president. And he had his own inconsistencies to answer for. His public declarations of belief in God and traditional values were diminished by the fact that he had come only recently to such public professions of belief and also by the memories of the wholehearted support he had given Clinton during the darkest moments of the Lewinsky scandal.

As the campaign moved into its closing weeks Gore's effort to recast his cultural profile faced its severest test in the three televised presidential debates. In these encounters he could not rely on Lieberman; he was on his own. In Bush Gore faced an adversary whom he far exceeded in experience and command of the issues. But Gore's real nemesis in the debates was not Bush but Clinton, whose reputation made him a phantom participant.

One reason that character dominated the cultural debate was that Gore was unwilling to engage Bush on another cultural issue for which the Democrats had laid the groundwork all through the year—gun control. Early in the campaign Gore placed gun control at the center of his presidential agenda, proposing such tough laws as licensing new handgun buyers, limiting gun purchases to one a month, and banning cheap and easily concealable handguns. Meanwhile, he hammered away at his anticipated Republican opponent, Bush, as a tool of the National Rifle Association (NRA).

Gore stuck to his guns on guns during his campaign for the Democratic nomination, in which he easily bested Bill Bradley. But in the fall, as the general election wore on, the issue took on a different cast. The political realities that had long frustrated gun-control advocates remained unchanged. Public opinion polls showed that a majority of Americans supported new gun-control laws. Most members of that majority, however, did not feel nearly as strongly about the issue as the gun owners did.

NRA advocates opposed controls and were willing to contribute to and work for political candidates to back up their views. One measure of the tepidness of public support of gun control was the polls, which showed that a majority agreed with the notion, vigorously promoted by gun owners and their Republican allies, that new gun laws would not be needed if the laws on the books would be enforced.

Moreover, as the polls showed, gun-control restrictions were unpopular among many of the swing voters both campaigns were targeting in the final weeks of the campaign. This was particularly true in battleground states such as Michigan, Missouri, Ohio, and Pennsylvania with a sizable bloc of hunters and other gun enthusiasts. To energize the pro-gun forces, the NRA launched a massive mobilization it called "Vote Freedom First," which, while not getting nearly as much attention as the Million Mom March, probably overshadowed that exercise in political impact. In Pennsylvania, for example, which boasted the second-highest number of gun owners in the nation next to Texas, more than 1,000 NRA supporters jammed a hotel ballroom in Monroeville to hear their president, Charlton Heston, tell them that by working to elect George W. Bush and other Republican foes of gun control, they had earned the right to be considered the direct descendants of America's revolutionary heroes.

"They won their freedom with bullets so that we could defend our freedom with ballots," Heston told the crowd at Al Monzo's Palace Inn. As a Culture War veteran, Heston knew just what ammunition to use. "That is the holy war which you in this room help wage and win. But instead of fighting the Redcoats, we're fighting the blue-blood elitists." Several in the audience told the *Washington Post* that they were not only going to vote Republican in November, but they were also volunteering on behalf of GOP candidates to make sure the next Congress did not put gun control on its docket.

In the face of this opposition, it was not surprising that Gore decided to backtrack. In the second presidential debate, he hastened to point out that he and Bush "agree on some things" and that he would "not do anything to affect the rights of hunters or sportsmen." Gore did refer to his support for closing a loophole allowing the unregulated sale of guns at gun shows, for establishing a three-day waiting period for gun buyers, and for mandatory trigger locks. But he made no mention—as gun-control advocates wanted—of a provision in a Bush-backed law in his own state that allowed Texans to carry concealed weapons while in such places as churches. Meanwhile, Bush was able to reiterate his basic position—what was needed was not new gun laws, but stricter enforcement of the laws on the books. "We need to say loud and clear to somebody, if you're going to carry a gun illegally, we're going to arrest you." He opposed, the Republican nominee made clear, any proposal for registration of guns. "I think the only people who are going to show up to register . . . are law-abiding citizens. The criminals are not going to show up and say, 'Hey, give me my ID card.'"

In the third debate Gore was even more pusillanimous. "I think that some common-sense gun safety measures are certainly needed with the flood of cheap handguns that have sometimes been working their way into the hands of the wrong people," he said. "But all of my proposals are focused on that problem, gun safety." Then he hurried to change the subject, using the remaining time he had been given to answer the gun question not to emphasize his differences with Bush on that issue but rather to puff his own record for "reinventing government."

Debate on the most sensitive cultural issue of all, abortion, was toned down, with both candidates trying to avoid getting singed by the overheated emotions on both sides. Gore accused Bush of intending to appoint federal judges who would overturn *Roe v. Wade*. But Bush denied that charge. "Voters should assume that I have no litmus test on that issue or any other issue," he said. While he viewed making abortions illegal "a noble goal," Bush added quickly, "I know we've got to change a lot of minds before we get there in America." In the meantime, he renewed his call for a ban on partial-birth abortions. Gore did not want to pick a fight on that issue. "I would sign a law banning that procedure, provided that doctors have the ability to save a woman's life or to act if her health is severely at risk," he said.

With this absence of argument about substantive cultural issues, the personalities of the candidates, or more explicitly, the cultural values the media somehow inferred from the way they conducted themselves in the debates, dominated discussion and appeared to have significant impact in the polls. In other words, the outcome of this incredibly close election was heavily influenced by these confrontations in which what mattered most was not what the candidates believed but how they behaved and what the media thought that meant.

The impact of the debates was distorted by the bias of the media, which wound up aiding Bush and damaging Gore. This one-sidedness ran counter to the traditional belief that the press tends to favor Democrats and liberals over Republicans and conservatives. But the slant in debate coverage had little to do with ideology; rather, it reflected the unwritten ground rules of political journalism, which impose an artificial set of standards on debate competition. Under these guideposts, Bush started off with an advantage because he was regarded as less experienced and less knowledgeable than Gore. Both Bush and Gore made errors in the debates, but Gore's cost him more because less was expected of Bush. In addition, the missteps Gore made took on extra significance in the judgment of the media because they were seen through the prism of Gore's link to Clinton and to Clinton's scandals.

The pattern was established with the first debate, October 3, when, as most pundits agreed, Gore dominated the exchanges between the two men, seeming more confident, more forceful, and better informed. A snap Gallup poll taken the night of the debate showed Gore the winner by a 48-to-41 score. And that initial impression seemed to endure for the next couple of days at least. A poll commissioned by *Time* gave Gore the edge by an average margin of more than 20 points on having "more to say on the issues" and having better "command of the facts."

But those scores did not stop the notion taking hold that Bush had somehow triumphed by merely surviving. "I think they held their own. They both did. And in the end, that has to favor Bush," contended CNN's Candy Crowley, a comment echoed by many of her colleagues. But a number of journalists, encouraged by Republican spinmeisters, advanced another analytic point, laden with cultural resonance, which turned Gore's apparent superiority to his disadvantage. This was the notion that while Bush came off gracefully as a good loser, Gore was a sore winner. "Mr. Gore seems to feel the need to pour it on—to offer not just his answer to a given question, but to show us everything he knows about the topic," wrote Bob Herbert, *New York Times* columnist. "The vice president's boorishness gets in the way of his message and almost certainly pushes some voters into a more favorable view of Mr. Bush, who benefits from a more conversational tone and the demeanor of an ordinary guy."

Conservatives leaped on the chance to depict Gore as the heavy-handed elitist browbeating Bush, the genial underdog. "If you looked at Al Gore, you thought back to the smartest kid in class who was always raising his hand and sighing audibly when you made a mistake trying to answer the teacher's question, showboating a little, being a goody two shoes," remarked conservative strategist Bill Kristol on Fox News Cable.

Even Gore's mannerisms, his tendency to grimace and sometimes sigh in seeming impatience during Bush's answers, became a major point of discussion among media critics. "The sighing kept Gore from winning the debate," *Time's* Margaret Carlson declared on CNN's "Inside Politics" on the day after the debate. Though Bush had answered questions "in a faltering, hesitant way," Gore was denied victory, Carlson contended, because "he has so many mannerisms—leading with the sigh, the bridge of sighs, that make people unable to embrace him as the winner."

The assault on Gore's mannerisms soon expanded to the broader and more critical area of his credibility. Gore's troubles started with the first question of the debate from moderator Jim Lehrer, who asked what he meant when he questioned whether Bush had the experience to be president. "I have actually not questioned Governor Bush's experience," Gore said inexplicably, "I have questioned his proposals." He then launched into a critique of Bush's plans for cutting taxes and overhauling Social Security. Unfortunately for Gore, he had been quoted in a page-one *New York Times* story the previous spring as charging that Bush's tax cut proposal "raises the question: Does he have the experience to be president?" Gore's lame explanation: "The point I was trying to make in that speech covered by the *Times* was that the tax cut proposal raises that question," but as he conceded: "Maybe that's a distinction without a difference."

Indeed.

But that was only the beginning of the opportunities Gore gave to the nitpickers who vetted his remarks that night and the next day. In complimenting Bush on his response to a series of disastrous fires and floods in Texas, Gore claimed that he had accompanied James Lee Witt, head of the Federal Emergency Management Agency, to Texas on an inspection trip. As it turned out, he had not. Gore's aides later said that the vice president had in fact done an aerial inspection of the region on his own, had been briefed on the damage by federal officials, and had often traveled with Witt to disaster sites. Thus, they claimed, he had made an honest and understandable error.

But Bush said the problem was not in the details but in the larger picture. "If there's a pattern of just exaggeration and stretches to try to win votes, it says something about leadership as far as I'm concerned, because once you're the president, you can't stretch," he claimed. Much of the media seemed to agree with him, and by amplifying the notion of Gore as a serial exaggerator they gave Republicans a cultural club with which they pounded Gore on a regular basis, often sounding as if they had been trained in clinical psychology. Gore suffered from "a credibility problem," contended Richard Cheney, and had an "uncontrollable desire" to exaggerate. Former Wyoming Senator Richard Simpson diagnosed Gore's misstatements as "not just slips of the tongue" but "disturbing traits of exaggeration and prevarication."

Bush made mistakes during the debates, too. For one thing, during the first debate Bush claimed that Gore had outspent him in their contest for the White House. As Gore pointed out later, Bush had spent twice as much as Gore. On more substantive grounds, Bush airily promoted his plan to partly privatize Social Security by diverting up to $1 trillion into private accounts as an all-gain, no-pain proposition. Scoffing at Gore's warnings that benefits could be threatened, Bush said, "A promise made will be a promise kept." But ultimately, sooner or later, as retirement analysts point out, the $1 trillion shift would mean that benefits would either have to be cut or taxes raised. To the media, obsessed with behavioral nuance, Bush's inconsistencies and contradictions were a bit more technical and thus less meaningful than Gore's missteps.

It seemed to matter not to the journalists that Gore's errors were particularly trivial since he had very little to gain by either mistaken utterance; he could have stuck to the truth without losing any ground. Nevertheless, it was Gore's errant ways which had become the dominant story line. And so the few mentions of Bush's dissembling were drowned out by the barrage directed at the vice president, which persisted through the entire two-week debate period, influencing Gore's own strategy in the subsequent debates. On the eve of the second debate, the *New York Times* let the world know that Gore's aides had forced him to watch the "Saturday Night Live" lampoon of his first performance. "They wanted the message to sink in that he had better watch his performance in the debate tonight and not come on too strong." Gore "seemed to get the message," the *Times* reported.

There was no doubt about that. In fact Gore absorbed the supposed lesson of the first debate so faithfully that he seemed to have sunk into a torpor for the first half of the encounter. He finally stirred himself only as time was running out to mount a vigorous attack on Bush's record governor of Texas. But the impact of his diatribe was eroded when he felt constrained to apologize for his "getting some of the details wrong" the previous week. Not surprisingly, his ratings in the polls plummeted. According to the Gallup poll, Gore, who had dropped 8 points behind Bush after the first debate and then recovered to catch up right before the second debate, once again tumbled into a tailspin. He managed to recover some of that ground by the third debate, abandoning attempts to change his personality and going after Bush hammer and tongs. But the best he could get for his efforts was a draw in the snap polls right after the debate, and in the judgment of most pundits.

Overall, the debates were a disaster for Gore and probably cost him the election. All the efforts that he and Lieberman had made to wrap themselves in religion and morality were unable to overcome the reaction to Gore's behavior under the television lights. Gore's exaggerations, as meaningless as they were, gained importance because they reminded the media and the voters of Clinton and his breaches of the truth. Even Gore's mannerisms took on importance because they conveyed hypocrisy. As a result, the public's negative reaction to Clinton's betrayal of the middle-class values he espoused was transferred to Gore.

Of course not all Americans felt that way. Indeed, the country was sharply divided among those who were influenced in their political decisions by their reaction to Clinton's behavior and those who dismissed Clinton's conduct as purely personal. This conflict greatly complicated Gore's strategic planning. Some Democrats urged him to call on the president to help him by campaigning in such key states as Michigan and Pennsylvania where polls showed the race was close. Clinton had been invited to some districts in these states by Democratic candidates involved in competitive races for Congress. But Gore's advisers concluded that campaigning by the Clintons would make undecided voters less likely to vote for Gore, would give ammunition to Republicans to mobilize their own voters for Bush, and thus would do more harm than good. They told Clinton to concentrate on efforts to motivate black and Hispanic voters to get to the polls and to limit his travel to states that the vice president was deemed likely to win.

Just as Gore's chances could be affected by voters' attitudes about Clinton, Bush's campaign could have suffered from voters' feelings about a group of his allies, the Christian conservatives. Bush kept this possibility at bay. It was clear that he wanted to keep the Christian Right at arm's length—until Election Day. From the moment he clinched the nomination by defeating McCain, with vital support from the religious Right, Bush maintained his distance from Pat Robertson and his comrades. He also soft pedaled his commitment to some of their favorite but more controversial issues, such as abortion.

For their part, conservative leaders went out of their way to find things about Bush they could like. "By the time Bush got to Philadelphia they saw him as one of their own," David Keene, head of the American Conservative Union, told me. "And then he gave an explicitly conservative acceptance speech." Eager for victory, the conservative leaders mostly held their tongues during the campaign, avoiding the sort of righteous rhetoric in which they had indulged in the past.

There is no evidence that Bush or his aides directly asked the Christian conservatives to keep a low profile. But they did not really need to say anything. Bush's attitude was made clear from the speaker list at the Republican Convention. The Christian conservatives were conspicuous by their absence, along with such conservative firebrands as House Republican whip Tom DeLay. "It was Democrat-lite in Philadelphia," grumbled Pat Robertson. The New Right leaders drew the obvious conclusion and realized they had little choice but to accept Bush's decision. "Our view was it was Bush's campaign to win or lose. He didn't want us in the campaign so if he felt he could win without us that was his call," said right-wing activist Paul Weyrich.

In part conservatives were willing to accept this subordinate role more or less graciously because they had reason to believe Bush was on their side on the issues that mattered most. And it was not just the substantive issues, it was the emotional appeal of Bush's startling invocation of Christ back in February at the debate in Iowa. But the main reason for their compliance was their antipathy to Clinton. Unable to defeat Clinton in two presidential elections and one impeachment struggle, they now saw a chance to at least prevent his chosen heir from succeeding him in the White House, and they were willing to sacrifice their pride to make good on that opportunity.

Thus in September, when Clinton's government gave the green light for approval of the new abortion pill RU-486, Robertson backed away from denouncing the pill even though the Christian Coalition's annual conclave in Washington gave him a perfect forum for doing so. Instead, Robertson described the approval as a Clinton scheme to hurt Bush by stirring up controversy over abortion. "I think it's a trap for Bush, and I think he ought to stay out of it, and I will too," Robertson told reporters. "Right now, to play this campaign on abortion would be a tragic mistake. Voters, by a vast majority, are more concerned about other issues."

Bush himself turned down an invitation to address the conference, a traditional stamping ground for GOP politicians and presidents. Instead he submitted a six-minute videotaped address that he used to remind the hundreds of activists on hand what the stakes were in the election. "I need your help," he declared to warm applause. "This may be the closest election in 40 years. If we work together, we will give America a fresh start after a season of cynicism."

Having finessed one potential cultural crisis with the Christian Coalition, Bush was caught off guard by another threat in the closing days of the campaign when word got out that he had been convicted of driving under the influence of alcohol in 1976. This was twenty-four years earlier. But the more serious offense, given the attention paid to Gore's wanderings from the truth during the debates, would have seemed to be Bush's withholding of this information, even though reporters had asked him whether he had ever been guilty of such an offense. As an excuse, Bush explained that he wanted to protect his twin daughters from embarrassment. This rationale, of course, echoed the claims of President Clinton's admirers that he had lied to the country and to a grand jury about his affair with Monica Lewinsky to spare his wife and daughter.

But if any members of the media noticed the similarity, no one called attention to it. Instead many reporters seemed confounded by Bush's attempt to turn the finger of blame away from himself to whoever it was who had leaked the truth about him. The DUI story turned out to be a two-day wonder, petering out by the Sunday morning talk shows. "Arguably the biggest hit to the Bush camp came Friday night on the late-night talk shows, when Jay Leno opened his monologue with this: 'What's new with George Anheuser Bush,'" reported the *National Journal.* Meanwhile, as he campaigned on the Saturday before the election, his past transgression apparently forgotten, Bush trumpeted the importance of presidential character and integrity in what the *New York Times* called "a defiant rebuttal" of the disclosures of the past week.

In the end, the exit poll results made clear the impact of the cultural backlash against the Clinton presidency. Sixty percent of the voters disapproved of Clinton personally, and this segment of the electorate voted for Bush by a nearly three-to-one margin. About 20 percent of the voters approved of Clinton's job performance but disliked him personally, and one-third of these voted for Bush. Ten percent of the voters said their main reason for the vote was to support Clinton, and Gore got about nine out of ten of their votes. But nearly twice as many said their reason for voting was to oppose Clinton, and Bush got nine out of ten of their votes. In some ways the cultural divide was reminiscent of the bitter urban-rural conflict that marked national politics in the 1920s. Gore got better than 60 percent of the city vote. Bush got roughly the same percentage of the rural and small-town vote.

In the closing weeks of the campaign Pat Robertson questioned Bush's standoffish approach to the religious Right. "It's a dangerous strategy just to ignore your base," he warned. But no one could say that the base did not come through for George W. Bush, as a poll conducted by the University of Akron Survey Research Center demonstrated. White churchgoing evangelicals—largely Baptist, Assemblies of God, Pentecostal, and nondenominational worshippers—gave Bush a stunning 84 percent of their vote, compared to only 70 percent for Bob Dole in 1996, and made up two-fifths of Bush's total vote. And the evangelicals led an alliance of white Protestants that provided three out of every five votes Bush got.

In an election in which he lost the national popular vote by 500,000—less than one half of one percent of the more than 100 million ballots cast and counted—and won an electoral vote majority by an eyelash, the tides of the Culture War had swept Bush into the White House. Now he faced the question of how to govern as these currents swirled around his young presidency.

CHAPTER

15

THE FORTY YEARS' WAR

Two days after the September 11, 2001, terrorist assault on the World Trade Center and the Pentagon, Jerry Falwell went on Pat Robertson's *700 Club* show to offer the television audience his explanation for the tragedy. Angered over the corruption of America's morals and values, Falwell contended, the Almighty had lifted the protection he had previously bestowed on the nation, allowing "the enemies of America to give us probably what we deserve."

"Jerry, that's my feeling," Robertson replied.

Encouraged, Falwell warmed to his theme. "The abortionists have got to bear some burden for this because God will not be mocked," he said.

And when we destroy 40 million little innocent babies, we make God mad. I really believe that the pagans, and the abortionists, and the feminists, and the gays and the lesbians who are actively trying to make that an alternative lifestyle, the A.C.L.U., People for the American Way, all of them who have tried to secularize America, I point the finger in their face and say, 'You helped this happen.'

To which Robertson responded, "Well, I totally concur, and the problem is we have adopted that agenda at the highest levels of our government."

During his long and controversial career as one of the Christian Right's leading crusaders Falwell had often indulged himself in utterances designed to call attention to himself and to infuriate his adversaries. But never before had anything he said stirred such a thunderclap in response, a reaction that was close to unanimously negative. If nothing else demonstrated how far Falwell had gone out on the wrong limb it was the attacks unleashed upon him by his longtime ideological and cultural allies. "Suggestions of this kind are one of the reasons why all conservatives get tarred and feathered with this extremist, bigoted, racist, sexist, homophobic label or image that isn't true," declared Rush Limbaugh, the voice of conservative talk radio. President Bush, striving to unite a stricken country, made a point of distancing himself from Falwell's comments. "The president believes that terrorists are responsible for these acts," said a White House spokesman. "He does not share those views, and believes that those remarks are inappropriate."

It took only a few days for Falwell himself to take the hint. "This was insensitive, uncalled for at the time and unnecessary as part of the commentary on this destruction," he said. "I apologize that . . . I singled out for blame certain groups of Americans." As for Robertson, he now claimed that his previous endorsement of Falwell's comments had resulted from confusion on his part. Falwell's remarks, he said, were "frankly, not fully understood" by him or the show's other hosts. And upon further reflection, he considered them "severe and harsh in tone" and "totally inappropriate."

But the retractions were not enough to satisfy the targets of their remarks. Feminist and gay leaders were unwilling to surrender the opportunity to hit back at the Christian Right. "We fear what he has said emboldens religious extremists in the United States," said Katherine Spillar, executive director of the Feminist Majority organization, of Falwell's comments. Particularly affronted were leaders of the gay community. "I'm a forgiving person, but I don't forget," said Gwenn Baldwin, director of the Los Angeles Gay & Lesbian Center. "We shiver when we hear words like his." Ralph Neas, head of People for the American Way, the Left's leading collector and disseminator of information on cultural issues, spoke more in sorrow than in anger, pronouncing himself "deeply saddened" that Falwell and Robertson had "chosen the path of division rather than unity."

The awkward attempts by Robertson and Falwell to recant demonstrated that the outbreak of America's war on terrorism had forced an alteration in the rules of engagement for America's forty-year-long Culture

War. And for a time the cultural conflicts that had raged for the past four decades might seem to be overshadowed by the national anguish and anxiety produced by the suicidal onslaught of September 11. But there was plenty of reason to believe that these schisms ran too deep for the reduction in the level of cultural conflict to be anything more than temporary.

As outlandish as they seemed to many Americans, Falwell's and Robertson's remarks were based in theology familiar to and accepted by many conservative evangelical Christians, such as George W. Bush, who believe the Bible teaches that God withdraws protection from nations that violate his will. "Any time you get away from God, you do become vulnerable," James Robison, an evangelist whose counsel is often sought by the president, observed about the events of September 11. "If it is a parent who stays out all night, the children become vulnerable and are left to fend for themselves. Bad judgment always leaves the door open to perpetrators of pain."

Whether or not Bush believes that Americans had made their country more vulnerable by straying from the Lord's way, his election assured that the Forty Years' War would be extended well into the twenty-first century. Indeed, the extent of Bush's personal and political commitment to the cause of cultural conservatism was driven home right after his election, even before he took office, by the way he picked his attorney general.

Initially, the all but certain holder of that position seemed to be Bush's good friend and fellow governor, Marc Racicot of Montana. Racicot had vaulted to national attention during the prolonged recount of the 2000 presidential balloting, a process that left the nation bewildered and the electoral process gridlocked. Normally a good natured and easygoing man, Racicot became infuriated about the way the crucial ballot recount was being conducted in Florida, where Bush's chances of being inaugurated the forty-third president hung on the thread of only a few hundred votes. Racicot, as he told Bush and the other guests at dinner in the governor's mansion in Austin, was convinced the Democrats were trying to steal the election from Bush by manipulating the recount process. Most particularly, he was furious at Democratic efforts to challenge the legality of absentee ballots filed by Floridians in the Armed Services abroad. In Florida, Democratic lawyers were arguing that many of these ballots had been filed too late for the statutory deadline. To Racicot, it seemed outrageous that Democrats would deny the franchise to men and women in uniform on what he insisted was as a mere technicality. This was something Bush should blow the whistle on—loud, Racicot argued.

The more Racicot fumed, the angrier he became, until finally, Bush, listening to this tirade, turned to an aide and said: "Why isn't he out there?" The next day he was. And in full cry. "Last night we learned how far the vice president's campaign will go to win this election," he told reporters at a press conference called for the specific purpose of allowing Racicot to vent his spleen. "The vice president's lawyers have gone to war in my judgment against the men and women who serve in our armed forces." Racicot's attack was so ferocious that when he reentered Bush headquarters after the press conference, Bush's aides gave him a standing ovation. On the following day Bush and his supporters had even more reason to cheer Racicot when Senator Lieberman, serving as a spokesman for the Gore campaign, urged the Florida Democrats who had challenged the military ballots to reconsider. "Al Gore and I don't want to ever be part of anything that would put an extra burden on the military personnel abroad who want to vote," Lieberman said.

The net result was to leave the Democrats stunned and on the defensive, helping to make it possible for Bush to pick up nearly 200 precious votes from the disputed absentee ballots. And Racicot continued his assault with more interviews and press conferences, becoming, as the *Los Angeles Times* put it, "the face of Republican outrage" against the supposed insidious tactics of the Democrats. His name, which he pronounced as if it were spelled "Roscoe," was soon on the lips of every politician and pundit involved in the recount battle. Given the high premium placed by Bush on personal loyalty, Racicot's thrust seemed likely to make certain something that most Republicans had already thought very probable: If Bush did hold his hair's breadth lead in the vote count, then Mark Racicot would get a very high post in the Bush presidency. As it turned out, instead Racicot would become the first casualty of the Culture War in the post-Clinton era. His downfall would lead to remobilization of the forces that had slugged it out on Capitol Hill over impeachment, touch off the fiercest struggle over a presidential nomination since the rejection of Judge Robert Bork, and send a wakeup call to anyone who thought the election might bring a lull in the Forty Years' War.

Such an outcome seemed highly improbable in the immediate wake of the election. Even before he took on the Democrats over the absentee ballots, Racicot had good reason to expect that he would be part of the next Republican administration in Washington. Racicot and Bush had come to be good friends after meeting at a conference for governors five years earlier, taking time out from their official duties to go fishing together. In December 1998, Racicot accompanied Bush, along with two other Republican governors, on a fact-finding trip to Israel. More recently, Racicot had been one of the principal organizers of the Republican governors' barnstorming tour of the country on Bush's behalf, conducted in the final weeks of the presidential campaign. Racicot was certainly eminently available for a federal appointment. Montana's term-limit law meant that his tenure as the state's governor would conclude with the end of his second term at the close of the year 2000.

Although there was some talk that Racicot might get the top job at the Interior Department, Bush and his aides were more interested in him taking another, more crucial post, that of attorney general. He had been Montana's attorney general for four years, and it was because of his legal skills that he had been summoned to Austin to help in the recount struggle. Moreover, despite his display of fierce rhetoric, Racicot was judged in his home state by Republicans and Democrats alike to be an amiable and evenhanded man, a politician whose home number was published in the Helena, Montana, phone book and whose banana bread recipe was posted on the Internet. In short, his Florida outburst aside, he seemed to fit in with Bush's oft-uttered campaign pledge to be a uniter, not a divider.

But a not-so-funny thing happened to Marc Racicot on his way to the Department of Justice. He ran into a Culture War buzz saw. The social conservatives had made a major contribution to Bush's success. They had restrained themselves during the campaign, avoiding doing or saying anything that might have embarrassed Bush or caused him to lose swing voter support. In short, they had allowed him to emphasize the compassionate part of compassionate conservatism. And then, on Election Day, they had turned out in force for Bush. The exit polls showed that. It could be argued that in such a close election they had provided Bush with his margin of victory. And now they wanted their share of the spoils.

Leaders of the Christian Right and cultural conservatives in general considered two cabinet appointments of top importance. One was Health and Human Services, for which they were confident that Bush would pick their favorite, Wisconsin Governor Tommy Thompson, a champion of welfare reform and school vouchers. But they regarded another position as even more important: This was the job of attorney general, which came with enormous legal and political clout as well as a national bully pulpit of its own. In addition to overseeing enforcement of the laws governing race relations, abortion, drug use, and immigration, not to mention supervision of the Federal Bureau of Investigation, the attorney general by custom has strong influence over presidential judicial nominations, including choices for the Supreme Court.

Along with all this, conservatives saw control of the Justice Department as a weapon to use in cleansing the government of the legal and moral corruption of the Clinton presidency. When conservatives thought of Janet Reno, they saw her as the attorney general who had refused to appoint independent counsels to investigate the campaign finance abuses of Clinton and Gore in 1996 and generally as a bulwark of permissiveness. "The whole question of the scandals that this Justice Department has either abetted or covered up is certainly a matter of a lot of concern to a lot of people," one Republican staffer on Capitol Hill told the *Los Angeles Times*. "The ability of somebody to tell the truth candidly would be in marked contrast to this administration. It'll be a breath of fresh air."

Yet some conservatives viewed Bush's impending choice for AG with apprehension, concerned that Bush might be too wedded to his campaign promises of conciliation to pick the sort of person they wanted. "He doesn't want to rock the boat," said Larry Klayman, chairman of Judicial Watch, a conservative legal foundation that had been one of President Clinton's harshest critics. "And from our standpoint, we're not real optimistic that whoever Gov. Bush appoints is going to be real strong."

Such misgivings were intensified by the talk of Racicot topping Bush's list of prospective attorneys general. The conservatives had heard all the stories about Racicot's congeniality and popularity. His approval rating in his home state—87 percent—was the highest of any governor in the country. He was famous also for his self-deprecating sense of humor. Asked about the athletic prowess he had demonstrated at his alma mater, tiny Carroll College in Helena, Montana, which had inducted him into its basketball hall of fame, Racicot typically quoted his father as telling him: "You may not be big, but you are slow." But when that sort of anecdotal evidence reached the ears of conservatives, it only hardened their conviction that Racicot was not who they wanted at justice. They were not interested in geniality, moderation, and pragmatism. They wanted zeal, conviction, and commitment to principle.

Looking at Racicot's record in Montana, they saw substantive evidence to reinforce their concern about his style. Racicot had failed to support school-choice programs. He explained that the idea made little sense in Montana because of its sparse population. He opposed abortion, but did not invest much time or effort in fighting for legislative curbs. What stuck in the craw of conservatives most, perhaps, was Racicot's 1998 support for extending hate-crimes laws to protect homosexuals, a stand he took after Matthew Shepard, a gay University of Wyoming college student, was beaten to death. It was not so much the issue itself, though most conservatives viewed hate-crime legislation as at best unnecessary and at worst an example of political correctness run amok. Rather, it irked conservatives that Racicot showed more enthusiasm for hate-crimes legislation than for antiabortion legislation.

If the flaws that conservatives found in Racicot's record seemed relatively minor, this was understandable. Because Racicot's main drawback, as far as the conservatives were concerned, was that they already had a man in mind to be attorney general who was about as different from Racicot as two white male Republican politicians from West of the Mississippi could be. This man was John Ashcroft, about to become an ex-senator from Missouri. Where Racicot was amiable in manner, Ashcroft was stern and dour, most of the time. Although, along with three other Republican senators, he belonged to a group called "The Singing Senators," an offshoot of his longtime sideline as a writer and performer of gospel music, Ashcroft was in deadly earnest, even about his singing. "John viewed music as a ministry," said an old Missouri friend who recalled hearing the future senator perform at church suppers and county fairs. "That was the way he ministered to people. He didn't preach."

Maybe not from a pulpit. But he often delivered what amounted to sermons at political events, another contrast with Racicot. Where the Montana governor went out of his way to avoid giving offense, Ashcroft seemed to go out of *his* way to rub people the wrong way with his self-righteousness. I saw Ashcroft's prickly approach to other politicians, members of his own party not excepted, demonstrated in a talk to the Political Action conference in Washington a few weeks after the Lewinsky scandal had erupted, when he declared that Clinton "had disgraced this country" and should leave office.

"I have been criticized for speaking out," he said at the time. "But to sin by silence makes cowards of all men. It is time to think less about politics and more about our country, think less about party and more about teaching our young people what is right and wrong," Ashcroft said. "There is danger in our party and there are some who believe that the shortest path to success is demise of our foes, that their scandal can be our victory," he added in a pointed reproof of his party's established leadership. "Nothing could be further from the truth. We've been told to settle for what we can get. This must end. We will no longer be satisfied with crumbs of appeasement that come from the banquet table of the party establishment. We need a standard-bearer who does more than grudgingly accept our agenda."

Ashcroft came by the moral fervor he expressed that day honestly. He was born and brought up in the Assemblies of God, the largest white-majority denomination in the Pentecostal faith, perhaps the most zealous and unrestrained of the evangelical faiths. And he was no ordinary foot soldier in the legions of salvation. His father, the Reverend J. Robert Ashcroft, had been one of the driving forces in shepherding Pentecostalism out of the social isolation its early-twentieth-century founders had favored.

Not that the Ashcrofts turned their backs entirely on tradition. On the day John Ashcroft was sworn in to the Senate in January 1995, his father knelt beside him in a friend's home and anointed his forehead, appropriating some Crisco from the kitchen cupboard for that purpose. As Ashcroft noted in his 1998 book, *Lessons from a Father to His Son,* Old Testament

Kings Saul and David were anointed in much the same way, and so even in the present day have been the kings and queens of England. For the most part, though, the Ashcrofts have sought to de-emphasize such old-fashioned Pentecostal ritualism in favor of modernity and conformity to the tastes of most middle Americans. Indeed, one of Robert Ashcroft's landmark accomplishments was convincing the denomination to give its Bible students a full liberal-arts education.

His son, born in 1942, went even further, forging a path into mainstream politics. After getting a bachelor's degree at Yale and a law degree from Chicago, he completed a stint teaching law at Southwest Missouri State. Then, he was appointed state auditor when he was still in his early thirties. He climbed steadily up the Missouri political ladder, becoming assistant attorney general of the state, then attorney general, then governor, moving on to the Senate in 1994.

In the Senate, Ashcroft's major accomplishment was his charitable choice initiative, incorporated into the welfare reform act of 1996, which served as the basis for the proposals by both Bush and Gore to rely more on faith-based organizations to provide social services to the poor. But to conservatives, far more important than Ashcroft's legislative accomplishments were his strong convictions on the role of law and government as evidenced by his rhetoric and his committee work. Unlike the two Democratic lawyers then resident in the White House, Bill and Hillary Clinton, who saw the law as an instrument for improving the plight of the disadvantaged and advancing the rights of minorities, the only minority that Ashcroft seemed to want to protect were the unborn, and toward that purpose he expended boundless energy and time.

In the Senate, Ashcroft sponsored the Human Life Amendment, which would have defined life as beginning at fertilization—barring not only abortion but also some forms of contraception. Ashcroft opposed Clinton's nomination of David Satcher as surgeon general because Satcher did not support a partial-birth-abortion ban. "If I had the opportunity to pass but a single law," Ashcroft once wrote, "I would fully recognize the constitutional right to life of every unborn child, and ban every abortion except for those medically necessary to save the life of the mother."

Some Missouri politicians believed that Ashcroft's hatred of abortion had influenced his long and vituperative opposition to the appointment of Ronnie White, Missouri's first black supreme court justice, to the federal bench. Although Ashcroft explained his opposition on grounds that White was "pro-criminal," he had another reason, some suspected, which he chose to keep to himself. This was a grudge he bore against White of several years standing, stemming from White's role while he was a state legislator, in killing an antiabortion bill championed by the then governor of Missouri, John Ashcroft.

On other culturally sensitive legal fronts, Ashcroft had little use for affirmative action, desegregation orders, or gay rights. He viewed the law mainly as a means of punishing wrongdoers, but gun control played only a small part in his anticrime agenda. He had campaigned for a 1999 Missouri referendum allowing the state's citizens to carry concealed weapons to protect themselves against lawbreakers. He had also cast his Senate votes against measures requiring safety locks on guns, banning assault weapons, and closing the gun-show loophole that allowed purchasers of guns at such shows to avoid the three-day background check otherwise required. Understandably, the National Rifle Association was one of his strongest financial backers.

Given this background, it was no wonder that by 1998, after only three years in the Senate, Ashcroft was being urged by James Dobson and other Christian conservative leaders to think of himself as presidential timber. And that when he heeded those urgings, the faithful responded. As he began gearing up for a presidential candidacy he got more money from religious organizations than any other source. His political action committee received what was probably the largest single contribution to any presidential prospect—$400,000 from the House of Lloyd, a direct sales company in Kansas City, Missouri, which espouses evangelical values. And as he stumped in New Hampshire and Iowa, grassroots activists flocked to his banner.

But the 1998 election in Missouri, even though he himself was not on the ballot, had a sobering impact on Ashcroft's incipient candidacy. Only a third of the citizens in his own state told exit pollsters they thought he would make a good president. Even worse news for Ashcroft came from

Missouri's popular Democratic governor, Mel Carnahan, who announced he would run for Ashcroft's Senate seat in 2000. This prospect meant that Ashcroft could not afford the luxury of pursuing a long-shot presidential candidacy on the assumption that if his White House hopes crashed he could easily gain reelection to the Senate. Ashcroft decided to play it safe, and in early 1999 he abruptly pulled out of the presidential race.

That experience did not dim his religious ardor. In May 1999 he accepted an honorary degree and delivered the commencement address at Bob Jones University, which the following year would become a center of controversy in the campaign for the Republican presidential nomination. "Unique among the nations, America recognized the source of our character as being godly and eternal, not being civic and temporal. America has been different. We have no king but Jesus," Ashcroft told the students.

For all of his credentials, Ashcroft would not have been available to be attorney general had it not been for a bad turn in his political fortunes in the 2000 election. Mel Carnahan had kept his word about challenging Ashcroft and was locked in a close contest with the Republican when, a few weeks before the election, Carnahan was killed in a plane crash. But his name stayed on the ballot, and his candidacy gained support when his widow, Jean Carnahan, agreed to accept appointment to the Senate if her late husband won the election. A frustrated Ashcroft was at a disadvantage, unable to attack either his dead opponent or his proxy, and lost a contest that was almost as close as the presidential election.

For Ashcroft, all this was a bitter pill to swallow. He had dropped out of the presidential race to defend his Senate seat against Carnahan and then wound up losing that seat anyway—to a dead man. But now circumstances changed in his favor. On December 12 a sharply divided Supreme Court, in one of the most controversial decisions in its long history, ended Al Gore's desperate efforts to continue the recount in Florida and in effect made Bush president. The future chief executive promptly began to turn his full attention to selecting a cabinet, and conservatives immediately began looking over his shoulder.

Actually social conservatives had been monitoring the Bush transition all through the recount process, trying to protect their interests. Realizing that Bush was preparing to pick Racicot as attorney general, the activists on the Right made it their objective to stop that from happening, and they began collecting evidence against him. The first blow against Racicot actually came from the inside when a memorandum prepared for the transition operation by a Princeton professor of politics named Robert George documented Racicot's "tepid record" on abortion, gay rights, and other social issues. George had been involved in a nomination battle once before, during the controversy over the selection of Clarence Thomas for the Supreme Court. An op ed piece he wrote for the *Washington Post* defending Thomas's belief in the natural law philosophy had been used by supporters of the nomination on the Judiciary Committee.

George's critique of Racicot, based largely on library research but supplemented by interviews with conservatives serving as consultants to the transition, was dispatched to Bush's chief political strategist, Karl Rove, in Austin. It reflected the view of many conservatives that on the issues that mattered most to them—abortion, school choice, and homosexuality—Racicot was a moderate to liberal Republican. Rove fought back. In a series of phone calls to Racicot's conservative critics, he rejected most of the criticisms. Anyhow, he said, Bush's mind was made up and the conservatives would have to live with the decision.

But even as he was beating back the George memorandum, Rove found he faced another attack on Racicot from the Right. This assault was spearheaded by the veteran activist Paul Weyrich, who, as history had demonstrated, was no man to trifle with when it came to nominations. In 1989 he had ruined the first President Bush's White House honeymoon by derailing the nomination of former Texas Senator John Tower as defense secretary. Having on several occasions seen Tower drunk and making advances to women other than his wife, Weyrich testified at Senate confirmation hearings that he had "serious reservations" about Tower's moral character. His opposition opened the way for critics from elsewhere on the political spectrum to probe into Tower's personal life, and ultimately the Senate rejected Tower's nomination.

Now, twelve years later, a new President Bush was about to enter the White House, and Weyrich and his comrades among conservative leaders had been busy gathering ammunition against Racicot. They had no thought yet of opposing his confirmation; rather, they were determined to prevent Racicot's name from ever getting that far. Their hand was greatly strengthened because they had a valuable conduit for getting their message across to Austin in Congressman Roy Blunt of Missouri, the man the *Weekly Standard* dubbed "the most influential Republican no one ever heard of." A fast-rising star on the Republican congressional firmament, he wore many hats. Most important was his role as chief deputy whip to Tom DeLay. And one of his responsibilities as DeLay's backup was to meet frequently with the Wednesday Group, the right-wing leaders who gathered on that day each week in Weyrich's office to keep in touch with each other and to make plans for dealing with the rest of the world.

It was a role to which Blunt was well suited. Conservatives could hardly have asked for anyone more sensitive to their concerns. Blunt fought the good fight not only at home, but abroad. From his post on the House International Relations Committee Blunt had championed legislation to penalize religious persecution abroad—an important issue for denominations like Ashcroft's Assemblies of God that have more members overseas than in the United States. Similarly, he fought against normalizing trade relations with China, arguing that "America should place her political principles above commerce." As go-between with the conservatives Blunt had come to be on good terms with Weyrich and had learned firsthand of conservative objections to Racicot.

In addition to being the liaison between the House leadership and the conservative movement, Blunt had another sensitive job—he was the Republican House leadership's envoy to the Bush transition, soon to be the Bush White House. "So," as Paul Weyrich told me, "he was in a position of being able to tell the Bush campaign what was on the minds of conservatives." Blunt was primed to do just that in a meeting with Bush and Cheney in Austin on Thursday, December 20. But just to reinforce the conservative's opposition, Weyrich called Blunt on Wednesday night, before he left, and right after the weekly gathering of conservative strategists, to bolster the case against Racicot.

In his meeting with Bush and Cheney, Blunt lived up to his name. Drawing on the public record and the comments of conservative leaders, he spelled out the case against Racicot, mainly that when it came to the causes that mattered most to conservatives he was notably lacking in zeal and enthusiasm. At this point, Racicot, who had been getting an earful of the conservative objections to his appointment, asked that his name be withdrawn, pleading the need to earn a private-sector income to provide for his family. Though it was said to be Racicot's decision to withdraw, by his own account, he had the assistance of the president-elect in making up his mind.*

Now Cheney and Bush told Blunt who their second choice was—Oklahoma Governor Frank Keating, who had achieved national fame in the wake of the disastrous bombing of the Oklahoma City federal building in 1995. Keating had pushed through the biggest tax cut in Oklahoma history and presented such an image of competent conservatism that he had been seriously considered as a possible running mate for Bush before he settled on Cheney. Keating had paid his dues battling for various right-wing causes. Surely the conservatives could not object to Keating.

But they could and would, Blunt told them. Like Racicot, Keating was viewed as lacking in enthusiasm for opposing abortion and fighting other social conservative battles. Weyrich also considered him to have been intemperate in his criticism of conservatives on some issues because, for one, he had said it was tantamount to bigotry to favor English-only teaching in schools. And on top of all this, Weyrich, a man with a strong libertarian streak, viewed ex-FBI agent Keating as having been too willing to let the police run roughshod over the rights of individuals, particularly in the aftermath of the federal building bombing.

In addition, Bush transition officials had learned that Keating had received cash gifts totaling about $250,000, earmarked for his children, over a period of ten years from former Wall Street financier Jack Dreyfus, founder of the Dreyfus mutual funds. The two men had first met when Keating was Ronald Reagan's associate attorney general. At that time,

---

*A year later Racicot would answer the president's call to become national chairman of the Republican Party. Conservatives regarded the post as not significant enough in terms of making policy to protest the move.

Dreyfus was trying to get federal officials to adopt Dilantin, a mood-altering drug he believed could help control violent federal prisoners. Although the gifts were not illegal and Dreyfus had no financial interest in Dilantin, the extent of Dreyfus's generosity, which Keating had never publicly disclosed, was bound to cause trouble for him if he were chosen to be the nation's number-one law enforcement official. That did it for Keating.

By this time Bush and Cheney were becoming frustrated and weary. Their Thursday meeting was dragging on, and the president-elect wanted to announce his choice of attorney general before the week was out. So far, all they had to show for their efforts were two candidates shot down.

Politics was in Roy Blunt's blood and breeding. His father was a state representative and Blunt himself had entered politics at the tender age of twenty-three as a county clerk. He had not been through all that and come all this way without developing an acute sense of timing. Sizing up the weariness that gripped Bush and Cheney, Blunt allowed himself the privilege of coming to their rescue. He had just the man to fill the spot at justice. Here was someone, Bush could rest assured, with whose credentials conservatives would not quarrel. To the contrary, they would be ecstatic. This was a man who said the right things, not because he wanted to please, but because he believed them. Blunt would have been happy to put forward the name of such a man in any case, and it certainly made him no less happy that he came from Blunt's own state of Missouri. Bush slept on the suggestion Thursday night. On Friday, he announced that his choice as attorney general would be John Ashcroft.

The result was the fiercest battle of the Culture War since the struggle over Clinton's impeachment two years before. Only this time it was the cultural liberals who were on the attack, while the Right was defending the principal figure in the controversy. Afterward, Bush's lieutenants put out word to the press that Bush believed his nominee would win confirmation easily because Ashcroft was fresh from his term in the Senate, and senators tend to support other members of the club, present or former. Given what had happened to his father's nomination of former Senator John Tower, he should have known better.

This time there would be no Weyrich blowing the whistle on the nominee from within the GOP's own house. After all, Weyrich and the rest of the conservatives could hardly have been happier. They rushed to support Ashcroft. But the other side hurried just as eagerly to the attack. Among Democratic senators, significantly, some of the most ardent opponents were those senators who would have to face a reelection campaign in 2002 or were considering a run for the White House. That included not only liberals like John Kerry of Massachusetts but conservative Democrats like John Edwards of North Carolina and Evan Bayh of Indiana. Their opposition was in good measure a reflection of the political muscle of their party's organized interest groups, which viewed Ashcroft as a threat to their cultural concerns.

Not surprisingly, they chose to cast their objections to Ashcroft in broader, less self-interested terms. The nomination posed a particularly difficult problem for "centrist Democrats" like himself, Bayh acknowledged in a *Washington Post* op ed piece, "because we have a strong desire to work with President Bush." But Ashcroft's nomination threatened the goals of consensus and harmony that moderates sought, Bayh explained. "An Ashcroft Justice Department will perpetuate divisiveness, partisanship and gridlock," Bayh warned. "By championing his own convictions and causes," Bayh said, "Ashcroft would encourage in others the unyielding extremist they perceive in him."

But the most compelling motivation for Bayh's stand against Ashcroft was made clear by the vocal and widespread outrage of Democratic interest groups. No one was angrier than blacks. "We hoped for a period in which there would have been healing gestures," said Wade Henderson of the Leadership Conference on Civil Rights. "Instead we got an in-your-face repudiation of that very concept."

Women's groups also had a hard time controlling their resentment. "I find his record very clear; that he has misused his power to advance his own political agenda and his own career," said Patricia Ireland, head of the National Organization for Women. "As attorney general of Missouri he sued NOW and tried to do away with our right to free speech and to say we had to stop calling for a boycott of the states that hadn't ratified the Equal Rights Amendment."

Taking a leaf from the liberals' strategy book for Clinton's defense during the impeachment battle, conservatives resorted to a populist argument to fend off the assault on Ashcroft. Clinton had been duly elected by the American people, the liberals had pointed out while the president was under assault; whatever one might think of his personal conduct, the scandal was not enough to undo the verdict reached in a presidential election. Similarly, Ashcroft's defenders pointed out that the chief executive had won the election (never mind the narrowness and dubiousness of his victory); therefore, he had the right to select his own cabinet even if others might disagree with the views of his choices. "George Bush selected him and there is a presumption that, unless there's something egregiously wrong, that he has the right to his own team," American Conservative Union chairman David Keene said in supporting the Ashcroft nomination. "The policies that John Ashcroft follows—the agenda that he sets, the priorities he pursues as attorney general will be the Bush administration's priorities."

But consistency has never been a restraint for either side in the Culture War. The truth is that Keene looked at things differently when he was on the other side of the fence, challenging the nominees of a Democratic president. Keene and the ACU were among the right-wing interest groups that had helped to kill Clinton's nominations of former Colorado State Treasurer Sam Brown as U.S. ambassador to a UN post as well as of Morton Halperin as assistant secretary of defense for peacekeeping and democracy. Both were deemed too radical—Brown because of his background as an anti–Vietnam War activist, Halperin because he had defended leakers of secret documents, criticized the CIA, and condemned the U.S. invasions of Grenada and Panama. "We opposed both the nominations of Sam Brown and Mort Halperin because we felt that the public was being asked to ratify their view of society," Keene explained at the time. "And they had made no change in terms of rhetoric or any other way from their activities in the 1960s." As Keene looked at things when Clinton was in the White House: "The President makes political appointments to pursue political objectives and his political objectives are legitimate fodder to argue about."

Like Keene and his fellow conservatives in the Clinton years, the cultural interest groups of the Left had no intention of walking away from a fight with a president over cultural differences. Such fights are the lifeblood of these organizations. They help to energize their members, enlist new recruits, and, not incidentally, fatten their treasuries. For the groups on the Left the Ashcroft nomination was a badly needed shot in the arm coming after the anguish of Gore's defeat in the presidential elections, a defeat confirmed by the conservative Supreme Court majority that they knew was likely only to become larger and stronger in the four years ahead.

Spearheading the assault against Ashcroft was People for the American Way, under the direction of Ralph G. Neas, who ten years earlier, as head of the Leadership Conference on Civil Rights, had helped to bloody Judge Bork's nose. Hoping for a similar result with Ashcroft, Neas's group issued a two-part, 65-page dossier on the nominee that amounted to a sweeping indictment of his actions and pronouncements during the course of his political career. Starting with his Missouri years, the report condemned him for, among other things, leading the fight in the courts to restrict the right to abortion, opposing school desegregation, and resisting efforts to impose health and safety rules on church-run day care centers. As for Ashcroft's Senate record, the report denounced him for blocking not only the federal court confirmation of Justice Ronnie White but also numerous other nominations of minority-group members and women; for sponsoring the Human Life constitutional amendment, which would not only have all but obliterated the right to abortion but also banned widely accepted forms of contraception; and for opposing the proposed Hate Crimes Act.

In addition to condemning Ashcroft for his address at Bob Jones University, the report also unearthed the fact that Ashcroft had been interviewed in 1998 by the magazine *Southern Partisan,* a publication dedicated to refusing to let the Lost Cause die. In his interview Ashcroft praised the publication, which often rationalizes slavery and finds kind words for white separatism and David Duke, for working to "set the record straight" against the attacks of historical "revisionists." Praising *Southern Partisan* for its steadfast defense of "Southern patriots" like Robert E. Lee, Stonewall Jackson, and Jefferson Davis, Ashcroft added: "Traditionalists must do more. I must do more. We've all got to stand up and speak in this respect, or else we'll be taught that these people were giving their lives, subscribing their sacred fortunes and their honor to some perverted agenda."

All this was grist for the mill of Ashcroft's foes in the ranks of Senate Democrats and among interest groups, some of whom broadened and intensified the attack. The Institute for Public Accuracy, a liberal think tank, revealed that in articles rebutting what its editors viewed as unfair attacks on slavery, *Southern Partisan* had once declared that "massive evidence suggests that slave families were rarely separated," claiming, "Efforts were made uniformly across the South to keep families together." Even worse, *Southern Partisan* also sold T-shirts celebrating the assassination of President Abraham Lincoln. The shirt's front was emblazoned with John Wilkes Booth's notorious last public words: *"Sic Semper Tyrannis"* ("Ever Thus to Tyrants"), while the back bore a statement made by Thomas Jefferson: "The tree of liberty must be refreshed from time to time with the blood of patriots and tyrants," illustrated with droplets of red blood. Furthermore, the institute revealed, just such a shirt was worn by Timothy McVeigh when he was arrested for blowing up the Oklahoma City federal building.

Naturally the forces on the Right rose to meet the challenge. Thomas Jipping, director of the Center for Law and Democracy and an official of Weyrich's Free Congress Foundation, released a report refuting the critique of Ashcroft as "a fraud" relying on "incomplete, inaccurate and misleading information."

Conservatives also counterattacked. Warning that the "radical left" was framing the debate over Ashcroft, right-wing direct mail specialist Richard Viguerie decried "the left wing special interests that are pushing congressional Democrats farther and farther from the mainstream of American politics. Congressional Democrats, it seems, no longer work for their constituents. Now they work for the NAACP, NOW, and NARAL." One point that Viguerie made liberals would have privately conceded: "The fight over Ashcroft isn't really about Ashcroft; it's about future Supreme Court nominations," he said. "The liberals," Viguerie charged, "wanted to prepare themselves for the battles they expected to wage against Bush's choices for the high courts." What they also wanted to accomplish, though Viguerie did not mention it, was to fire a warning shot over the bow of Bush's ship of state—to make him aware that if he did pick someone for the high court with Ashcroft-like credentials he would face an even tougher struggle.

Denouncing the influence of liberal interest groups did not stop conservatives from mobilizing their own forces for the battle. In the first week of the Senate confirmation hearings, Weyrich's Free Congress organization announced that more than 260 grassroots organizations had joined the coalition supporting Ashcroft. "This broad based support for Senator Ashcroft dwarfs his left-wing opposition," claimed Thomas Jipping. In truth, after the sound and fury of the preliminary rhetorical battle the actual confirmation proceedings seemed like an anticlimax. Though the stakes were high in this confrontation pitting the two opposing forces in the Culture War against each other, the lack of suspense about the outcome deprived the scenario of much of its potential drama.

Even Ashcroft's staunchest foes privately conceded at the outset that they had little hope of blocking his nomination. With the Senate divided 50–50, any chance of defeating Ashcroft depended on at least a few Republican votes opposing his confirmation. But there was small prospect of any defections. Among the Democrats, though, several of the conservatives had indicated they would support the nomination. Ashcroft himself did a great deal to blunt the attack against him on the first day of hearings when he pledged to enforce all the laws, even the laws he opposed. "I understand that being attorney general means enforcing the laws as they were written, not enforcing my personal preferences," he told the Senate Judiciary Committee. "It means advancing the national interest, not advocating my personal interest." Democrats on the committee openly expressed skepticism about that promise, in view of Ashcroft's passionate advocacy of a number of positions that challenged the existing statutes. But to undermine the force of Ashcroft's pledge, his opponents would have to demonstrate that his past utterances and actions were so extreme that he could not be trusted to keep his word. And such a task would be almost impossible to achieve.

In the end, Ashcroft prevailed by a 58–42 vote, the narrowest margin for any attorney general in memory, and his opponents took comfort from the hope that the closeness of the vote would serve to curb Bush's conservative impulses. But as the first president in more than a century, and only the fourth in history, to win office while getting fewer votes than his opponent, Bush was not one to worry overly much about slender majorities. Within ten days of his inauguration, and before the Senate had gone on record on the Ashcroft nomination, he launched another Culture War initiative.

In keeping with his campaign rhetoric, but in a move without precedent in the history of church-state relationships in this country, he created an office in the White House that would enable religious organizations to receive government funds to provide services to the poor and downtrodden. "When we see social needs in America," Bush said, "my administration will look to faith based programs and community groups which have proven their power to save and change lives." Since Al Gore had championed the same faith-based approach in his campaign for the White House, Democrats were slow to question or oppose what the president had done. Indeed, Gore's running mate, Joe Lieberman, seemed to give his tacit endorsement of the idea by appearing with Bush at a faith-based community center in Washington at which the legislative proposals to implement his plan were presented.

Anyway, the Democrats were in a poor position to challenge Bush's initiatives on culture and morality because of President Clinton's conduct in the twilight of his White House tenure. The outgoing president's greedy acceptance of gifts in his last days of office, but most particularly his pardon of fugitive commodities trader Marc Rich, outraged political leaders in both parties and embarrassed a good many Democrats.

Among those ensnared in the final Clinton presidential scandal was Eric Holder, the deputy attorney general who had incurred the wrath of the White House by opening the door for Kenneth Starr to plunge into the Lewinsky affair. Holder had done what he could to mend his fences with the White House, in part through his subsequent conduct toward Starr, seeming, in Starr's view, to try to subtly undermine the independent counsel's investigation. Having survived the Lewinsky affair, Holder's future in the Washington legal community once again seemed bright.

But in the last few hours of the Clinton presidency, Holder once again, as with the Lewinsky case, was forced into making a decision—this time on the requested pardon for Marc Rich, whose former wife had contributed heavily to the Democratic Party and to the Clinton presidential library. It was in the eyes of many an application that had no merit and no supporters, except for those who had been beneficiaries of Rich's largesse, who in fact were mounting a potent campaign on his part. Confronted with another test of conscience, Holder fell back on his favored strategy—calculated ambiguity. "Neutral, leaning toward favorable," was the way he described his judgment on the Rich case.

It was a nice try, but Holder leaned a little too far for his own good. Clinton later cited his opinion as one of the reasons he granted the pardon, and Holder himself said that if he had focused on the matter properly what he should have said was: "Don't do this Mr. President." But it may well have been too late for Holder to once again rescue himself. "A lot of well-meaning people get involved and they put on a lot of pressure" during Clinton's pardon deliberations, Democratic Senator Diane Feinstein of California said. "And a lot of other well-meaning people get involved in that—I think Mr. Holder is one of them, for example—and something like this can really ruin their entire career."

But most of the condemnation that the pardon inspired, much of it from Democrats, was focused on the president himself. Representative Barney Frank of Massachusetts, one of Clinton's staunchest defenders during impeachment, said he found it "appalling" that Clinton's pardon of Rich was "so insensitive to what is right and wrong. It damages him, and that's going to harm his ability to be useful to the causes he believes in." Another Clinton impeachment defender, Democratic Senator Pat Leahy of Vermont, was no less angry. "It was a terrible pardon," he said. "It was inexcusable. Here was a man who was involved in a huge swindle and has shown absolutely no remorse," Leahy said of Rich, the beneficiary of Clinton's mercy. "Usually," Leahy added, "pardons go to those who have paid at least some penalty for their crime. Rich's penalty? He's been living a life of luxury in exile in Switzerland and Spain."

The last Democratic president, Jimmy Carter, who for a time had helped give the Democrats the moral upper hand in politics, called the pardon "disgraceful." Carter's former White House chief of staff, Hamilton Jordan, was even more scathing in his denunciation, not only of

Clinton but of the former First Lady and newly elected senator from New York, Hillary Rodham Clinton. He described them both, in an article written for the *Wall Street Journal*, as "grifters," a term coined during the Great Depression to describe the con artists who traipsed around the land, swindling the poor and the uneducated. How to explain these blunders by two such supposedly astute politicos? Jordan put the blame on the outcome of the Lewinsky affair. "I believe they developed a feeling of invincibility and even arrogance after his impeachment trial, when the Clintons confused their short-term victory with the sense of national exhaustion and disgust that followed the scandal."

But as the wave of public dismay and disgust over the pardon demonstrated, the First Couple were not the only Democrats to delude themselves because of the impeachment acquittal. Many others in the land came to believe that a new national social consensus had developed that amounted to a super-sophisticated sort of double standard. As the most prominent prophet of this reputed new outlook, sociologist Alan Wolfe, explained it in a book called *One Nation, After All*, Americans "believe in the importance of leading a virtuous life but are reluctant to impose values they understand as virtuous for themselves on others." The heart of this new morality was its flexibility. Many Americans reject "morality writ large," Wolfe argued, in the form of sweeping pronouncements from any institution such as government. What they prefer is "morality writ small," a code of conduct that establishes clear expectations but also acknowledges what Wolfe views as the messy choices of daily life.

This new consensus left conservatives out in the cold. They sought to focus on the immorality of Clinton's behavior—what he had done, and lying about what he had done; most Americans, in contrast, were willing to dismiss the significance of the president's actions because he lied about sex, not about a fundamental decision of state. Or so Wolfe explained it. In his view this distinction was a sign of healthy maturity. Conservatives wanted to judge Clinton by his sins; Wolfe argued that it was wiser and fairer to consider not just Clinton's transgressions but his triumphs, thus creating a moral code forgiving enough to make America truly "one nation, after all."

It is easy to understand why Clinton's supporters found this theory attractive. It justified their political support for a president who had betrayed some of the most fundamental of American cultural values, including those he often invoked himself. But two years after Clinton's acquittal, in the wake of his pardon of Rich and his other excesses, it also became easy to see where his supporters went wrong. Just as Clinton's foes miscalculated the way the public would react to the disclosure of the president's sins, his defenders misinterpreted the public response to the Lewinsky scandal. A majority of Americans, it turned out, did not accept the president's behavior as simply a private indiscretion. Instead they rejected the only remedy that was offered to them, impeachment, because it was inconvenient to them and because they mistrusted the motives of the people who sought to drive the president from office. Given the opportunity of a new election, about half of them were willing to use that chance to express their disapproval by rejecting Clinton's chosen successor.

But even further off the mark, in the light of the election results, than the underestimation of public resentment of Clinton was the notion of America as "one nation" holding fast to a moral consensus. In his budget message to the Congress in the first weeks of his presidency, George W. Bush said an artist could paint "two very different pictures of our country." Bush was referring mainly to economic differences reflected in the layoffs and rising energy prices that warned of recession, on one hand, and the budget surpluses and technological advances that showed the nation's strengths, on the other hand. But one could also paint a country divided just as starkly along cultural grounds, as the social critic Gertrude Himmelfarb did in her book *One Nation, Two Cultures*. She depicted one culture shaped by the 1960s, rather harshly, as permissive, secular, and bent on individual gratification. The other culture, drawing its beliefs from the 1950s but also from the earlier decades of the twentieth century, she portrayed as God fearing, moralistic, and devoted to traditional values, particularly the importance of the family.

But the closeness of the 2000 election result and the sharp and variegated cleavages that the vote produced provided evidence that the "two cultures" conceived of by Himmelfarb were even more fragmented than her analysis suggested. Cultural commentator Terry Teachout pointed out that the exit polls reflected not only sharp divisions along religious lines—63 percent of voters attending church more than once a week voted for

Bush while 61 percent of non-churchgoing voters voted for Gore—but differences in a number of other cultural categories. Seventy percent of Republican voters were married, compared to only 52 percent of Democratic voters. Among the 4 percent of self-acknowledged homosexual voters, 70 percent backed Gore. Among gun owners, who made up nearly half the electorate, three out of five voted for Bush, and among non–gun owners, about the same ratio backed Gore.

These demographic divisions were reinforced by a geographic demarcation. Nearly all of the states won decisively by Bush were contiguous, making up an arc that swept down from the Rocky Mountains to cut across the Great Plains, then through the Midwest and South. By contrast, except for California and Washington, most of Gore's states were in two urban clumps—one in the Northeast, the other in the Midwest.

In broad outline these two Americas seem roughly similar to the two nations that confronted each other when Al Smith, the hero of the burgeoning cities, and William Jennings Bryan, defender of the values and traditions of the countryside, fought for the soul of the Democratic Party in 1924, a battle that dragged on for 103 ballots and ruined the party for the rest of the decade. But the dramatic changes of the past half century have altered the makeup of these two cultural realms without lessening the tension between them. The denizens of Gore's metropolis work in factories, as did Al Smith's followers. But many also work for government agencies and belong to labor unions, and a good many others are representative of the new highly educated and commensurately compensated information class that did not even exist in Smith's time. Bush Nation, in contrast, is made up of the old Bible belt, recently redubbed "the country music belt," terrain that would have been familiar ground to Bryan. But its shrinking rural and small-town populations have been supplemented by residents of the rapidly expanding exurbs that have sprung up where the older suburbs ran out of room and economic resources, both phenomena not even imagined in Bryan's time.

Just as immigration contributed to the cultural tensions of early twentieth-century America, a new influx from overseas has heightened those conflicts at the outset of the twenty-first century. "What Alexis de Tocqueville saw in America," John F. Kennedy once wrote, "was a society of immigrants, each of whom had begun life anew, on an equal footing. This was the secret of America: a nation of people with the fresh memory of old traditions who dared to explore new frontiers." In 1965, in part prodded by Kennedy's rhetoric, the United States abandoned the quota system that for nearly half a century had preserved the overwhelmingly European character of the nation and ushered in the largest wave of immigration since the turn of the century.

These newcomers were not from the Old World but from the Third World, especially Asia and Latin America, putting nations such as Mexico and Vietnam near the top of countries of origin while the old leader, Great Britain, fell well down the list. Of the more than 15 million immigrants who arrived in the last two decades of the twentieth century, fewer than 2 million came from Europe. For them to adapt to their new home, and for the established citizenry to adjust to them, has been a long and often jarring process. While it is true that in the past each succeeding wave of Irish or Germans or Greeks has caused disruption, as *Time* magazine acknowledged, it is also true that the disparities among Korean merchants, Russian Jews, Hmong tribesmen, French socialites, and Haitian boat people have been greater than the United States or any other country has ever confronted.

The impact of change was demonstrated most dramatically in the nation's largest state, California, where in 2000 the Census Bureau reported that non-Hispanic whites no longer constituted a majority of the population. In the preceding decade the state's Asian and Latino populations had each increased by about a third, while the white population actually dropped. Some of the state leaders sought to put the best face on the change. "It is my hope that we can all see our state's diversity as a cause for celebration and not consternation," said Lieutenant Governor Cruz Bustamante, the state's highest-ranking Hispanic elected official. "If there's no majorities, then there's no minorities," he said. "Maybe now we can all call each other Californians."

Actually, in the start of the new century there is no longer any telling what Americans are likely to call each other, or themselves either. The 2000 census showed that nearly 7 million Americans out of 281 million described themselves as multiracial, and the number of interracial couples quadrupled over the previous decade. The presence of these disparate groups and subgroups, each striving for success and identity, makes it impossible not only to achieve one national cultural consensus but even to establish cohesion and harmony within the two main polarized segments that make up twenty-first-century America.

But wait, things are even more complicated. For the individuals who make up these warring cultural universes are themselves walking and breathing aggregates of cultural contradictions. When sociologists James Davison Hunter and Carl Bowman analyzed the results of a national survey they conducted in the fall of 2000 to find out what cultural values actually mean to Americans, they discovered it was hard to sort out the responses. Though nine in ten interviewed put a high premium on "sacrificing your own interests for the good of others," the same percentage said that "protecting your own interests" is a salutary trait. Eight in ten survey respondents agreed that "following your own conscience" is a mark of strong character. But an even greater number—nine in ten—said that "obeying those in positions of authority" is a good character trait.

"The contradictions continued when Americans were asked about specific moral issues," Hunter and Bowman wrote in an analysis of the survey results. Again and again, Americans identified specific behaviors that are important aspects of good character—only to say, in the same polling interview, that they thought it would be all right for someone to go in the opposite direction. Yet when all was said and done the vast majority clung to the idea that character mattered, rejecting the statement that "character is just a nice word with little real meaning."

Drawing on their survey data the researchers divided Americans into no fewer than five separate classifications based on their view of morality for themselves and for society. Reading from Right to Left, more or less, the groups are traditionalists, who tend to be religiously conservative and live in the South and Midwest; neo-traditionalists, who are a bit less conservative and dwell in the South and on the West Coast; pragmatists, who are still fairly conservative but more tolerant of homosexuality, divorce, and other departures from conventional moral standards, who live mostly in cities; communitarians, who tend to be skeptical of traditional values but are willing to subordinate their own gain and pleasure for the sake of the common good, who also live mostly in urban areas; and finally, permissivists, who as their name suggests are lenient about moral standards, hedonistic, and live on the East and West Coasts. Despite these labels Hunter and Bowman said it would be a mistake to link the beliefs of these groups to ideological differences because "all the clusters are represented across the ideological spectrum." The fault lines dividing citizens according to their economic and political beliefs do not conform to the nuanced distinctions between individuals and groups based on their cultural attitudes.

This complexity helps explain why the political impact of cultural conflict is hard to gauge and even harder to manage. And no wonder, after the murderous rampage at Columbine High, as Americans erupted in a frenzy of questions their anxious mood sent the nation's politicians into a frenzy of their own. Was the problem too many guns on the streets? Not enough God in the schools? Too much violence in the media? Not enough prevention programs? The coddling of juvenile delinquents? Straining for answers, the U.S. House of Representatives in just one day in the post-Littleton spring found itself debating measures to curb gun sales, to allow public schools to teach the Ten Commandments, and to ban the distribution of violence-laden films and videos. Even some of the lawmakers confessed to doubts about the relevance of what they were doing. "We've got an answer for just about everything," joked Missouri Republican Representative Jo Ann Emerson, a single mother of a teenage girl and a cosponsor of a successful resolution to condemn the "pointless brutality" of the entertainment industry. "But we're not going to solve the problem of youth violence here in Congress. You can't legislate behavior."

"To be honest, I don't know what the solution is, and neither does anyone else," said Representative Kay Granger, a Texas Republican. "I think we're all too anxious to be seen as doing something." But moments later, she took to the House floor to deliver an impassioned plea for new restrictions on media violence.

So, it is not surprising, given their eagerness to tap into the public mood, that political leaders often wind up looking like hypocrites. Thus, as the 2000 presidential campaign neared its climax, Al Gore, in the midst of denouncing Hollywood for profiting off violence and sensationalism, set off to a multimillion-dollar fund-raiser in New York's Radio City Music Hall arranged by Harvey Weinstein, distributor of *Pulp Fiction*. That tidbit was too juicy to be ignored by Lynne Cheney, who besides being the wife of Bush's running mate had made a reputation for herself as a crusader for conservative values while presiding over the National Endowment for the Humanities during the presidency of Bush the elder. "Shouldn't people of stature go to Harvey Weinstein and ask him to pledge that in the future he will not fund works that debase our culture and corrode our children's souls?" she asked. Alluding to Gore and Lieberman's expected attendance at the Radio City affair, she said pointedly: "I would ask them please to deliver this message."

The campaign for the White House in 2000 made a powerful case for the potency of cultural issues but left both sides in a quandary as to how best to exploit their appeal. The Democrats, having lost the presidency, could probably attribute some of the blame to their unconvincing mimicry of the Republican themes of faith and morality. "Although Al Gore is actually a very religious man, most people did not know that about him. Then his faith suddenly appeared on the radar screen, and it surprised a lot of people," said John Green, University of Akron specialist in religion and politics. "People seemed to see it as something odd." If the Democrats are going to become more credible in discussing morals and values, they need to do it in terms more consistent with their own heritage and ideology. *Tikkun* editor Michael Lerner, for all the exasperating murkiness of his conceits, suggested a potentially constructive approach in his book *The Politics of Meaning* setting forth notions that for a while caught the fancy of Hillary Rodham Clinton. Lerner urged, for example, that the Democrats promote a pro-family agenda that, in addition to offering such traditional liberal nostrums as child care and a living wage, combats the cynicism and selfishness prevalent in modern American culture by catering to the psychological and spiritual needs of families.

But the Republicans are in no position to gloat or coast in the competition for cultural advantage. After all, though he captured the White House, Bush lost the popular vote by half a million. And when it came to talking about faith, Bush had credibility problems of his own with black

Protestants and Hispanic Christians, most of whom cast their ballots for Democrat Gore. Moreover, the key cultural initiative of his presidency, the program for supporting faith-based social welfare, soon ran into trouble, not only from civil libertarians worried about breaching the church-state barrier but also from religious leaders concerned that it would undercut the spirituality of the churches it enlisted. "If government provides funding to the thousands of faith-based institutions but, under a tortured definition of separation of church and state, demands in return that those institutions give up their unique religious activities, then not only the effectiveness of these institutions but possibly their very raison d'etre may be lost," warned Pat Robertson. If the president is to fulfill his promise of conservatism leavened with compassion, he may have to find a nonsectarian way to deliver the compassion, another conundrum to compound the difficulties of cultural politics.

What does seem clear is that politicians in both parties need to remember the main lessons that emerge from the great clashes of the Forty Years' War, from the streets of Chicago to the pulpits of South Carolina: The line that separates the victors from the vanquished is often blurred, and any triumph has a limited political shelf life. Thus, Paul Weyrich, bemoaning the acquittal of President Clinton, threw in the sponge in the Culture War in the winter of 1999, complaining that political victories did not pay dividends on the cultural battlefields. But two years later he was back on top of the heap, able to help torpedo the candidacy of one prospect for attorney general and help advance another.

Cultural conservatives had swallowed the bitter pill of silence during the campaign—of having to accept Bush's judgment that they were more liability than asset—and yet had emerged smelling like roses. "Yes, we all voted heavily for Bush and we are glad he won and we are cooperating with his administration," Weyrich told me. And so the conservatives could exult in the knowledge that John Ashcroft, pillar of Pentecostalism, ruled the Justice Department and a new ministry of faith in the White House was ready to do the Lord's work with the poor. But even as they rejoiced, cultural conservatives had to recall that only two years earlier, the cultural liberals, the heirs of the Sixties revolution, had cheered what they took to be their own vindication in the impeachment struggle.

And conservatives and liberals both had to realize that conflicts severely testing each side lay ahead. These problems would no doubt be complicated by the ethnic tension inevitable in America's new multiracial society. Ethnicity would play a role in any number of dilemmas facing society, such as the showdown anticipated in the Social Security system between the rising number of retirees and the dwindling number of workers. The elders receiving the benefits will overwhelmingly be white, while most working persons paying for them won't be. And, of course, the dilemma of how best to handle bilingualism in the public schools will continue to be discussed. Unlike past generations of immigrants, who believed they had to learn English quickly to survive, many Hispanics now maintain that they must speak their own language to preserve their ethnic and cultural identity, viewing efforts to make English the sole official language as threatening their heritage.

Cultural conflict, framed by racial and ethnic differences, simmers almost everywhere in national life, from inner-city mean streets to leafy college campuses, with tensions not limited to the polar simplicity of white versus nonwhite. Hispanic political leaders have learned to switch their endorsements back and forth between white and black factions, offering support wherever there has seemed to be the most to gain for their own people. And their clout has increased dramatically with their numbers; the 2000 census showed that the Hispanic population, driven by new immigration, has grown by more than 60 percent since 1990, reaching approximate parity with blacks as the nation's largest minority. For their part, blacks, who have waited the longest in the fight for equality, resent being outstripped in wealth and status by the newer groups of Asians and Hispanics. Two months after the city was devastated by terrorism, the struggles of blacks and Hispanics competing against each other and whites for political power so weakened New York's Democratic Party that the nation's largest and most Democratic city elected a Republican mayor, Michael Bloomberg, who had never held public office before.

As the New York election result demonstrated, even the outbreak on September 11, 2001, of a shooting war, the first to spill American blood on American soil since the Civil War, could not end the continuing cultural tension. To be sure, in the immediate aftermath of the terrorist attack an aura of nationalism suffused with religiosity seemed to pervade the land. "We're a nation of patriots," President Bush told an assemblage of high-school students decked out in red, white, and blue. Suddenly the Stars and Stripes sprouted everywhere, in store windows, on front porches, and on auto antennas. "God Bless America," popularized by the buxom Kate Smith on the eve of World War II, seemed to have supplanted the "Star Spangled Banner," and a CD compilation of patriotic and religious songs bearing the title of the old Irving Berlin anthem soared to the top of the charts. Even more heartening to cultural conservatives, public schools around the land joined in an outpouring of prayer on the theory that the nation's need for healing and togetherness overshadowed the Supreme Court's firm stand against school prayer. "People in time of crisis are drawn to their faith," declared John Burrus, an Oklahoma school official, as he joined in leading a stadium-wide prayer at a post–September 11 football game. "They turn their eyes to God and their country."

But it turned out that many Americans were still not prepared to erase the line between the two. As the first shock of the terrorist assaults faded, the vast majority of public schools soon turned the clock back, resuming their compliance with the restrictions on prayer imposed by a long series of judicial orders going back to the Sixties. For their part, though, cultural conservatives were not prepared to surrender the ground they had so recently seemed to regain. Noting that the American Civil Liberties Union had complained about a California elementary school that had posted the motto "God Bless America" on a campus marquee, the American Center for Law and Justice vowed to defend any community facing a similar challenge. And Arkansas Republican Governor Mike Huckabee proclaimed October "Student Religious Liberty Month," firing off a letter urging school districts to allow students to pray.

Other chinks in the facade of cultural unity soon began to develop. Though in the immediate aftermath of the attacks African Americans rallied behind the president and commander-in-chief, opinion surveys indicated support for the war varied along racial lines. No fewer than 50 percent of the blacks interviewed in a *Washington Post* survey said they opposed a military response to the terrorist attacks, while 90 percent of the overall population backed the idea. The lack of enthusiasm among blacks reflected their collective experience with a culture and government that has always been firmly controlled by whites. "White patriotism is a patriotism of ownership of the state," said Ronald Walters, a University of Maryland political scientist and former campaign adviser to the Reverend Jesse Jackson. "Black patriotism is one of ambivalence; it is patriotism that has suffered."

One reason for this skepticism was that Bush's attempt to frame the struggle against Osama bin Laden and his terrorist cohorts as a manichaean battle between good and evil ran afoul of reality. As malignant as everyone agreed that bin Laden was, the United States found itself obliged to deal with other nations also involved in evildoing in order to destroy bin Laden. And having condemned the terrorists for murdering innocent civilians in order to accomplish their goals, Americans had to cope with the fact that their own armed forces, as they struck back, however inadvertently, also killed civilians who were just as innocent as the victims buried in the World Trade Center towers and the Pentagon.

Questions about the validity of Bush's rationale for the war, and the wisdom of his single-minded absorption with the battle against terrorism, were raised by religious as well as secular leaders. Thus, when the synod of Catholic bishops from around the world condemned terrorism and the "perversion of religion for violent purposes," their statement also included a pointed appeal to "remember those corners of the world which receive no media coverage and where our brothers and sisters are dying from famine and lack of medicine." Similarly, the bishops of the United Methodist Church, Bush's own denomination, issued a statement of their own implicitly criticizing the American war effort. "Violence in all of its forms and expressions is contrary to God's purpose for the world," said the bishops, who offered no exception in their condemnation for the U.S. military response to the September 11 attacks. The bishops' criticism came on the heels of a statement by their denomination's social-issues board saying that terrorists must be brought to justice but that "War is not an appropriate means of responding to criminal acts against humanity" and "Military actions will not end terrorism."

In the meantime, the Bush administration's insistence on conformity—notably illustrated by White House Press Secretary Ari Fleischer's admonition, in response to criticism of the military effort against terrorism, that Americans "need to watch what they say, watch what they do"—stirred bitter reminders of past denunciations of the antiwar protest and the counterculture by the Johnson and Nixon administrations. These parallels were underlined by the dominant role played in the effort to curb domestic terrorism by the Bush administration's leading culture warrior, John Ashcroft. Though Bush named former Pennsylvania governor Tom Ridge to head the newly created Office of Homeland Security, it was Ashcroft who was the true point man on the domestic front. From the outset Ashcroft vowed he would use every available means to detain or deport those he considered terrorist threats, and the attorney general proved to be as good as his word.

Within a few weeks of the 9/11 attacks Ashcroft established new rules to allow the FBI to eavesdrop on suspected terrorists and their lawyers, ordered the interrogation of more than 5,000 young men, mostly from the Middle East, and proposed a system of secret military tribunals for trying accused terrorists. Indeed, so ham-handed was Ashcroft in his disregard for constitutional liberties that his actions caused qualms even among some conservatives, such as Georgia Representative Robert L. Barr, an early instigator of Clinton's impeachment. But no one needed to question where Ashcroft's heart guided him on the ideological spectrum. In the midst of his terrorism probe, and the nationwide scare over anthrax, Ashcroft demonstrated his loyalty to the right-to-life cause by torpedoing an assisted suicide law that had been recently passed by Oregon voters. In the face of the law's provisions allowing terminally ill patients to take lethal drugs with medical approval, Ashcroft commanded federal drug agents to prosecute physicians who prescribed them.

Moreover, the attorney general showed an apparent willingness to sacrifice the effectiveness of his crackdown on terrorism to uphold the beliefs of his cultural conservative supporters, particularly opponents of gun control. Over the protests of congressional Democrats, Ashcroft refused to allow the FBI to compare the names of suspected terrorists against federal gun purchase records compiled under the Brady gun control law.

Ashcroft also exacerbated underlying cultural tensions by his conspicuous zeal in prosecuting the so-called American Taliban, John Walker Lindh, the twenty-one-year-old Californian so resentful of his own country that he had taken up arms on the side of the Al Qaeda and Taliban terrorists. Because of his countercultural lifestyle while growing up, conservatives sought to make this wretched youth a belated poster child for the excesses of the Sixties. That effort was abetted by no one less than President Bush, who airily referred to Lindh as "some misguided Marin County hot-tubber," a wisecrack for which he was ultimately forced to apologize when residents of the bucolic county north of San Francisco voiced their outrage.

Still Ashcroft pressed the case against Lindh, who was charged in a ten-count federal indictment with conspiring to kill Americans, with all the attorney general's might and main. The attorney general's enthusiasm for this task disturbed even some who generally supported the administration's effort to deal with the insidious threat of terrorism driven home by the September 11 onslaught. Jim Hoagland, widely respected foreign policy columnist of the *Washington Post,* referred to "growing concern that Attorney General John Ashcroft, who seizes every opportunity to go before the cameras to prosecute in public one lamentable-to-despicable American youth who joined the Taliban is playing at politics, not justice."

And so the conflicts mount and fade and new tensions build, as the tide of battle ebbs and flows. Meanwhile, in a warning to conservatives who might be lulled into complacency or moderation by their recent successes, Justice Clarence Thomas cautioned against excessive civility in public discourse. "In the effort to be civil in conduct, many who know better actually dilute firmly held views to avoid appearing 'judgmental,'" Thomas complained. In this way, he admonished a warmly approving audience of conservative intellectuals, "We sometimes allow our critics to intimidate us.

> Active citizens are often subjected to truly vile attacks; they are branded as mean-spirited, racist, Uncle Tom, homophobic, sexist, etc. To this we often respond (if not succumb), so as not to be constantly fighting, by trying to be tolerant and non-judgmental—i.e., we censor ourselves. This is not civility. It is cowardice, or well-intentioned self-deception at best.

Conservatives seemed to take Justice Thomas's aggressive coaching to heart. Even the war on terrorism did not seem to abate the fervor of many on the Right when it came to cultural controversies, and the start of Bush's second year in the White House produced a flurry of skirmishes. Secretary of State Colin Powell's advocacy of the use of condoms among the "sexually active" to prevent the spread of AIDS prompted Ken Connor, head of the conservative Family Research Council, to denounce Powell's comments as "reckless and irresponsible," and "a slap in the face" to the president's core constituency.

The National Religious Broadcasters, an organization of 1,400 self-described Christian broadcasters, forced their president, Wayne Pederson, to quit soon after Pederson publicly lamented that "evangelicals are identified politically more than theologically" and warned that "we get associated with the far Christian right and marginalized." Explaining Pederson's abrupt departure, Glenn Plummer, chairman of the group, said: "There are land mines in our association and Wayne basically ripped a wire on one of those land mines."

In a move that seemed certain to accelerate the politicization of religion already under way as a result of the 2000 candidacies of Gore, Lieberman, and Bush, and Bush's presidency, a Republican lawmaker introduced a measure to override limits on church political activity. North Carolina Republican Representative Walter B. Jones's bill would allow churches to endorse candidates and spend money to elect them without fear of losing their tax-exempt status. Barry Lynn, head of Americans United for Separation of Church and State, contended the legislation would "open a gigantic new loophole for funding candidates without public scrutiny."

In this fractious environment, as conservatives and liberals geared up to contend with each other in the Bush presidency, both knew in their hearts that over time the iron rule of the Culture War, shaped by the struggles of the past forty years that had seen the creation and smashing of icons on both sides, and the rise and fall of the likes of Abbie Hoffman and Richard Daley, Richard Nixon and Jimmy Carter, Pat Robertson and Bill Clinton, was bound to prevail again. Success almost always leads to excess. And everything that goes around in the Culture War would, as always, come around.

NOTES

These notes provide the sources for the material presented in this book, except for information based on my own reporting, which I have indicated as such in the text, and events and statements that are a matter of public record, were widely reported, and are readily accessible.

Abbreviations used in the notes:

NYT: New York Times
WP: Washington Post
LAT: Los Angeles Times

CHAPTER 1: "DOES THE TRUTH MATTER?"

Page

3   Holder's phone call: Michael Isikoff, *Uncovering Clinton* (New York: Crown, 1999), p. 293.

4   Common gossip: Susan Schmidt and Michael Weisskopf, *Truth at Any Cost: Ken Starr and the Unmaking of Bill Clinton* (New York: HarperCollins, 2000), p. 140.

5   Bennett a free-wheeler: Isikoff, *Uncovering Clinton*, pp. 274–275.

6   "People were afraid": *LAT*, Sept. 6, 1997.

7   "Jackie, this is Eric": Schmidt and Weisskopf, *Truth at Any Cost*, p. 31.

7   "I called *you*": Stephen Braun et al., "Pathway to Peril," Chapter 3, *LAT*, Jan. 31, 1999.

8   "An ongoing enterprise": Ibid.

8   "Does the truth matter?": Associated Press, Dec. 12, 1998.

9   "Impose a theocracy": Author's interview with Alan Dershowitz, Jan. 7, 1999.

10   "Men still talk": Joseph Bensman and Bernard Rosenberg, "Mass Media and Mass Culture," in Philip Olson, ed., *America as a Mass Society* (New York: The Free Press, 1963).

13   Greenberg's findings: Stanley Greenberg, "Report on Democratic Defection," prepared for the Michigan House Democratic Campaign Committee, April 1985.

13   What Clinton told Dukakis: Transcript of address by Bill Clinton, Chautauqua Institution, June 28, 1991.

14   Atwater's "savage caricature": Stanley Greenberg, "From Crisis to Working Majority," *American Prospect*, Fall 1991.

18 "Our internal mantra": George Stephanopoulos, *All Too Human: A Political Education* (Boston: Little, Brown, 1999), p. 415.

18 The clerical pulpit: *NYT,* March 10, 1994.

CHAPTER 2: GOD'S OWN GUERRILLA

21 "I paint my face": Barbara Slavin, "Ralph Reed: Onward Christian Soldier Politics," *LAT,* May 1, 1995.

21 "Mirror image of the New Left": Dan Balz and Ronald Brownstein, "God's Fixer: Christian Coalition Leader Ralph Reed Has a Strategy," *WP,* Jan. 28, 1996.

21 "Ability to connect": Slavin, "Ralph Reed."

23 Comparison with Barry Goldwater: David Von Drehle and Thomas B. Edsall, "Life of the Grand Old Party," *WP,* Aug. 14, 1994.

25 "So strong was their grip": Norman Lear, "Religious Right Was There All Along," *LAT,* Aug. 28, 1992.

25 "We had religious warfare": Susan Estrich, "The Changing Face of the GOP," *LAT,* Aug. 23, 1992.

25 "If there was a cat that died": Balz and Brownstein, "God's Fixer."

25 Challenge to conventional wisdom: James L. Guth, John C. Green, Lyman A. Kellstedt, and Corwin E. Smidth, "God's Own Party," *The Christian Century,* Feb. 17, 1993.

26 An army of clerics: Peter Steinfels, "Beliefs: God at the Inauguration," *NYT,* Jan. 23, 1993.

26 Nearly every Sunday: Peter Steinfels, "The President's Church: Pastors Want Clinton in Their Flocks," *NYT,* Dec. 7, 1992.

26 Prevailing upon evangelicals: Gustave G. Niebuhr, "Not All Presidential Advisers Talk Politics," *NYT,* March 18, 1997.

27 Charges by Larry Nichols: *WP,* June 27, 1994.

28 An equally passionate response: William J. Bennett, "Credit the Christian Right," *WP,* June 26, 1994.

29 Further energize the Right: John C. Green, James L. Guth, Lyman A. Kellstedt, and Corwin E. Smidth, "Evangelical Realignment," *The Christian Century,* July 5, 1995.

31 Role of conservative Christians: Balz and Brownstein, "God's Fixer."

32 Rivaling traditional powerhouses: *NYT,* Sept. 10, 1995.

32 Double the majority: Green et al., "Evangelical Realignment."

32 Reacted with "foreboding": Nina Easton, *Gang of Five: Leaders at the Center of the Conservative Crusade* (New York: Simon & Schuster, 2000), p. 290.

34 "Clinton has hammered away": *WP,* Sept. 14, 1996.

CHAPTER 3: THE MINISTER'S SON

38 The "solicitous general": Jeffrey Rosen, "Kenneth Starr: Trapped," *NYT,* June 1, 1997.

38 Mikva's description: Michael Winerip, "Ken Starr Would Not Be Denied," *NYT,* Sept. 6, 1998.

39 "Sense of moral certainty": David Jackson and Pete Slover, "Starr Search," *Dallas Morning News,* Aug. 2, 1998.

39 "We just started him from babyhood": Winerip, "Ken Starr Would Not Be Denied."

40 "A very fundamentalist church": "Ken Starr: The Eye of the Storm," *A&E Biography*, Sept. 12, 1998.

40 "A quick warm way": Ibid.

42 A $50,000 severance payment: *LAT*, Aug. 6, 1994.

44 "Able to stand back": Marcia Coyle, "Starr Potential," *National Law Journal*, Sept. 25, 1989.

43 The Bob Jones University Case: Ibid.

43 A studious silence: Winerip, "Ken Starr Would Not Be Denied."

44 Complaining about Fried: *WP*, May 6, 1989.

48 Starr rejected the protest: *LAT*, Aug. 11, 1994.

48 "He had a duty": Winerip, "Ken Starr Would Not Be Denied."

48 "He thought he could parachute in": Winerip, "Ken Starr Would Not Be Denied."

49 The "immaculate conception": *LAT*, Aug. 9, 1997.

50 "No room for white lies": Winerip, "Ken Starr Would Not Be Denied."

CHAPTER 4: DAY OF JUDGMENT

51 Bennett's meeting with Holder: Stephen Braun et al., "Pathway to Peril," Chapter 3, *LAT*, Jan. 31, 1999.

52 "Someone needs to work the case": Susan Schmidt and Michael Weiskopf, *Truth at Any Cost: Ken Starr and the Unmaking of Bill Clinton* (New York: HarperCollins, 2000), p. 32.

52 "Specific and credible" charges: Ibid., p. 34.

57 Reed's and Bauer's comments: *LAT*, Feb. 14, 1998.

59 "Disturbingly complicit": Barbara Ehrenreich, "The Week Feminists Got Laryngitis," *Time*, Feb. 8, 1998.

60 Starr breathed easier: Ibid., pp. 140–141.

61 "No story there": R. W. Apple, "Changing Morality: Press and Politics," *NYT*, May 6, 1987; author's interview with R. W. Apple, Sept. 15, 1999.

62 Ickes scurried around: Peter Baker, *The Breach: Inside the Impeachment and Trial of William Jefferson Clinton* (New York: Scribner, 2000), p. 65.

63 "Substantial and credible information": *The Starr Report: The Official Report of the Independent Counsel's Investigation of the President* (Rocklin, Calif.: Forum), p. 35.

63 The largest single portion: John C. Green, "Religion and Politics in the 1990s," in Mark Silk, ed., *Religion and American Politics: The 2000 Election in Context*, Pew Program on Religion and the News Media, Trinity College, Hartford, Conn.

65 DeLay's background and style: Eric Pianin and Kevin Merida, "How GOP's Enforcer Propelled the Process," *WP*, Dec. 16, 1998; Melinda Henneberger, "Impeachment: The Whip," *NYT*, Dec. 17, 1998.

65 Hyde's background and style: Kevin Merida, "The Judiciary Chairman's Trying Times," *WP*, Dec. 14, 1998; Stephen Braun, "Hyde Was Driving Force Behind Day of Reckoning," *LAT*, Dec. 20, 1998.

67 Bennett was booed: Author's interview with William Bennett, Jan. 11, 1999.

67 The "extreme" language: John Judis, "Political Witch Hunts, Then and Now," *New Republic*, Jan. 25, 1999.

67 Baldwin's tirade: *Hotline*, Dec. 16, 1998; Richard John Neuhaus, "Bill Clinton and the American Character," *First Things*, June 1999.

68   "Like the Weather Underground": *LAT,* Feb. 7, 1999; *LAT,* Dec. 17, 1998.

68   Demonstration in Los Angeles: *LAT,* Dec. 17, 1998.

69   New York demonstration: Pia Nordlinger, "Clinton's Intellectuals," *Weekly Standard,* Dec. 29, 1998; *NYT,* Dec. 15, 1998.

72   Senators denounced Clinton: Eric Schmitt, "The President's Acquittal: The Rebuke," *NYT,* Feb. 13, 1999.

72   Weyrich's reaction: *WP,* Feb. 18, 1999.

CHAPTER 5: ROOTS OF UPHEAVAL

77   "Woodstock nation": Abbie Hoffman testimony, trial transcript, Famous American Trials website, www.law.umkc.edu/ faculty/projects/trials/Chicago7.

78   *The Best Years:* Joseph Goulden, *The Best Years: 1945–1950* (New York: Atheneum, 1976).

78   "General euphoria": Ibid., p. 9.

79   "Expanding affluence": David Halberstam, *The Fifties* (New York: Villard, 1993), p. x.

80   Sloan Wilson, *The Man in the Grey Flannel Suit* (New York: Simon & Schuster, 1955); William H. Whyte, *The Organization Man* (Garden City, NY: Doubleday, 1957); David Riesman, with Nathan Glazer and Reuel Denney, *The Lonely Crowd* (New Haven: Yale University Press, 1950); C. Wright Mills, *White Collar* (New York: Oxford, 1951).

81   "It became very difficult": Abbie Hoffman, *Soon to Be a Major Motion Picture* (New York: Perigree, 1980), p. 14.

82   Fears of youngsters: *LAT,* Aug. 4, 1985.

83   Organizers poured in: Ibid., pp. 53–54.

84   Reaction to use of troops: *NYT,* Sept. 26, 1957.

85   "Between justice and injustice": William Manchester, *The Glory and the Dream: A Narrative History of America, 1932–1972* (Boston: Little, Brown, 1976), p. 741.

86   Greensboro sit-in: *Time,* March 14, 1960.

86   Freedom rides: Manchester, *The Glory and the Dream,* pp. 934ff.

87   "The first crashing intimation": Stephen Macedo, *Reassessing the Sixties* (New York: Norton, 1997), p. 5.

88   "Cultural miscegenation" Todd Gitlin, *The Sixties: Years of Hope, Days of Rage* (New York: Bantam, 1993), p. 39.

88   Allen Ginsberg, *Howl and Other Poems* (San Francisco: City Lights, 1956).

88   Port Huron statement: Charles Kaiser, "Blowin' in the Wind," in Thomas B. Allen and Charles O. Hyman, eds., *We Americans: Celebrating a Nation, Its People, and Its Past* (Washington, D.C.: National Geographic, 1999).

89   Folk song revival: *Time,* July 19, 1963.

CHAPTER 6: EVE OF DESTRUCTION

91   The Worcester peace march: Abbie Hoffman, *Soon to Be a Major Motion Picture* (New York: Perigree, 1980), pp. 70–75.

92   "We *shall* overcome": *Public Papers of the Presidents, Lyndon Johnson, 1965* (Washington, D.C.: National Archives and Record Service, 1966), p. 2830.

93   SDS protest plans: Gitlin, *The Sixties: Years of Hope, Days of Rage* (New York: Bantam, 1993), pp. 178–182.

94   Two major stories: *Time,* Jan. 7, 1966; *Time,* Jan. 6, 1967.

95   Badge of rebellion: Jules Archer, *The Incredible Sixties: The Stormy Years That Changed America* (New York: Harcourt, 1986), pp. 77ff.

96   Passing the joint: Gitlin, *The Sixties,* p. 213.

97   Hailing "The Yellow Submarine": Ibid., p. 209–210.

97   "Throw in your cards": Richard Goodwin, *Remembering America: A Voice from the Sixties* (Boston: Little, Brown, 1988), p. 389.

98   Organizing the MOBE: Maurice Isserman and Michael Kazin, *America Divided: The Civil War of the 1960s* (New York: Oxford, 2000), p. 185.

98   Central Park march: Archer, *The Incredible Sixties,* p. 57.

98   Newark and Detroit riots: Ibid., pp. 35–36.

99   Gitlin wrote a friend: Gitlin, *The Sixties,* p. 267.

99   "Just as Che needed Fidel": Hoffman, *Soon to Be a Major Motion Picture,* pp. 127–129.

100   McNamara's reaction: Robert McNamara, *In Retrospect: The Tragedy and Lessons of Vietnam* (New York: Times Books, 1995), pp. 303–305.

100   "The YIP is a party": *Time,* April 5, 1968.

100   Lippman's warning: Walter Lippman, "The Democrats in 1968," *Newsweek,* Jan. 1, 1968.

100   Tet offensive: "Hanoi Attacks," *Newsweek,* Feb. 12, 1968.

101   Press coverage of Tet: Don Oberdorfer, *Tet: The Turning Point in the Vietnam War* (New York: Da Capo, 1984), p. 160.

102   "A perilous course": "The Fight to Dump LBJ," *Newsweek,* March 25, 1968.

102   LBJ drops out: Lyndon B. Johnson, *Vantage Point: Perspectives on the Presidency, 1963–1969* (New York: Holt, 1971), p. 435.

102   Uprising at Columbia: Isserman and Kazin, *America Divided,* p. 229; Gitlin, *The Sixties,* pp. 306–307.

102   Shutting down SFSU: Archer, *The Incredible Sixties,* p. 62.

103   Rioting in wake of King's death: Isserman and Kazin, *America Divided,* p. 227.

103   Nominating a pig: Hoffman, *Soon to Be a Major Motion Picture,* p. 144.

CHAPTER 7: THE GUARDIAN

106   Daley as middle-class guardian: David Farber, *Chicago '68* (Chicago: University of Chicago Press, 1988), pp. 119ff.

107   "The essentials of Tammany Hall": Nathan Glazer and Daniel P. Moynihan, *Beyond the Melting Pot: The Negroes, Puerto Ricans and Jews* (Cambridge: MIT Press and Harvard University Press, 1957), pp. 224–227.

108   Daley's childhood and law school years: Mike Royko, *Boss: Richard J. Daley of Chicago* (New York: New American Library, 1971), pp. 30–53.

110   Daley's marriage: Adam Cohen and Elizabeth Taylor, *American Pharaoh: Mayor Richard J. Daley* (Boston: Little, Brown, 2000), p. 63.

111   Daley's rise: Royko, *Boss,* pp. 56–79.

112   Influence of Joseph P. Kennedy: Richard Whalen, *The Founding Father: The Story of Joseph P. Kennedy* (New York: New American Library, 1964), p. 379.

113   Winning Illinois in 1960: Cohen and Taylor, *American Pharaoh,* pp. 265–272.

114   "Do you drink a lot?": Frank Sullivan, "Private Glimpses of a Public Giant," *Chicago Tribune,* Feb. 26, 1989.

114   "Not in some resort center": Royko, *Boss,* p. 172.

115 "Not in Chicago": Farber, *Chicago '68*, p. 117.
116 No blank ammunition: Royko, *Boss*, p. 164.
117 "No one is going to take over the city": Farber, *Chicago '68*, p. 122.
117 Attacking the peace marchers: Royko, *Boss*, p. 175.

CHAPTER 8: THE WHOLE WORLD IS WATCHING

119 Worries about a bloodbath: Todd Gitlin, *The Sixties: Years of Hope, Days of Rage* (New York: Bantam, 1993), p. 323.
119 Daley mobilizes: Daniel Walker, *Rights in Conflict: Report to the National Commission on the Causes and Prevention of Violence* (New York: Bantam, 1968), pp. 95–116; "Boss Daley's Fatherly Fist," *Newsweek*, Sept. 9, 1968.
120 Daley's welcome: Lewis Chester, Godfrey Hodgson, and Bruce Page, *An American Melodrama: The Presidential Campaign of 1968* (New York: Viking, 1969), p. 506.
120 Early trouble in Lincoln Park: Walker, *Rights in Conflict*, p. 129; David Farber, *Chicago '68* (Chicago: University of Chicago Press, 1988), p. 181.
121 Hayden's comments: Farber, *Chicago '68*, p. 183.
122 Violence in Grant Park: Walker, *Rights in Conflict*, p. 184.
122 "The whole world is watching": Farber, *Chicago '68*, p. 187.
123 Action returns to Lincoln Park: Walker, *Rights in Conflict*, pp. 192ff.
123 A new front in Grant Park: Farber, *Chicago '68*, p. 192.
124 Failure of the delegate challenges: Chester, Hodgson, and Page, *An American Melodrama*, pp. 553–558.
125 Trying to ease the tension: Walker, *Rights in Conflict*, pp. 212–213.
125 Poorly disguised police: Ibid., p. 217.
126 Trouble brews in Grant Park: Ibid., pp. 220ff.
126 Convention debate on Vietnam: Chester, Hodgson, and Page, *An American Melodrama*, pp. 525ff.
127 Humphrey pleaded with Boggs: Hubert H. Humphrey, *The Education of a Public Man* (Garden City, N.Y.: Doubleday, 1976), pp. 289–290.
128 Defeat of the peace plank: Ibid., p. 535.
128 Delegates sing "We Shall Overcome": Ibid., pp. 579–581.
128 Events took hold: John Schultz, *No One Was Killed: Documentation and Meditation, Chicago—August 1968* (Chicago: Big Table Publishing, 1969), p. 170; Farber, *Chicago '68*, pp. 194–199; Gitlin, *The Sixties*, pp. 326–336; Walker, *Rights in Conflict*, pp. 236–246.
130 Tear gas in Humphrey's suite: Theodore White, *The Making of the President, 1968* (New York: Atheneum, 1969), pp. 296–299.
131 Ribicoff vs. Daley: Gitlin, *The Sixties*, p. 334; Chester, Hodgson, and Page, *An American Melodrama*, pp. 584–585.
131 No choice but to join us: Gitlin, *The Sixties*, pp. 134–135.

CHAPTER 9: "UNBLACK, UNYOUNG, AND UNPOOR"

133 "The quality issue": Theodore White, *The Making of the President, 1964* (New York: New American Library, 1966), pp. 264–266.
133 New York murder rate: Ibid., p. 366.
134 "They've changed the law": *Wall Street Journal*, June 27, 1962.

134   "Violence in our streets": Richard Scammon and Ben Wattenberg, *The Real Majority,* rev. ed. (New York: Primus, 1992), p. 37.

135   "What's happening to us?": White, *The Making of the President, 1964,* p. 367.

136   "Equivalent of Christ's crucifixion": Paul D. Erickson, *Reagan Speaks: The Making of an American Myth* (New York: New York University Press, 1985), pp. 25–29.

136   "Observe the rules or get out": Lou Cannon, *Reagan* (New York: Perigree Books, 1982), pp. 113–114.

136   Nixon on the courts: Lewis Chester, Godfrey Hodgson, and Bruce Page, *An American Melodrama: The Presidential Campaign of 1968* (New York: Viking, 1969), pp. 462–463.

137   "We hear sirens in the night": Jules Witcover, *The Resurrection of Richard Nixon* (New York: Putnam, 1970), pp. 357–358.

138   Wallace's campaign: Chester, Hodgson, and Page, *An American Melodrama,* pp. 279–293.

139   "The better I come across": Richard Nixon, *RN: The Memoirs of Richard Nixon* (New York: Grossett and Dunlap, 1978), p. 303.

139   Nixon's aides handpicked the exchanges: Witcover, *The Resurrection of Richard Nixon,* pp. 238–239.

139   Explaining law and order: Joe McGinnis, *The Selling of the President: 1968* (New York: Trident, 1969), p. 71.

140   Defending "square" virtues: Nixon, *RN,* p. 354.

141   "Undercut the credibility": Ibid., p. 405.

141   Analysis of Nixon's speech: Herman Stelzner, "The Quest Story and Nixon's Nov. 3, 1969, Address," *The Quarterly Journal of Speech,* April 1971.

142   Hersh's view: Seymour M. Hersh, *The Price of Power* (New York: Summit Books, 1983), pp. 130–131.

142   On the Left: Charles Reich, *The Greening of America* (New York: Bantam, 1971).

142   A new consciousness: Ibid., pp. 4ff.

142   A grouchier mood: Scammon and Wattenberg, *The Real Majority.*

143   "The social issue" Ibid., pp. 36ff.

143   "You have got to feel it": "The Middle Americans," *Time,* Jan. 5, 1970.

143   *Time* paid tribute: Ibid.

144   The main skirmish lines: Scammon and Wattenberg, *The Real Majority,* p. 81.

144   "Impudent snobs": Jules Witcover, *White Knight: The Rise of Spiro Agnew* (New York: Random House, 1972), p. 305.

145   "Rotten apples": Ibid., p. 309.

145   No "long-haired brats": "The Middle Americans."

145   "You see these bums": Nixon, *RN,* p. 454.

146   Four die at Kent State: Jules Archer, *The Incredible Sixties: The Stormy Years That Changed America* (New York: Harcourt, 1986), pp. 1–3.

146   Campuses erupted: Maurice Isserman and Michael Kazin, *America Divided: The Civil War of the 1960s* (New York: Oxford, 2000), p. 270.

146   Nixon's response: William Safire, *Before the Fall: An Inside View of the Pre-Watergate White House* (New York: Doubleday, 1975), p. 62.

146   *Newsweek* poll: *Newsweek,* May 18, 1970.

146   Hard hats' reaction: Isserman and Kazin, *America Divided,* p. 270; Todd Gitlin, *The Sixties: Years of Hope, Days of Rage* (New York: Bantam, 1993), p. 414.

146   Days of Rage: Archer, *The Incredible Sixties,* p. 181.

147   Some 250 major bombings: Gitlin, *The Sixties,* p. 401.

147   Townhouse blast: Ibid., p. 400.

147   Democratic rule changes: Robert Shogan, *None of the Above: Why Presidents Fail and What Can Be Done About It* (New York: New American Library, 1982), pp. 118–121, 139–144.

147   Guidelines for minorities: Eddie N. Williams and Milton D. Morris, "The Electoral Process and Minorities," in James A. Reichley, ed., *Elections American Style* (Washington, D.C.: Brookings, 1987), p. 146.

148   Doubling of black delegates: Ibid., p. 147.

148   Increase in women and greening of convention: Theodore White, *The Making of the President, 1972* (New York: Atheneum, 1973), p. 177.

149   Picturesque California: Ibid., p. 176.

149   Meany's reaction: Ibid., p. 178.

149   Platform debate: Ibid., p. 180.

149   Vote on homosexual plank: Colleen McGuiness, ed., "National Party Conventions: 1831–1988," *Congressional Quarterly,* 1991, p. 123.

150   "Beyond the political and cultural limits": White, *The Making of the President, 1972,* p. 180.

150   "Pulled the mask off": Ernest R. May and Janet Fraser, eds., *Campaign '72: The Managers Speak* (Cambridge: Harvard University Press, 1973), p. 129.

151   Nixon's self-revealing analysis: Nixon, *RN,* pp. 514–515.

152   Nixon's southern strategy: Shogan, *None of the Above,* p. 157.

152   "A new lease on life": Nixon, *RN,* p. 717.

153   "The final judgment": Nixon, *RN,* p. 967.

CHAPTER 10: THE RETURN OF THE RIGHTEOUS

159   Carter at prayer breakfast: Robert Shogan, *Promises to Keep: Carter's First 100 Days* (New York: Crowell, 1977), p. 36.

160   Evangelicals had found a foothold: Kenneth Woodward, "Born Again!" *Newsweek,* Oct. 25, 1976.

160   *Christianity Today* ad: William Martin, *With God on Our Side: The Rise of the Religious Right in America* (New York: Broadway Books, 1996), p. 153.

161   A direct challenge: Kenneth Woodward, "Politics from the Pulpit," *Newsweek,* Sept. 6, 1976.

161   Ford vs. Carter on abortion: Jules Witcover, *Marathon: The Pursuit of the Presidency, 1972–1976* (New York: New American Library, 1977), pp. 63, 588, 220.

162   "An urgent priority": Martin, *With God on Our Side,* p. 155.

162   "An unprecedented opportunity": Ibid., p. 157.

163   "People were uneasy": Jonathan Moore and Janet Fraser, eds., *Campaign for President: The Managers Look at '76* (Cambridge, Mass.: Ballinger, 1977), p. 134.

163   "To the point of absurdity": Ibid., p. 134.

163   *Playboy* interview: Robert Scheer and Barry Golson, "Jimmy Carter: A Candid Conversation," *Playboy,* November 1976.

163 Reaction to interview: Witcover, *Marathon*, pp. 603, 607.

165 "Those living in sin": Shogan, *Promises*, p. 135.

166 Phyllis Schlafly: Susan Fraker, "A Kitchen Crusader," *Newsweek*, July 25, 1977.

167 The battle of Houston: Merrill Sheils et al., "A Women's Agenda," *Newsweek*, Nov. 28, 1977.

167–168 Robertson and Falwell reaction: Martin, *With God on Our Side*, p. 166.

168 "It's all gone our way": *WP*, Nov. 19, 1978.

169 Tax-exempt controversy: Martin, *With God on Our Side*, p. 169.

170 "Bureaucrats out of touch": Connaught Marshner, e-mail to the author, April 6, 2001.

170 IRS modifies guidelines: *WP*, Dec. 12, 1978.

170 Family Conference controversy: Melinda Beck, "A Family Meeting Turns into a Feud," *Newsweek*, June 16, 1980.

171 "The water is six feet deep": *LAT*, Nov. 6, 1980.

172 Viguerie's view: Leslie Bennetts, "Conservatives Join on Social Concerns," *NYT*, July 30, 1980.

172 "Enough is enough!": Ibid.

173 Coining the "moral majority": Martin, *With God on Our Side*, p. 200.

173 "Get this man out of the White House": Ibid., p. 189.

CHAPTER 11: THE CITY ON A HILL

175 "The baby smiles": Peggy Noonan, *What I Saw at the Revolution* (New York: Ivy, 1991), p. 154.

176 "It was a good life": Ronald Reagan, with Richard G. Hubler, *Where's the Rest of Me?* (New York: Duell, Sloan & Pearce, 1965), p. 20.

176 "A presumption of good will": Lou Cannon, *Reagan* (New York: Perigree Books, 1982), p. 24.

176 "A foot in the air": Reagan, *Where's the Rest of Me?* p. 11.

176 "A city upon a hill": James C. Roberts, ed., *A City upon a Hill: Speeches by Ronald Reagan Before the Conservative Political Action Conference, 1974–1978* (Washington, D.C.: American Studies Center, 1989), p. 11.

177 Sacred to evangelicals: William Andrew Moyer III, *Battle for the City on the Hill: Evangelical Interpretations of American History, 1960–1996*, doctoral dissertation, George Washington University, 1998, p. 10.

177 Reagan's embellishment: Ibid., pp. 283–284.

177 Yankelovich's findings: Daniel Yankelovich, "American Values, Change and Stability," *Public Opinion*, December/January 1984.

178 Reagan "more humanized": Richard Williamson, letter to the author, Aug. 16, 1989.

178 First test: *NYT*, Aug. 18, 1980.

179 The two-day conclave: *WP*, Aug. 24, 1980.

180 "We plan to reverse that": Allan J. Mayer, "A Tide of Born Again Politics," *Newsweek*, Sept. 15, 1980.

180 "Not voting is a sin": Ibid.

181 Weyrich's caution: *WP*, Aug. 24, 1980.

181 "God isn't a right-winger": Mayer, "A Tide of Born Again Politics."

181 Criticism of evangelicals: Ibid.
182 Falwell shrugs off criticism: Ibid.
182 Dobson's reaction: Cal Thomas and Ed Dobson, *Blinded by Might: Can the Religious Right Save America?* (Grand Rapids: Zondervan, 1999), pp. 15–17.
183 "A lady on the Court": Ibid., p. 586.
184 The New Right smolders: *WP,* July 21, 1981.
184 Contending against the Democrats: *WP,* May 17, 1982.
186 Graveyard for the New Right: *WP,* Jan. 31, 1984.
187 The improved misery index: Scott Keeter, "Public Opinion in 1984," in Gerald Pomper, ed., *The Election of 1984: Reports and Interpretations* (Chatham, N.J.: Chatham House, 1985).
189 The administration claimed: Robert Shogan, background paper, *Obstacle Course: The Report of the Twentieth Century Fund Task Force on the Presidential Appointment Process* (New York: Twentieth Century Fund, 1996), pp. 125–126.
189 To mobilize support: Ethan Bronner, "Passing Judgment," *Boston Globe* magazine, Aug. 27, 1989.
190 "A man who would throw the book": Bronner, *Battle for Justice* (New York: W. W. Norton, 1989), p. 226.

CHAPTER 12: "THE CHRISTIANS ARE COMING"

193 Doug Wead's late night at the office: William Martin, *With God on Our Side: The Rise of the Religious Right in America* (New York: Broadway Books, 1996), pp. 265–267.
195 "A flood tide of revival": *LAT,* March 4, 1986.
196 "A home run": *WP,* May 28, 1986.
197 "A tidal wave": Ibid.
197 "The Christians have won": Ibid., July 31, 1986.
197 "The Christians are coming": David S. Broder, "A Tug to the Right," *WP,* June 1, 1986.
198 Robertson's childhood: *Current Biography Yearbook,* 1987.
199 Enjoying the Big Apple: Pat Robertson, *Shout It from the House Tops,* rev. ed. (Virginia Beach, Va.: Christian Broadcasting Network, 1986), p. 1.
199 "Life was empty": Ibid., p. 2.
200 Robertson transformed: Ibid., pp. 7–8.
201 CBN's growth: *LAT,* March 4, 1986.
201 "It was a miracle": Ibid.
201 "I think that, too": Robertson, *Shout It from the House Tops,* p. 116.
202 "I know God's will": *WP,* Sept. 19, 1986.
203 Backing from other evangelical leaders: *WP,* Oct. 27, 1986.
204 Robertson under fire: *WP,* Sept. 18, 1986.
205 Barone's complaint: Michael Barone, "Why Ridicule Someone's Religion?" *WP,* Sept. 21, 1986.
205 The evangelical empire: Richard N. Ostlin, "Power, Glory—And Politics; Right-wing Preachers Dominate the Dial," *Time,* Feb. 17, 1986.
205 A roll in the hay: Larry Martz, "God and Money," *Newsweek,* April 6, 1987.
205 New revelations: *LAT,* Dec. 26, 1987.

206   Robertson pressed on: Martin, *With God on Our Side*, p. 276.

206   Elwell takes charge in Iowa: Ibid., p. 277.

207   "Wounded very badly": Lawrence I. Barrett, "Pat Robertson's Spirit Filled Crusade," *Time*, Sept. 28, 1987.

207   Negative poll ratings: Ibid.

208   Epps's view: Garrett Epps, "Voices of '88: A Surprising New Politics of Protest: Robertson's Evangelicals," *WP*, Feb. 14, 1988.

209   Sanny Thompson's efforts: John Balzar, "Robertson in Iowa," *LAT*, Nov. 25, 1987.

210   "An enormous boost": *LAT*, Feb. 9, 1988.

210   Robertson's tiffs with network anchors: *NYT*, Feb. 10, 1988.

210   More troubles with the press: *WP*, Feb 12, 1988.

210   Exuding confidence in Bedford: *WP*, Feb 14, 1988.

211   Robertson's big spending: *NYT*, Feb. 23, 1988.

212   "An absurd charge": *LAT*, Feb. 25, 1988.

213   Finishing third in South Carolina: *WP*, March 6, 1988.

213   Super Tuesday results: *WP*, March 9, 1988.

213   "I should have kept my mouth shut": Ibid.

214   Keeping his candidacy alive: *WP*, March 25, 1988.

214   Robertson supporters at the convention: *LAT*, Aug. 16, 1988.

215   Kemp's proposals: Author's interview with Jack Kemp, May 8, 1991.

215   "More important things": *LAT*, Aug. 16, 1988.

CHAPTER 13: THE PRINCE OF COMPASSION

221   *Post* sounds alarm: *WP*, Jan. 10, 1999.

222   Pitfalls of polling: Richard John Neuhaus, "Bill Clinton and the American Character," *First Things*, June 1999.

222   Contradictions in polling data: John J. Miller, "No Need to Hide," *NYT*, Feb. 8, 1999.

222   *WP* survey: David Broder and Richard Morin, "Worries About Nation's Morals, . . . " *WP*, Sept. 8, 1998.

223   Olasky's role: Joan Didion, "God's Country," *New York Review Of Books*, Nov. 2, 2000; *LAT*, July 27, 2000.

223   Olasky's book: Marvin Olasky, *The Tragedy of American Compassion* (Washington, D.C.: Regnery, 1992).

223   "Recommended by Newt Gingrich": *LAT*, Aug. 22, 1995.

224   The Ashcroft amendment: *NYT*, Oct. 22, 2000.

224   "A lot of gin and tonics": *LAT*, July 27, 1988.

225   Father-son comparison: Richard T. Cooper, "To the Manner Born, Bush Finds His Own Way," *LAT*, July 30, 2000.

229   Bush at Andover and Yale and young manhood: Ibid.

230   Bush's service record: Walter Robinson, "Questions Remain on Bush's Service," *Boston Globe*, Oct. 31, 2000.

232   "It was a Mercedes": Nicholas D. Kristof, "Learning How to Run: A West Texas Stumble," *NYT*, July 27, 2000.

232   Religious involvement: Hanna Rosin, "Applying Personal Faith to Public Policy," *WP*, July 24, 2000.

233   "A life changing moment": www.beliefnet.com, Oct. 15, 2000.

234   "I've done something": Laurence I. Barrett, "Junior Is His 'Own Bush Now,'" *Time,* July 31, 1989.

235   "If it works": Robert Shogan, "Bush May Be Tonic the GOP Needs," *LAT,* July 27, 1998.

236   "The next bold step": *LAT,* June 13, 1999.

236   "My first goal": "Hardball with Chris Matthews," June 14, 1999, CNBC transcript.

236   "A message to my own party": *WP,* July 23, 1999.

237   "Government is not the enemy": *LAT,* July 23, 1999.

237   Ralph Reed's view: quoted in E. J. Dionne, "In Search of George W.," *WP Magazine,* Sept. 19, 1999.

238   "When we put our hand on the Bible": *Washington Times,* June 15, 1999.

239   Bauer on abortion: *LAT,* Jan. 23, 2000.

239   "Would that be right?": *LAT,* Jan. 31, 2000.

240   Forbes's frustration: *LAT,* Jan. 23, 2000.

241   "Christ, because he changed my heart": *NYT,* Dec. 14, 1999.

241   Keyes's complaint: Bill Press, "A Presidential Debate Is for Speeches, Not Sermons," *LAT,* Dec. 17, 1999.

242   "Almost like a surrogate": *NYT,* Aug. 31, 1999.

242   McCain's restraint: Frank Rich, "Save Us from Our Saviors," *NYT,* Sept. 11, 1999.

243   "He will not listen to reason": *NYT,* Oct. 2, 1999.

243   Meghan McCain and abortion: *LAT,* Jan. 27, 2000.

245   Weyrich letter: *WP,* Feb. 18, 1999.

245   "I am the Right": *WP,* Feb. 3, 2000.

246   McCain fought back: David Broder, "God Appears to Be a Republican," *LAT,* Feb. 18, 2000.

246   "If McCain wins": Ibid.

247   Bush's apology: *LAT,* Feb. 28, 2000.

247   McCain on the offensive: *LAT,* Feb. 29, 2000.

248   Super Tuesday exit polls: *NYT,* March 8, 2000; *WP,* March 8, 2000.

CHAPTER 14: THE FAITH THAT FAILED

252   As even Gingrich acknowledged: *WP,* March 21, 1999.

252   The *Love Story* flap: Margaret Carlson, "Stretches and Sighs," *Time,* Oct. 16, 2000; *LAT,* Dec. 15, 1997.

252   "One of our greatest presidents": *WP,* Dec. 21, 1998.

252   Clinton's poll problems: Kathleen Kenna, "Americans Beset with 'Clinton Fatigue,'" *Toronto Star,* June 29, 1999.

253   Demonstrating "Clinton fatigue": Pew Research Center for the People and the Press, "Public Votes for Continuity and Change," March 1, 1999.

253   Gore seeks separation: *NYT,* June 17, 1999.

254   "Allergy to faith": *LAT,* May 25, 1999.

254   "A dead-end debate": Peter Steinfels, "Al Gore Reveals the Roots of His Faith," *NYT,* May 29, 1999.

254 "A real smorgasbord": Melinda Henneberger, "Spiritual Seeker," *NYT,* Oct. 22, 2000.

255 Gore's book: Albert Gore, *Earth in the Balance* (Boston: Houghton Mifflin, 1992).

255 "It's very personal": ABC News, "World News Tonight," Sept. 13, 1999. Transcript #99091307-j04.

255 "Almost cheapens faith": *NYT,* Dec. 15, 1999.

255 Sniping from Republicans: "Good Morning America," March 8, 1999, ABC News transcript.

256 "My abilities match the national moment": *WP,* March 4, 2000.

257 Gauges of social conditions: Karl Zinsmeister et al., "Is America Turning a Corner?" *The American Enterprise,* January 1999.

258 "Not as well liked": *NYT,* May 16, 2000.

258 White males reject Gore: *WP,* May 12, 2000.

258 Million Mom March: *LAT,* May 15, 2000.

259 Bush's edge with married voters: *LAT,* May 11, 2000.

260 "A black spot": *Boston Globe,* June 18, 2000.

260 "Occupy the land with character": *WP,* Aug. 4, 2000.

260 "Few . . . missed the allusion": *NYT,* Aug. 4, 2000.

261 Lieberman background: *NYT,* Aug. 8, 2000; *WP,* Aug. 8, 2000.

261 "Power to shape our culture": Michael Barone and Grant Ujifusa, *The Almanac of American Politics, 2000* (Washington, D.C.: National Journal, 1999), p. 346.

262 Lieberman's speech to the Senate: *NYT,* Sept. 4, 1998.

262 "I was angry": "Meet the Press," NBC News, Sept. 6, 1998, Federal News Service transcript.

263 Ross Baker's comments: *LAT,* Sept. 11, 1998.

263 Impact on the polls: Michael Kelly, "A Calculated Risk," *WP,* Aug. 9, 2000.

263 "A daring choice": *Chicago Tribune,* Aug. 8, 2000.

264 "A Jew on the ticket": *NYT,* Aug. 7, 2000.

265 Ardent kiss: *WP,* Aug. 22, 2000.

265 The decade-long argument: *LAT,* Aug. 20, 2000.

266 Screeching halt: *LAT,* Aug. 18, 2000.

267 The role of faith: Joseph Lieberman, *In Praise of Public Life* (New York: Simon & Schuster, 2000), pp. 139–141.

267 Anxiety among Jewish leaders: Catherine Decker, "Lieberman Mix of Faith, Politics Sets Off Clash," *LAT,* Aug. 30, 2000.

267 Lieberman in Detroit: *NYT,* Aug. 28, 2000.

268 "Received with alarm": *NYT,* Aug. 27, 2000.

269 "Inappropriate and even unsettling": Decker, "Lieberman Mix of Faith."

269 "Very supportive": *WP,* Sept. 10, 2000.

270 Gore and Lieberman attack: Ronald Brownstein, "Gore Outflanks Bush," *LAT,* Sept. 12, 2000.

270 Weinstein's event: *WP,* Sept. 14, 2000.

270 A stinging editorial: *NYT,* Sept. 12, 2000.

271 A rap on the knuckles: *LAT,* Sept. 21, 2000.

272 Gore's early gun-control stance: *NYT,* July 6, 2000.

272   Polls on gun control: *WP,* April 13, 2000.

273   Heston sounds off: *WP,* Oct. 20, 2000.

273   Gore backtracks: Debate transcript, *NYT,* Oct. 12, 2000.

274   Even more pusillanimous: Debate transcript, *NYT,* Oct. 18, 2000.

274   Gore did not want a fight: Debate transcript, *NYT,* Oct. 4, 2000.

275   Gore wins in polls: Nancy Gibbs, "Where Is the Love," *Time,* Oct. 16, 2000.

275   "They held their own": *Hotline,* Oct. 4, 2000.

275–276 A sore winner: Bob Herbert, "Gore Piles On," *NYT,* Oct. 5, 2000.

276   "Goody two shoes": "Fox Special Report," Oct. 3, 2000, Fox News transcript #100305cb.254.

276   "The bridge of sighs": "Inside Politics," CNN transcript #00100400V15, Oct. 4, 2000.

276   Gore's troubles started: Debate transcript, *NYT,* Oct. 4, 2000.

276   "A distinction without a difference": "Inside Politics," CNN transcript #00100400V15, Oct. 4, 2000.

277   The inspection trip: Ibid.

277   "You can't stretch": Ibid.

277   Republicans pound Gore: *WP,* Oct. 7, 2000.

277   Bush's claim on campaign spending: *NYT,* Oct. 6, 2000.

277   Bush's claim on Social Security: *NYT,* Nov. 2, 2000.

278   Gore "gets the message": *NYT,* Oct. 11, 2000.

279   Clinton had been invited: *NYT,* Oct. 28, 2000.

280   "It was Democrat-lite": "Face the Nation," Oct. 1, 2000, CBS News, Federal Document Clearing House transcript.

280   "That was his call": Paul Weyrich, e-mail to the author, Feb. 12, 2001.

280   "I think it's a trap": *LAT,* Sept. 30, 2000.

280   "If we work together": *LAT,* Oct. 1, 2000.

281   A two-day wonder: Vaughn Ververs, "Timing Is Everything," *National Journal,* Nov. 6, 2000.

281   "A defiant rebuttal": *NYT,* Nov. 4, 2000.

282   "A dangerous strategy": "Face the Nation," Oct. 1, 2000, CBS News, Federal Document Clearing House transcript.

282   University of Akron Poll: "How the Faithful Voted," Ethics and Public Policy Center, Washington, D.C., March 2001, No. 10; also see Ethics and Public Policy Center, press release, Jan. 25, 2001.

CHAPTER 15: THE FORTY YEARS' WAR

283   "Probably what we deserve": *WP,* Sept. 18, 2001.

283   "We make God mad": *NYT,* Sept. 15, 2001.

284   Limbaugh's reaction and Falwell apology: *LAT,* Sept. 23, 2001.

284   Robertson disavowal: *WP,* Sept. 18, 2001.

284   Response from liberals: *LAT,* Sept. 23, 2001.

285   "You do become vulnerable": *NYT,* Sept. 15, 2001.

285   Racicot's resentment: Evan Thomas and Michael Isikoff, "Shootout in the Sun," *Newsweek,* Nov. 27, 2000.

286   Lieberman's response: David Von Drehle et al., "For Bush Camp, Some Momentum from a Memo," *WP,* Jan. 31, 2001.

286   "The face of Republican outrage": *LAT,* Nov. 22, 2000.

286   Racicot's ties to Bush: Ibid.

288   Conservatives' view of Justice Department: *LAT,* Dec. 22, 2000.

288   Intensified misgivings: Joshua Green, "How Ashcroft Happened," *The American Prospect,* Feb. 26, 2001.

289   "You may not be big, but you are slow": *LAT,* Nov. 22, 2000.

289   More enthusiasm for hate-crimes laws: Mike Allen, "Montana Gov. Didn't Have Right Stuff," *WP,* Jan. 2, 2001.

290   "He didn't preach": Laurie Goodstein, "Moderato Non Troppo," *NYT,* Jan. 14, 2001.

290   Father and son: David Van Bieman, "The Roots of His Faith," *Time,* Jan. 22, 2001; John Ashcroft, *Lessons from a Father to His Son* (Nashville, Tenn.: Thomas Nelson, 1998).

291   The Human Life Amendment: Mitch Frank, "Confirmation Fight," *Time,* Jan. 22, 2001.

291   "The right to life of every unborn child": Van Bieman, "The Roots of His Faith."

292   Another reason to oppose White: Howard Fineman and Michael Isikoff, "Right from the Start," *Newsweek,* Jan. 22, 2001.

292   Urged by Christian Right: David Johnson and Neil A. Lewis, "Religious Right Made Big Push to Put Ashcroft in Justice Department," *NYT,* Jan. 7, 2001.

292   A sobering impact: Michael Barone and Grant Ujifusa, *The Almanac of American Politics 2000* (Washington, D.C.: *National Journal,* 1999), p. 926.

293   Ashcroft at Bob Jones: *LAT,* Jan. 13, 2001.

294   The first blow: "How Ashcroft Won," *Weekly Standard,* Jan. 1, 2001; *WP,* Jan. 2, 2001.

294   Weyrich's role in Tower's defeat: Author's interview with Paul Weyrich, Feb. 14, 1989.

295   Blunt's background: Barone and Ujifusa, *Almanac,* p. 950.

295   Weyrich called Blunt: Paul Weyrich, e-mail to author, Feb. 19, 2001.

295   Blunt's meeting in Austin: Ibid.

296   Keating's other problems: Michael Isikoff, "Why Keating Didn't Cut It," *Newsweek,* Jan. 15, 2001.

298   A problem for centrists: Evan Bayh, "The Wrong Man," *WP,* Jan. 19, 2001.

298   "Healing gestures": Fineman and Isikoff, "Right from the Start."

298   Patricia Ireland's opposition: "Inside Politics," Jan. 15, 2001, CNN transcript #01011500V15.

299   "The right to his own team": Ibid.

299   Opposition to Brown and Halperin: *USA Today,* Nov. 17, 1993; *Washington Times,* Oct. 13, 1993.

299   "Legitimate fodder": David Keene interview with author, Aug. 9, 1994.

300   A two-part, 65-page dossier: People for the American Way, "Special Report: The Case Against the Confirmation of John Ashcroft As Attorney General of the United States," The Senate Years, 2001; the Missouri Years, Jan. 13, 2001.

300   *Southern Partisan* interview: *Southern Partisan,* 2nd quarter, 1988, p. 28, cited in People for the American Way: "Special Report," p. 16.

301   The *Southern Partisan* T-shirt: Institute for Public Accuracy, Washington, D.C.; ipa@accuracy.org, press release, Jan. 15, 2001.

301 "Incomplete, inaccurate and misleading": Free Congress Foundation, press release, Jan. 17, 2001.

301 Fighting the "radical left": Richard Viguerie's Conservative HQ, press release, Jan. 19, 2001.

302 "Broad based support": Free Congress Foundation, press release, Jan. 19, 2001.

302 Ashcroft blunts attack: *NYT,* Jan. 17, 2001.

303 Bush's faith-based initiative: *NYT,* Jan. 29, 2001.

303 Lieberman's tacit endorsement: *LAT,* Jan. 31, 2001.

304 Eric Holder's pardon problems: Peter Slevin, "A Rush to Judgment," *WP,* March 1, 2001.

304 Frank calls it "appalling": *WP,* Feb. 14, 2001.

304 Views of Leahy: E. J. Dionne, ". . . And the Gifts That Keep on Giving," *WP,* Feb. 6, 2001.

304 Carter call it "disgraceful": *New York Daily News,* Feb. 22, 2001.

305 The "grifters": Hamilton Jordan, "The First Grifters," *Wall Street Journal,* Feb. 20, 2001.

305 "Reluctant to impose values": Alan Wolfe, *One Nation, After All"* (New York: Viking, 1998); Ronald Brownstein, "The Right Swings the Wrong Way," *LAT,* Dec. 28, 1998.

306 "Two very different pictures": *NYT,* Feb. 28, 2001.

306 Himmelfarb's book: Gertrude Himmelfarb, *One Nation, Two Cultures* (New York: Vintage, 2001); "One Nation Fairly Divisible," *The Economist,* Jan. 23, 2001.

306 Even more fragmented: Terry Teachout, "Republican Nation, Democratic Nation," *Commentary,* Jan. 1, 2001.

307 Seventy percent of Republican voters married: Gertrude Himmelfarb, "Two Nations or Two Cultures?" *Commentary,* Jan. 1, 2001.

308 "The secret of America": Otto Friedrich, "The Changing Face of America," *Time,* July 8, 1985.

308 Fewer than 2 million from Europe: U.S. Census Bureau, *Statistical Abstract of the United States,* 119th ed. (Washington, D.C.: Government Printing Office, 1999), p. 11, Table 8.

308 "We can all call each other Californians": *WP,* Aug. 31, 2000.

308 Nearly 7 million multiracial: *WP,* March 13, 2001; Dec. 29, 2000.

309 Complexities of character: Richard Morin, "Does Character Really Count?" *WP,* Feb. 25, 2001; James Davison Hunter and Carl Bowman, "The Politics of Character," Institute for Advanced Studies in Culture, University of Virginia, 2000.

310 Lawmakers' doubts: *WP,* June 18, 1999.

311 "Please deliver this message": *WP,* Sept. 14, 2000.

311 "Something odd": "How the Faithful Voted," Ethics and Public Policy Center, Washington, D.C., March 2001, No. 10.

311 A Democratic family agenda: Michael Lerner, *The Politics of Meaning: Restoring Hope and Possibility in an Age of Cynicism* (New York: Addison-Wesley, 1999), p. 58.

312 "Their very raison d'etre may be lost": Pat Robertson, "Mr. Bush's Faith-Based Initiative Is Flawed," *Wall Street Journal,* March 12, 2001.

313 Approximate parity with blacks: *NYT,* March 8, 2001.

313 New York mayor's race: *NYT,* Nov. 8, 2001.

314   "A nation of patriots": *WP,* Nov. 2, 2001.

314   An outpouring of prayer: *NYT,* Oct. 20, 2001.

314   God and country: Jodie Morse, "Letting God Back In," *Time,* Oct. 22, 2001.

314   War support varied along racial lines: *WP,* Oct. 6, 2001.

315   Warnings from the bishops' statement: *NYT,* Nov. 10, 2001.

315   Fleischer's admonition: *NYT,* Oct. 30, 2001.

316   Ashcroft's new rules: *WP,* Nov. 29, 2001.

316   Assisted suicide law: *WP,* Nov. 7, 2001.

316   Disregarding gun ownership data: *WP,* Dec. 7, 2001.

317   Bush had to apologize: *LAT,* Feb. 28, 2002.

317   "Growing concern:" Jim Hoagland, "Assessing the War Honestly," *WP,* Feb. 14, 2002.

317   "This is not civility": Clarence Thomas, address to American Enterprise Institute, Feb. 13, 2001, AEI transcript.

318   Powell's advice on condoms: *WP,* Feb. 16, 2002.

318   Pederson forced to quit: *WP,* Feb. 21, 2002.

318   New rules for churches: *WP,* Feb. 17, 2002.

INDEX